Research, Innovation and Entrepreneurship in Saudi Arabia

This book provides valuable insights into the Kingdom of Saudi Arabia (KSA) through a comprehensive examination of Vision 2030, an ambitious economic plan by the KSA to reinvent and diversify its economy from a heavy dependence on hydrocarbon to knowledge-based resources.

Research, Innovation and Entrepreneurship in Saudi Arabia: Vision 2030 discusses how this initiative will assist the government in achieving its envisioned goals by creating a culture of research, innovation and entrepreneurship. It studies the current state of the field as well as new policies and reforms in Saudi Arabia which encompass education systems, ICT infrastructure and a vibrant innovation landscape that includes academia, the public and private sectors and civil society. The authors present a number of real-life case studies as a model of inspiration for cross-sector development. The book provides a source of inspiration for other nations in studying the KSA's determined and ambitious plans as a country in a transitioning journey from a natural resources–based economy towards a knowledge-based country with considerable diversification in all sectors.

This book is a useful reference for students, researchers and policy and decision-makers in understanding Saudi innovation and the economic diversification ecosystem.

Muhammad Khurram Khan is currently working as Professor of Cybersecurity at the Center of Excellence in Information Assurance (CoEIA), King Saud University, Kingdom of Saudi Arabia. He is founder and CEO of the Global Foundation for Cyber Studies and Research, an independent, non-profit and non-partisan cybersecurity think-tank registered in Washington D.C. which explores and addresses global cyberspace challenges from the intersecting dimensions of policy and technology.

Muhammad Babar Khan received his masters in media sciences from Iqra University, Pakistan, in 2015. He is working for a renowned think tank, Global Foundation for Cyber Studies and Research, USA, as a research analyst and media advisor and is currently pursuing another masters in international relations and a PhD in media studies.

Routledge Studies in Innovation, Organizations and Technology

For more information about this series, please visit www.routledge.com/Rout ledge-Studies-in-Innovation-Organizations-and-Technology/book-series/ RIOT

Research, Innovation and Entrepreneurship in Saudi Arabia

Vision 2030

Edited by
**Muhammad Khurram Khan
and Muhammad Babar Khan**

Routledge
Taylor & Francis Group

LONDON AND NEW YORK

First published 2020
by Routledge
2 Park Square, Milton Park, Abingdon, Oxon OX14 4RN

and by Routledge
605 Third Avenue, New York, NY 10017

First issued in paperback 2021

Routledge is an imprint of the Taylor & Francis Group, an informa business

Publisher's Note
The publisher has gone to great lengths to ensure the quality of this reprint but
points out that some imperfections in the original copies may be apparent.

Disclaimer: Since this is an edited book, therefore, contents presented in all
respective chapters are the sole responsibility of the contributing authors.
Editors of this book don't represent their social, national and political views
in the chapters authored by contributing authors.

British Library Cataloguing-in-Publication Data
A catalogue record for this book is available from the British Library

Library of Congress Cataloging-in-Publication Data
A catalog record for this book has been requested

ISBN 13: 978−1−03−223714−5 (pbk)
ISBN 13: 978−1−138−48853−3 (hbk)

DOI: 10.4324/9781351040020

Typeset in Bembo
by Apex CoVantage, LLC

Printed in the United Kingdom
by Henry Ling Limited

Contents

Figures

Tables

Biographies of editors

Muhammad Khurram Khan is currently working as Professor of Cybersecurity at the Center of Excellence in Information Assurance (CoEIA), King Saud University, Kingdom of Saudi Arabia. He is one of the founding members of CoEIA and served as the manager of R&D from 2009–2012. He, along with his team, developed and successfully managed the cybersecurity research program of CoEIA, which made the center one of the best centers of excellence in the region.

He is founder and CEO of the Global Foundation for Cyber Studies and Research (www.gfcyber.org), an independent, non-profit and non-partisan cybersecurity think tank in Washington D.C., USA, which explores and addresses global cyberspace challenges from the intersecting dimensions of policy and technology.

Prof. Khurram is the editor-in-chief of a well-reputed international journal, *Telecommunication Systems*, that has been published by Springer for over 26 years, with a recent impact factor of 1.707 (JCR 2019). Furthermore, he is on the editorial board of several international journals, including *IEEE Communications Surveys & Tutorials*, *IEEE Communications Magazine*, *IEEE Internet of Things Journal*, *IEEE Transactions on Consumer Electronics*, *Journal of Network & Computer Applications* (Elsevier), *IEEE Access*, *IEEE Consumer Electronics Magazine*, *PLoS One*, *Electronic Commerce Research*, *IET Wireless Sensor Systems*, *Journal of Information Hiding and Multimedia Signal Processing*, *International Journal of Biometrics* and so on. He has also played the role of guest editor of several international journals of IEEE, Springer, Wiley and Elsevier Science. Moreover, he is one of the organizing chairs of more than five dozen international conferences and a member of technical committees of more than ten dozen international conferences. In addition, he is an active reviewer of many international journals as well as research foundations in Switzerland, Italy, Saudi Arabia and the Czech Republic.

Prof. Khurram was the recipient of the King Saud University Award for Scientific Excellence (Research Productivity) in May 2015. He was also a recipient of the King Saud University Award for Scientific Excellence (Inventions, Innovations, and Technology Licensing) in May 2016. He secured the Outstanding Leadership Award at the IEEE International

Conference on Networks and Systems Security 2009 in Australia. Additionally, he received a certificate of appreciation for outstanding contributions in Biometrics & Information Security Research at the AIT International Conference, June 2010, in Japan. He was awarded a Gold Medal for the Best Invention & Innovation Award at the 10th Malaysian Technology Expo 2011, Malaysia. Moreover, in April 2013, his invention won a Bronze Medal at the 41st International Exhibition of Inventions in Geneva, Switzerland. In addition, he was awarded the best paper award from the *Journal of Network & Computer Applications* (Elsevier) in December 2015.

He has published more than 350 research papers in journals and conferences of international repute. In addition, he is a holder of ten US/PCT patents. He has edited seven books/proceedings published by Springer-Verlag and the IEEE. He has secured several national and international competitive research grants in the domain of cybersecurity. He has played a leading role in developing the BS Cybersecurity Degree Program and Higher Diploma in Cybersecurity at King Saud University. His research areas of interest are cybersecurity, digital authentication, IoT security, cyber policy and technological innovation management.

He is a fellow of the Institution of Engineering and Technology (IET) (UK), fellow of the British Computer Society (BCS) (UK), fellow of the FTRA (Korea), senior member of the Institute of Electrical and Electronics Engineers (IEEE) (USA), senior member of the IACSIT (Singapore), member of the IEEE Consumer Electronics Society, member of the IEEE Communications Society, member of the IEEE Technical Committee on Security & Privacy, member of the IEEE IoT Community, member of the IEEE Smart Cities Community and member of the IEEE Cybersecurity Community. He is also the vice chair of the IEEE Communications Society Saudi Chapter. He is a distinguished lecturer of the IEEE.

His detailed profile can be visited at www.professorkhurram.com

Muhammad Babar Khan received his MS in media sciences from Iqra University, Pakistan, in 2015. He is working for a renowned think tank, Global Foundation for Cyber Studies and Research, USA, as a research analyst and media advisor.

He has had many publications in Higher Education Commission (HEC) and well-reputed international journals. He also has many research papers in the pipeline which will be accepted by journals shortly. He holds patents and has done industrial designs which have been granted by the Intellectual Property Organization, Pakistan.

Currently he has received another masters in international relations and is pursuing a PhD in media studies.

Contributors

Muhammad Babar Khan, Iqra University, Pakistan

Ibrahim Babelli, Ministry of Economy and Planning, Saudi Arabia

Irfan Hameed, Iqra University, Karachi, Pakistan

Sadia Iqbal, Help International Welfare Trust, Karachi, Pakistan

Kamran Khan, Khadim Ali Shah Bukhari Institute of Technology, Karachi, Pakistan

Muhammad Khurram Khan, King Saud University, Saudi Arabia

Mohammad Nurunnabi, Prince Sultan University, Riyadh, Saudi Arabia

Preface

The purpose of this book is to share the vision and insights of the Kingdom of Saudi Arabia (KSA). Vision 2030 is comprehensive in all aspects, and in light of this, the Kingdom is well on its way to transforming from an oil-based economy to a knowledge-based economy. KSA is geographically the fifth-largest state in Asia and the second-largest state in the Arab world, and it has become the world's largest oil producer and exporter, with the world's second-largest oil reserves and sixth-largest gas reserves. However, it is a fact that creating a Saudi knowledge-based economy is a challenging task, as oil and gas are the major pillars of economic growth, but the country has a strong, long-term plan to overcome any challenges ahead in this. Saudi Arabia has set a plan to reduce dependency on oil and diversify its economy by developing public-sector services, but the economy of Saudi Arabia is the least diversified in the Gulf nations, under the shadow of the economic development visions of the Gulf Cooperation Council (GCC). This book highlights vision statements on sustainable economic development plans for GCC countries. The vision pillars of every state have been addressed in detail and present a detailed comparative study of why aggressive steps have been taken to break the long-term established link between the fate of the Saudi economy and conditions in the global market for oil. Likewise, Saudi Arabia's economic development vision is based on three pillars:

- A vibrant society
- A thriving economy
- An ambitious nation

All these themes combine to form a hub for the best economic growth among all the nations of the entire GCC. In order to accomplish Saudi Arabia's Vision 2030 and to identify the challenges through appropriate mechanisms for follow-up and performance evaluation, the National Transformation Program (NTP) 2020 was launched in 2016 with the goal of giving Saudi Arabia a leading position in all fields and to figure out the general direction, policies, goals and objectives to accomplish the goals for the 2030 vision. To expedite this transformation, the Kingdom is investing more in entrepreneurship education, schools, colleges, universities, globalization, women's education and empowerment, infrastructure, tourism, renewable energy, enabling the R&D workforce, health services and recreation.

Saudi Arabia is on the cusp of a new era: an era marked by transformation in the will, in the economy, in the process and in the way we do things. The King Abdullah University of Science and Technology (KAUST), with its innovative Industrial Collaboration Program (KICP), is working towards fostering strong ties with local, global and regional businesses that possess a keen interest in building up entrepreneurship links and participating in the Kingdom's transition to a knowledge-based economy. KAUST is playing a vital part in recruiting the best intellectuals from within and outside the Kingdom globally to participate in scientific research. The main aim of its effort is to invite and retain excellent Saudi and international students and provide all the necessities for them. As a result, the Kingdom can achieve economic development and attract foreign investment. The most important initiative taken by the government in Vision 2030, which identified numerous areas and offered benefits from the concerted investment of government resources and national engagement, is again an important aspect of effectively governing an ambitious nation. This goal is to bring everyone onto the same page, from government agencies to citizens and the private sector, in order to deepen their communication channels. Each agency's programs, plans and relevant performance indicators are comprehensively analyzed, along with detailed studies and benchmarks for effective decision-making which will prove fruitful for decades to come and assist Saudi Arabia to achieve Vision 2030.

Saudi Arabia has worked hard to restructure its funds, and now its focus is on refining the funds' investment capabilities, which will enable it to further manage a much broader portfolio of new and current assets. Saudi Arabia aims to transform these funds into the world's largest sovereign wealth fund and, to the same end, is working on a comprehensive plan to achieve the long-awaited goals which will prove fruitful for Vision 2030.

This program intends to build up new strategic partnerships globally with economic partners for the Kingdom in the twenty-first century. This is essential in order to align with the national vision and become a trade hub connecting three continents: Asia, Africa and Europe.

Last, we would like to say from the bottom of our heart that this book is an endeavor to look at the substance of Vision 2030 of Saudi Arabia to set up its effectiveness regarding the objectives of manageability. Our gratitude goes to those who have offered encouragement on the project, and sincere thanks are also due to our supportive and capable authors and academic colleagues.

1 Kingdom of Saudi Arabia

The land of opportunities

*Muhammad Babar Khan, Irfan Hameed
and Kamran Khan*

Historical background

King Abdul-Aziz Al-Saud founded the Kingdom of Saudi Arabia (KSA), commonly known as Saudi Arabia, which is located in southwestern Asia. Saudi Arabia covers a significant fraction of the Arabian Peninsula, with an area of 2149.7 (in thousands) square kilometers [1]. The World Bank reported that the population of the Kingdom is 33.70 million in the year 2018. The growth rate of the population is 3.5%, the fastest growth rate in the world [2]. The population living in the Kingdom of Saudi Arabia is diverse; the majority (90%) are Arabs, and the remaining 10% are of Asian and African origin [3]. The kingdom of Saudi Arabia has 13 governing provinces, including over 5,000 villages and cities. The metropolitan cities include Jeddah, the central port on the Dammam and the Red Sea, and Riyadh, the capital city, which is located in the middle of the country and is the major city on the Arabian Gulf.

Population

The land area in Saudi Arabia totals 2,149,690 square kilometers or 829,999.94 square miles. In relation to the total population of the country, this is 15.61 individuals per square kilometer, or 6 people per square mile. Of Saudi Arabia's population, 83.33% live in municipal areas, means that there are several sizeable cities in the Kingdom. The capital city of Saudi Arabia is Riyadh with over 7.5 million people and Jeddah is the second largest city, with 3,976,400 citizens. The holy city of Mecca and Medina have approximately the same population, between 1 and 1.6 million. Within different age groups, the 0–14 group makes up the median amount of population, with 32.4% of the total. The middle age group, 15–64, has the highest share in the total population, about 64.8%. The 65+ age group makes up under 2.8% of the total population. The male-to-female gender ratio at birth is 1.05. For the age group of under 15, this ratio is 1.05; for the 15–64 age group, it is 1.03 and for the age group of 65+, it is 1.03. The total population mean male-to-female ratio is 1.21 [4].

Geography

The Kingdom of Saudi Arabia covers around 80% of the Arabian Peninsula. The majority of the country's borders with Oman, United Arab Emirates and the Republic of Yemen are disputed, which is why the actual size of the country remains unknown. Per the statistics of the Saudi government, it is estimated that the country's area is 2,217,949 square kilometers. Some other sources differ between 2,149,690 and 2,240,000 square kilometers. It is also noted that less than 1% of the total area is ready for cultivation. Saudi Arabia is covered by seven countries and three different bodies of water. The western side of the Gulf of Aqaba and the Red Sea form a coastal border of almost 1800 km which drains towards south of Yemen and then follows the mountain ridges for approximately 320 km to near Narjan. The Saudi border is on the southeastern side of Narjan and is still undecided. The borders of Saudi Arabia became an issue in the early 1990s, when oil was discovered in the area of Saudi Arabia when Yemen, on behalf of foreign companies, explored oil for commercial use. Saudi Arabia is confined by Jordan, Iraq and Kuwait from the northern side. The boundary encompasses almost 1,400 kilometers, from Aqaba on the western side, and extends towards Ras al Khafi on the Persian Gulf. Jordan and Saudi Arabia agreed on terms in 1965 in which an exchange of small territories was agreed upon, in which Jordan was given extra land near Aqaba, which is a port. In 1922, Abd al Aziz ibn Abd ar Rahman Al Saud signed a pact called Moammara with British delegates representing Iraqi interests in which the boundary was defined between the future Saudi Arabia and Iraq. Per the regulations, the border in Abd al Aziz's territories of Najd and the eastern side of the provinces and the British colony of Kuwait was first controlled by Al Uqair in 1922. To avoid territorial disagreements, another diamond-shaped zone of about 5,790 kilometers was created which is south of Kuwait. Furthermore, Saudi Arabia and Kuwait signed a pact in 1965 which divided lands geographically, with each country administering half the resources. Saudi's oceanic entitlements constitute 12 nautical miles of its coast. There are also many islands and sea beds beyond the 12 nautical mile limit [5].

Culture

Saudi culture and religion are predominantly Islamic. Islam is followed by all Saudis, and they conduct their own political, legal, personal and economic lives per the principles of Islam. Saudi Arabia is the birthplace of Islam, so millions of Muslims visit Saudi Arabia every year. The majority of the population living in the Kingdom of Saudi Arabia is Sunni; however, there are significant numbers of Shia living on the eastern side of the coast and some other minority sects near the Yemen border. Muslims firmly believe in the second pillar of Islam, which is to pray five times a day, at dawn, noon, afternoon, evening and sunset. Since Friday is considered the holy day for Muslims, the culture is defined such that all businesses are shut down on Fridays, and the day is considered part of the weekend. Throughout the holy month of Ramadan, Muslims living in the Kingdom of Saudi Arabia are required to fast from dawn to dusk and are allowed to work for five to six hours per day. Per Saudi law and culture, non-Muslims are not allowed to drink, smoke and eat in the public during the month of Ramadan. However, non-Muslims are allowed to follow their religions outside the holy cities of the Muslims. The major celebrations that take place over all of Saudi Arabia that are specifically for Muslims are Eid-ul-Fitr after the holy month of Ramadan, which is on the first of Shawwal; Eid-ul-Adha, the day of animal sacrifice for Muslims, is at the end of Hajj and is a pilgrimage in honor of Prophet Ibrahim (A.S); and September 23 is considered Saudi National Day. Tribal and family culture are the basis of the social culture. As their family names suggest, different tribes of Saudis are conscious about their clan, heritage, extended family and nuclear family. Saudis are very responsible and cautious about their families. Their families are usually large, and there are joint family systems in extended families. Family members are close to each other, and Saudis are usually very hospitable when it comes to helping needy people or supporting anyone. Social divisions are only experienced between local and foreigners. Attitudes, beliefs and practices are commonly shared across economic divisions, which is considered the bridge which strengthens the relation between kinship and religion. Contemporary literature and classical Arabic poetry are always highly valued. Recitation of verses from the Holy Quran as well as poetry are commonly practiced at weddings and other major Saudi events. The novel has been popular among men and women because of influential writers from Egypt and the levant. Saudis are fond of painting, folks dancing and sculpture. Dancing with swords is a cultural representation of Saudis in their major events [6].

Climate

Saudi Arabia has a warm, dry desert climate with very high temperatures in most parts of the country. The southern part of the country has a reasonable temperature which can be less than 10 degrees Celsius in summers. During winter, the temperatures are moderate, but the nights are cold, the temperature sometimes dropping to the freezing point. Rainfall is most common on the Red Sea in March and April, and the rest of the country has low rainfall [7].

Education in Saudi Arabia

Saudi Arabia is spread out over an area of over 2 million square kilometers and has 13 administrative provinces [8]. Moreover, the population recorded in 2016 was approximately 32,430,000, with males and females making up 55.2% and 44.8%, respectively, and a large part of the population falls into the age bracket of 15–64 years [9]. Saudi Arabia follows a gender segregation policy throughout its public sector, which also includes universities; however, King Abdullah

University of Science and Technology and the health segments are excluded from this policy **[10]**.

Most of the higher education universities in the Kingdom of Saudi Arabia are public sector, which play a significant role in the development of the country **[11]**. Nonetheless, further research validates that although the country heavily relies on the revenue generated from oil, Saudi Arabia faces the same challenge that China has been facing which comes from economic diversity, and this challenge has made the quality of skills and knowledge a high priority **[10]**. Moreover, in view of the increasing population and the economy's growing demand, King Abdullah's scholarship program was developed in 2005 with a purpose to send students abroad to satisfy job market needs and fulfill the growing demand **[9]**.

The current status of higher education in Saudi Arabia

In 2005, when King Abdullah bin Abdul Aziz took the throne, there were only 7 public educational institutions (universities), but in 2015, this number increased to 28, with 9 private institutions. Although there was a steep decline in the prices of oil, a budget of $229.3 billion was announced in 2014, with $57.9 billion allocated for the education sector. This budget included distributions of approximately $3.28 billion for the renovation and finishing of the university campuses operating in the country **[12]**.

Several Saudi scholars have identified a deep connection between Islam and education in Saudi Arabia. It has been found in various studies that Saudi Arabia follows the Islamic philosophy towards education and that the root of the education system can be found in the principles of Islam **[13, 14]**. Moreover, scholarship-oriented policies have always been a part of the strategy of education designed by Al-Sauds **[15]**. Today, Saudi Arabia encourages and shows hospitality towards students who come from abroad to study in the Kingdom. The total number of non-locals who secured a scholarship to study at universities in Saudi Arabia was approximately 32,000 as of 2015. In addition, when one talks about the development and the existing status of Kingdom's education sector, then King Abdullah deserves significant credit because he was the one who came up with the scholarship program and the current government has expanded it exponentially with a great emphasis on research and development **[12]**. It is worth mentioning here that Saudi Arabia has the fifth-highest percentage of students acquiring their education abroad, and the most frequently chosen field of specialization by students is social sciences, engineering, health and basic sciences **[11]**.

Organizational structure

As per **[16]**, the Supreme Council of Higher Education (SCHE) remained the topmost authority governing higher education in the Kingdom of Saudi

Arabia and the King was the chairperson of the council, while other members included the rectors of the institutions and ministers and legislators from other institutions. The main focus of the Supreme Council of Higher Education was to govern the higher education system at the national level and harmonize educational policies with the policies and strategies of the country.

According to [16], the most significant achievement of the Supreme Council of Higher Education is the development of integrated higher education regulation and policy. The unified policies include those for the faculty, researchers, examinations and employment. The council had the responsibility of tackling an extensive array of issues which included the hiring of faculty and approval of textbooks, curricula, scholarships and policies related to admission and graduation. However, a major issue facing higher education institutions (HEIs) in the Kingdom of Saudi Arabia was their association with other governmental bodies because universities didn't have a complete hold on the employment system, and they had to follow the central employment system established by the government [16]. However, the new system of universities has given them autonomy for making decisions, hiring staff, and explore new avenues of sustainability.

Challenges in higher education

The education system of Saudi Arabia has constantly been trying to make progress and has been facing some major challenges which include productivity and quality of research, accreditation and improvement in education excellence. These issues have been pointed out by numerous writers, including Mazi and Altbach and Smith and Abouammoh [17, 18].

According to Mazi and Altbach, research is the lone characteristic of an educational institution that can be measured on a cross-cultural basis [17, 19]. Hence, research is identified as the major concern for universities where Saudi Arabia is found to be lacking, but it is trying very hard to overcome this lack with the new indicators showing it as an emerging country by number of publications and patents. The quality of the publications is also improving steadily and it seems researchers in the local universities are paying attention to the impact of research. Moreover, a research study has proved that the productivity of research contributes to an educational institution's overall ranking; therefore, this is a major challenge for the universities in the Kingdom [20].

Entrepreneurial education

Entrepreneurship is considered crucial for the growth of a nation; therefore, countries focus on improving the entrepreneurial capabilities of students to enhance potential spillover to the economy [21]. Students must realize that being an entrepreneur is not as easy as it looks because an entrepreneur is always on the hunt to revolutionize and then respond to a need or gap and try to make the most of it [22].

Therefore, there is a strong need to guide youth towards entrepreneurship because the young often select their career path during their studies [21]. However, most of the youth in the Kingdom of Saudi Arabia prefer to work in public sector organizations, which is a major challenge. Likewise, there are social blocks that result in an interruption in entrepreneurship. Entrepreneurs often do not share their success stories to encourage the youth [23]. However, the new initiatives by the Saudi government and private sector organizations by establishing incubators, accelerators, venture funds, and other investment opportunities have attracted local talent to establish their own startups and businesses. The Kingdom has also made it simpler for the foreign entrepreneurs to establish their startups with the ease of doing business.

e-learning and distance learning

There are numerous concepts that relate to the contemporary style of learning, and when it comes to modern styles of learning, there are the concepts of e-learning and distance learning [24]. In e-learning, technology is required by the learner, which often includes videos, touch screens or other types of media. e-learning is used when the learner and the teacher are separated [25]. Distance learning, on the other hand, is a completely different concept. This concept is applicable in a formal setting where one party is present. It is normally used when the student cannot be physically present due to a reason like illness or distance [26]. Hence, there is a clear difference between the two terms; they are not the same thing, as assumed by many individuals.

However, it is not always true that they cannot happen in the same place because while e-learning refers to the method of the delivery of teaching, distance learning is teaching delivered to people who may be halfway across the world. Hence, there is no reason the teacher can't use multimedia tools or other technology to deliver teaching to students who are at a distance [27]. The Saudi government has taken the following great initiatives which are used for e-learning and distance learning.

The National Centre for e-Learning and Distance Learning

In light of the growth in the distribution of resources from the Ministry of Higher Education (MOHE) to improve the system of education, many educational institutions have started to enhance their Information and Communication Technologies (ICT) groundwork [8]. In addition, educational institutions in the Kingdom of Saudi Arabia have begun to incorporate the use of technology in their education system, especially the use of the internet to deliver learning to students. Hence, this has proved a convenient and effective method for the delivery of learning **[29]**.

In 2007, the MOHE formed a center for distance learning and e-learning called National Center for e-Learning and Distance Learning (NCeL). The establishment was aimed at facilitating the many projects focused on encouraging Saudi educational institutions to adopt or embrace the use of technological tools for the delivery of teaching **[28]**. Furthermore, the NCEL assists Saudi universities with the required technology and training to deliver sessions online. Hence, the National Center for e-Learning and Distance Learning has formed a center to provide support and counseling called the Saudi Centre for Support and Counselling (SANEED) that offers academic assistance, recommendation and facilitation to the beneficiaries of e-learning **[29]**.

Saudi Digital Library

The Saudi Digital Library (SDL) was established in 2010 by the Ministry of Higher Education. The library was formed with the mission of backing the system of education and fulfilling the needs of research scholars and faculty in higher education **[30]**. The Saudi Digital Library has over 300,000 complete electronic books (e-books) under numerous scientific specializations. Moreover, the SDL has subscriptions to more than 300 local, international and regional publishers. Many authors have highlighted a significant issue in such electronic projects: ease of use. It is argued that if the system is not user friendly, users will discontinue using the system and take their work elsewhere **[31]**. SDL is the largest digital library in the Kingdom where students or faculty can access information for the purpose of education. Hence, the user experience contributes significantly to the usage of the system **[34]**.

Saudi Electronic University

The state of Saudi Arabia has seen many periods of development and enhancement in various sectors, including the educational sector, which have brought about an affluent boom in the country. This rapid growth is reflected in the living standards of the citizens and manifests in government expenditure on the development and growth of sectors, including the education sector **[33]**. Such development can be seen in the formation of the Saudi Electronic University (SEU) ordained by the Council of Higher Education in 2011. It is the 25th government university that has adopted the contemporary approach towards learning, that is, e-learning and distance learning **[33]**. Hence, the SEU has a strong vision to effectively contribute to the development of a knowledge economy and to convey a pioneering message to the society of the Kingdom of Saudi Arabia.

e-learning status in Saudi universities

The concept of e-learning was embraced in the Kingdom of Saudi Arabia and further enhanced with the introduction of the technology of computers and the internet. In 2007, the IT and National Communication plan was set out, and it has been driving the incorporation of ICT at all levels of learning in the universities of Saudi Arabia [34].

Moreover, Saudi Arabia educational institutions started establishing centers for distance learning and e-learning in the early 21st century, and among the early institutes to adopt this concept were King Fahd University of Petroleum and Minerals in 2003 and King Faisal University in 2008 [35]. However, institutions across the KSA have experienced continuous challenges and difficulties regarding the incorporation of e-learning, and approximately 30% to 40% of students and faculty demonstrate a significant level of dissatisfaction with e-learning [36]. In addition, among these challenges, computer literacy is the major one. However, once KSA resolves these challenges, the education system may be able to enhance the outcomes from its investment in e-learning and improve its status at a global level.

Saudi Arabia's macroeconomy

The Kingdom enjoys the largest and richest economy in the Arabian Peninsula [37]. Large-scale public works by the government and a high inflow of foreign direct investment in the country enable the Kingdom to be a regional power; however, its economy is still based on oil and has strong government control over its major economic activities [38]. Oil contributes around 83% to total exports and government earning [39]. A recent report highlighted that the country has about 16% of the total petroleum reserves, which gives it a lead role in OPEC and also accounts for 87% of the revenue in the budget, that is, around 42% of the GDP, and contributes around 90% of export earnings [40].

Economic performance

Saudi Arabia's oil exports are facing tough competition from the United States of America's shale oil exports. This affects both a decrease in current account surplus to 34.22 billion USD from 72.33 billion USD and also an increase in the public debt to GDP ratio, which stood at 23.2% in 2019. The budget deficit is also expected to rise to 28.4% in 2020 and 33.6% in 2021. Inflation is also expected to grow due to a decrease in house rentals, as around 2 million foreign laborers have left the Kingdom since 2017 [41]. The main drivers of the macroeconomy are given subsequently and indicate the economic outlook of the Kingdom for the last 5 years, see table 1.1:

Table 1.1 Economic outlook of the Kingdom for the last 5 years

Main indicator	2016	2017	2018	2019 (e)	2020 (e)
GDP *(Billions USD)*	644.94	686.74	769.88e	795.58	815.32
GDP *(Constant Prices, Annual % Change)*	1.7	−0.9	2.2	2.4	1.9
GDP per Capita *(USD)*	20,318	21,096	23,187	23,491	23,602
General Government Gross Debt *(in % of GDP)*	13.1	17.2	19.4e	20.4	21.2
Inflation Rate *(%)*	2.0	−0.9	2.6	2.0	2.3
Unemployment Rate *(% of the Labor Force)*	5.6	6.0	0.0	0.0	0.0
Current Account *(Billions USD)*	−23.87	15.23	64.67	69.99	62.23
Current Account *(in % of GDP)*	−3.7	2.2	8.4	8.8	7.6

Source: IMF – World Economic Outlook Database, October 2018

To counter the growing worries about the economy's status quo, the Kingdom has launched a comprehensive development policy with the title Vision 2030 as a paradigm shift. The plan not only covers financial aspects, that is, fiscal consolidations and economic diversification, but also includes social beneficial areas. The leadership of the Kingdom has already taken steps on issues like allowing women to drive, opening entertainment outlets and movie theaters, economy diversification plans, and the introduction of value-added tax (VAT) on the services. The leadership believes that long-standing reforms are crucial for economic diversification, including labor reforms, opening the markets for foreign investors and privatization of public companies [42]. The authorities have implemented plans to reform water and energy prices after introducing value-added tax. Transparency is also ensured in public procurement and government spending. The Budget 2020 document stressed creating more jobs, economic diversification and generating more revenue through non-oil revenue. The government approved Budget 2020 on December 9, 2019 [43], which revealed that revenue was reduced due to oil price volatility and lower production, and hence expenditures for the upcoming years were lowered by 2.7% to 1,020 billion SAR. Although some reforms have taken place, the authorities in the Kingdom still face challenges, including the foreign direct investment (FDI) and unemployment. Dealing with the oil crises and other issues seems to have slowed down the progress of implementation of the reforms, which has also led to economic slow-down. However, the leaderships is determined to tackle these challenges which seems quite obvious by the new reforms and meeting the demands in global sluggish market.

Oil–gas–minerals

As discussed earlier, oil and gas are by far the most important sector of Saudi Arabia's economy. The sector contributes the maximum share to the earnings

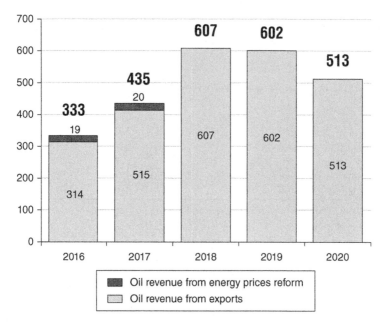

Figure 1.1 Revenue from oil exports/resources **[20]**

and GDP of the Kingdom and mostly runs on surplus. It is also an international tool for political and financial influence **[44]**. The Kingdom's law (Royal Decree No. A/90 dated 27/8/1412 H [1 March 1992]) gives powers to the government of Saudi Arabia to control all the wealth from the oil and gas sectors. Previously the Ministry of Petroleum and Mineral Resources and currently the Ministry of Energy, Industry and Mineral Resources dealt with the policies of oil and gas of the Kingdom. The economy of the Kingdom largely remained dependent on oil since its discovery. The economy was affected several times due to fluctuation of prices and more recently in 2014, when oil prices on the international market went under US$35 per barrel. The reserves of the Kingdom went to $750 billion in 2015 from $30 billion in 2003. In 2018, the Kingdom cut down production to achieve higher prices to meet structural and fiscal reforms.

The budget revealed that oil revenue is expected to decrease to SAR 513 billion from SAR 602 billion in 2020, mainly due to price volatility and growing competition. Considering this scenario, the focus is on Vision 2030 to diversify the kingdom's economy and move away from oil dependence. But presently, the role of oil and gas in the country's economy is inevitable. As far as the gas reservoir of the country is concerned, in February 2020, Saudi Aramco said that it has found 200 trillion cubic feet of gas reserves, and production will begin in early 2024. The country's minister for energy aims to make the country a gas exporter. Aramco plans to invest $110 billion in the gas reserves of Jafurah field. This means that with the reserves of gas overlooked due to oil supplies for more than half a century, the country aims to become gas exporter in the coming years [45].

The focus of the Kingdom's Vision 2030 is on economic diversification, import substitution and increase in exports. This will lead to a search for new industries other than oil to bring in investments so that the targets will be achieved. The mining sector of the Kingdom is one the government believes will contribute significantly to the GDP. Structural reforms are planned to invite private sector investment, create more jobs, review licensing processes, funding methods and so on. The country is rich in mineral resources, and to date, 48 minerals have been identified, including limestone, silver, zeolites, rock wool, olivine, marble, magnesium, pozzolan, high-grade silica sand, granite, gold, zinc and so on [48]. The extraction of these minerals is taking place at high speed, especially in high-demand industries, that is, steel and aluminum [45].

Public and private sectors

As the Kingdom's Vision 2030 is based on diversity of revenue streams, the main objective is to make the private sector more interesting and attractive for citizens. This will help create more opportunities for locals in the job market and will also create financial benefits for the economy. In the short run, this might be slow, but in the longer run, this will be compatible with the economy [46]. For decades, youth were given the opportunity to join the public sector with decent perks and benefits and ignore the private sector, which resulted in an increase in foreign workers in the private sector, and this contributes about 85% of the workforce in the private sector [47]. The new leaderships aims to fill the private sector with local employment up to 50% and cut down the size of the civil service. This radical change might bring social issues, but it will help reduce unemployment in the Kingdom using the National Transformation Programme (NTP). Through the NTP, the authorities are aiming to create a minimum of 450,000 jobs in the private sector for locals in non-oil areas such as tourism and mining, and, at the same time, the plan is to reduce civil servants by 20% to decrease the dominant role of the state [47]. The labor ministry is also studying labor regulations and effective measures to hire more Saudi locals in private businesses.

The budget document reveals that the Kingdom's economy is diversifying and has a positive outlook, especially in indicators like ease of doing business. The country moved up 30 places, reached 62 and scored 71.6 out of 100 in the ease of doing business index. This shows the implementation of Vision 2030 is moving in the right direction. The document shows that the non-oil private sector has shown improvements in 2019. It is pertinent to say that in the future, the main drivers of the Kingdom will be the non-oil sector if Vision 2030 is fully realized [43].

Macroeconomic development

The Kingdom of Saudi Arabia has taken several steps in light of Vision 2030 to diversify its revenue streams as stated earlier e.g. increased spending on infrastructure; widening the tax net, that is, imposing an excise tax on drinks and a levy on foreign workers to improve the efficiency of expenditures and opening up the country for foreign investors to invest in different sectors such as mining, technology, financial sector and so on. These prudent measures have been taken by the authorities of the Kingdom to increase non-oil revenues in the years to come; however, oil is undoubtedly the main contributor to the Kingdom's revenue at the moment [43]. Figure 1.2 shows the performance taken from the budget document of non-oil revenues that continue to grow.

The infographic suggests that in the last five years, the Kingdom has clearly tried to increase revenue streams other than oil. For 2020, non-oil revenues are expected to reach 38% of total revenues of the budget. The diversity in the revenue streams is in accordance with Vision 2030. Moreover, the education sector is taking the highest share of the budget, as the government has planned to invest SAR 193 billion, which is 18.9% of the budgeted expenditure. The main idea behind education is to increase the skills of the youth,

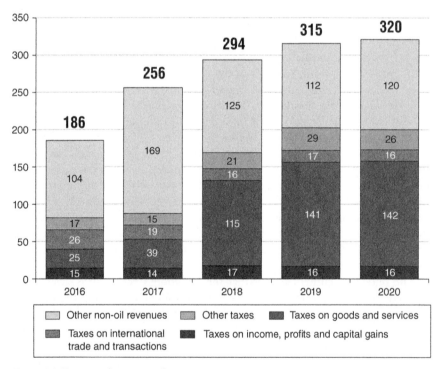

Figure 1.2 Revenue from non-oil resources

Source: KPMG's review on Saudi Arabia budget 2020 [20]

which will support industry and decrease unemployment. Moreover, capacity building of education staff is also a priority of the government to enhance the research culture and contribute to a knowledge economy. The second strongest sector in terms of expenditure is the military, which takes around 17.8% of the total expenditure budget. The country plans to invest in R&D initiative programs for defense assembly and production. Vision 2030 aims to localize defense expenditure by 50% by creating notable developments in the military-industrial sector. Healthcare remains the third largest sector to take a share of the expenditure budget, that is, 16.4%. As per Vision 2030, the government aims to privatize 295 health facilities and increase new skilled labor by creating more medical colleges. An e-health strategic framework is also planned to adopt digital information systems in the sector. The next major aim of the budget is to improve the infrastructure, including transport, desalination plants, strategic reservoirs, transmission pipelines, sewage plants and so on. The National Industrial Developing and Logistics Program (NIDLP) aims to improve the Kingdom's industrial capabilities to have a manufacturing base within the country **[43]**.

Conclusion

The Kingdom of Saudi Arabia is a land of opportunities with rich history and culture. As the biggest country and biggest economy on the Arabian Peninsula, the Kingdom is blessed with natural resources. The current leadership is determined to make a radical socioeconomical change in the country. It has potential for international investors to invest and make decent returns. With a Vision 2030 approach, the Kingdom's conventional policy to rely on oil will be changed, and the country will see revenue streams from non-oil resources. The policy implementations in education, research and innovation will also bring fruitful results for the job market and the economy.

References

1 World Bank 2018, World Development Indicators database, Saudi Arabia Country Profile, World Bank, viewed 12 March 2020, https://databank.worldbank.org/views/reports/reportwidget.aspx?Report_Name=CountryProfile&Id=b450fd57&tbar=y&dd=y&inf=n&zm=n&country=SAU

2 Onsman, A., 2010. Dismantling the perceived barriers to the implementation of national higher education accreditation guidelines in the Kingdom of Saudi Arabia. *Journal of Higher Education Policy and Management, 32*(5), pp. 511–519.

3 Alhawsawi, S., 2013. Investigating student experiences of learning English as a foreign language in a preparatory programme in a Saudi University (Doctoral dissertation, University of Sussex).

4 World Population Review, 2020. Saudi Arabia population, world population review, viewed on 3 March 2020, <http://worldpopulationreview.com/countries/saudi-arabia-population/>

5 Metz, H.C. ed., 1993. *Saudi Arabia: A country study* (Vol. 550, No. 51), Federal Research Division, Library of Congress, Washington, D.C.

6 Commisceo Global Consulting, 2019. *Deeply religious, culturally conservative and geographically challenging.* The kingdom of Saudi Arabia can be tough for foreigners, Commisceo Global Consulting, viewed on 3 March 2020, <www.commisceo-global.com/resources/country-guides/saudi-arabia-guide>

7 Weather & climate, Climate and Average Weather in Saudi Arabia, Weather & Climate, viewed on 3 March 2020, <https://weather-and-climate.com/average-monthly-Rainfall-Temperature-Sunshine-in-Saudi-Arabia>

8 Hamdan, A., 2013. An exploration into "private" higher education in Saudi Arabia: Improving quality and accessibility?. *The ACPET Journal for Private Higher Education*, 2(2), p. 33.

9 Alamri, M., 2011. Higher education in Saudi Arabia. *Journal of Higher Education Theory and Practice*, 11(4), pp. 88–91.

10 Hilal, K.T., 2013. Between the fears and hopes for a different future for the nation-states: Scholarship programs in Saudi Arabia and United Arab Emirates from a public policy standpoint. *International Journal of Higher Education*, 2(2), pp. 195–210.

11 Alharbi, E.A.R., 2016. Higher education in Saudi Arabia: Challenges to achieving world-class recognition. *International of Journal of Culture and History*, 2(4), pp. 169–172.

12 Pavan, A., 2016. Higher education in Saudi Arabia: Rooted in heritage and values, aspiring to progress. *International Research in Higher Education*, 1(1), pp. 91–100.

13 Alsubaie, A. and Jones, K., 2017. An overview of the current state of women's leadership in higher education in Saudi Arabia and a proposal for future research directions. *Administrative Sciences*, 7(4), p. 36.

14 Al-Sudairy, H.T., 2017. *Modern woman in the kingdom of Saudi Arabia: Rights, challenges and achievements.* Cambridge Scholars Publishing, Newcastle, U.K.

15 Pavan, A., 2017. Saudi Arabia approaching 2030: The shift from quantitative to qualitative ambitions in education, enhancing human development. *International Research in Higher Education*, 2(2), pp. 8–14.

16 Alkhazim, M.A., 2003. Higher education in Saudi Arabia: Challenges, solutions, and opportunities missed. *Higher Education Policy*, 16(4), pp. 479–486.

17 Mazi, A. and Altbach, P.G., 2013. Dreams and realities: The world-class idea and Saudi Arabian higher education. In *Higher Education in Saudi Arabia* (pp. 13–26). Dordrecht: Springer.

18 Smith, L. and Abouammoh, A., 2013. *Higher education in Saudi Arabia.* Dordrecht: Springer.

19 Rasheed, M.M., 2002. *The history of Saudi Arabia.* London: Cambridge University Press.

20 Rauhvargers, A., 2011. *Global university rankings and their impact* (p. 85). Brussels: European University Association.

21 Hameed, I. and Irfan, Z., 2019. Entrepreneurship education: A review of challenges, characteristics and opportunities. *Entrepreneurship Education*, 2(3–4), pp. 135–148.

22 Autio, E., Nambisan, S., Thomas, L.D. and Wright, M., 2018. Digital affordances, spatial affordances, and the genesis of entrepreneurial ecosystems. *Strategic Entrepreneurship Journal*, 12(1), pp. 72–95.

23 Mueller, S., 2011. Increasing entrepreneurial intention: Effective entrepreneurship course characteristics. *International Journal of Entrepreneurship and Small Business*, 13(1), pp. 55–74.

24 Zhang, D., Zhao, J.L., Zhou, L. and Nunamaker, J.F., 2004. Can e-learning replace classroom learning? *Communications of the ACM*, 47(5), pp. 75–79. https://doi.org/10.1145/986213.986216

25 Derouin, R.E., Fritzsche, B.A. and Salas, E., 2005. E-learning in organizations. *Journal of Management*, 31(6), pp. 920–940.

26 James, W.B. and Gardner, D.L., 1995. Learning styles: Implications for distance learning. *New Directions for Adult and Continuing Education, 1995*(67), pp. 19–31.

27 Moore, J.L., Dickson-Deane, C. and Galyen, K., 2011. e-learning, online learning, and distance learning environments: Are they the same? *The Internet and Higher Education, 14*(2), pp. 129–135.

28 Alharbi, A., 2013. *E-learning in the KSA: A taxonomy of learning methods in Saudi Arabia.* Auckland: Auckland University of Technology.

29 AlMegren, A. and Yassin, S.Z., 2013. Learning object repositories in e-learning: Challenges for learners in Saudi Arabia. *European Journal of Open, Distance and E-learning, 16*(1), pp. 115–130.

30 Alasem, A.N., 2013, October. Evaluating the usability of Saudi Digital Library's interface (SDL). In *Proceedings of the world congress on engineering and computer science* (Vol. 1, pp. 178–181).

31 Alasem, A.N., 2014. Measuring the usability of the interface of the Saudi Digital Library. In *Transactions on engineering technologies*. Edited by Haeng Kon Kim, Sio-Iong Ao and Mahyar A. Amouzegar (pp. 305–313). Dordrecht: Springer.

32 Taala, W., 2019. Impact of Saudi Digital Library (SDL) to Saudi research output: A review. *Open Access Library Journal, 6*(03), p. 1.

33 Alshathri, S. and Male, T., 2015. Students and instructors perceptions of blended learning in the first electronic university in the Arab world (Saudi Electronic University). British Education Studies Association Annual Conference 2015, Cardiff Metropolitan University (pp. 1–23).

34 Al-Masaud, K. and Gawad, A., 2014. Impediments of activating e-learning in higher education institutions in Saudi Arabia. *International Journal of Advanced Computer Science and Applications, 5*(4), pp. 12–18.

35 Al-Asmari, A.M. and Khan, M.S.R., 2014. E-learning in Saudi Arabia: Past, present and future. *Near and Middle Eastern Journal of Research in Education, 2014*(1), p. 2.

36 Alkhalaf, S., Nguyen, J., Nguyen, A. and Drew, S., 2011. *The potential role of collaborative learning in enhancing e-learning systems: Evidence from Saudi Arabia.* Australian Society for Computers in Learning in Tertiary Education, Hobart, Australia.

37 Hameed, I. and Irfan, Z., 2019. Entrepreneurship education: A review of challenges, characteristics and opportunities. *Entrepreneurship Education, 2*, pp. 135–148.

38 IndexMundi, 2019. Saudi Arabia economy. *IndexMundi*, viewed on 4 January 2020, <www.indexmundi.com/saudi_arabia/economy_overview.html>

39 SAMA, 2017. Saudi Arabian monetary authority: Annual statistics 2017, viewed on 12 February 2020, SAMA, <www.sama.gov.sa/en-US/EconomicReports/Pages/Yearly Statistics.aspx>

40 CIA, 2018. The world factbook. *CIA*, viewed on 2 March 2020, <www.cia.gov/library/ publications/the-world-factbook/fields/207.html>

41 Nordea, 2020. Saudi Arabia: Economic and political overview. *Nordea*, viewed on 1 March 2020, <www.nordeatrade.com/en/explore-new-market/saudi-arabia/economical-context>

42 Dr. Sara Bazoobandi, 2019. The future of economic reforms in Saudi Arabia. *Les clés du Moyen-Orient*, viewed on 3 March 2020, <www.lesclesdumoyenorient.com/ The-future-of-Economic-Reforms-in-Saudi-Arabia-by-Dr-Sara-Bazoobandi>

43 Dr. Abdullah Al Fozan, 2019. Kingdom of Saudi Arabia budget report. *KPMG*, viewed on 2 March 2020, <https://assets.kpmg/content/dam/kpmg/sa/pdf/2019/Kingdomof Saudi%20Arabia2020BudgetReport.pdf>

44 Shearman & Sterling LLP, 2016. *Saudi Arabia: Oil and gas in the kingdom of Saudi Arabia – An overview.* Mondaq Ltd, viewed on 2 March 2020, <www.mondaq.com/saudiarabia/

Energy-and-Natural-Resources/532740/Mining-In-The-Kingdom-Of-Saudi-Arabia-An-Overview>

45 Cronin, S., 2020. Who flares, wins: Saudi Arabia bets big on gas again. *Arab News*, viewed on 2 March 2020, <www.arabnews.com/node/1631786/business-economy>

46 Omar Al-Ubaydli, 2019. Why Saudi Arabia should consider increasing some public sector salaries. *Al Arabiya English*, viewed on 4 March 2020, <http://english.alarabiya.net/en/views/news/middle-east/2019/06/09/Why-Saudi-Arabia-should-consider-increasing-some-public-sector-salaries.html>

47 Kerr, S., 2016. Privatising Saudi Arabia's public sector. *Financial Times*, viewed on 4 March 2020, <www.ft.com/content/4dc29106-bff6-11e6-9bca-2b93a6856354>

48 Shearman & Sterling LLP, 2016. *Saudi Arabia: Mining in the kingdom of Saudi Arabia – An overview*. Mondaq Ltd, viewed on 2 March 2020, www.mondaq.com/saudiarabia/Energy-and-Natural-Resources/532740/Mining-In-The-Kingdom-Of-Saudi-Arabia-An-Overview

2 Economic development vision of the Gulf Cooperation Council

Muhammad Babar Khan, Sadia Iqbal and Irfan Hameed

The economic development of any country depends on three cornerstones, namely research, innovation and entrepreneurship [1]. All the countries under the umbrella of the Gulf Cooperation Council have collectively taken up a decision to rejuvenate their economies and bring in a revolution which will benefit their homelands as well as their people. Their first priority was to transform from a natural resources-based economy to a knowledge-based economy, and to this end, they have taken steps to reform their higher education systems and research institutions [1]. This has led to great interest in GCC countries in establishing research and innovation centers along with entrepreneurship programs to give them an edge to transfer their knowledge and tech-savvy skills from universities to industries [1]. For innovation and economic growth, various things are of great importance, including the digital world. The key ingredient in the digital world is the internet, and smart cards serve as an intermediary between people's physical and digital identities. Additionally, these smart identity cards link citizen's trust and confidence in online transactions strongly together, and this is the most crucial ingredient for the growth of the digital economy [2].

The GCC has six countries under its wings, and each has different components as part of its Vision 2025 or Vision 2030. Though all are striving to shift from an oil-based economy to a knowledge-based economy, each encapsulates its own strategies, which shall be reviewed in the upcoming literature review.

Oman's economic development vision

Oman's Vision 2020 came into existence after many developments in its plan, starting from a five-year plan (1976–1980). The Omani economy eventually gained a head start toward a steady development plan with the vision to transform its economy which resulted in Vision 2020. Before Vision 2020, Oman was always a middle-income economy that was highly dependent on oil resources, but Vision 2020 had very diversified plans, which changed the entire canvas of Oman's economy [3]. In terms of development, its economy now has a variety of diversification, industrialization and privatization, resulting in more job opportunities for young Omanis heading out on career paths. Sultan Qaboos

Bin Saeed made it a point that Vision 2020 outline the economic and social goals which revolve around the economic and financial stability of the country, reforming the government's role in the economy, encouraging more participation of the private sector, Omani economic globalization, human capital development for the Omani workforce and bringing diversity into economic and national income sources [3]. All these components are the stairs Oman needs to climb in order to reach a better economic development destination, and that is what it is striving for.

A major component of Oman's long-term diversification strategy is commonly known as the industrial sector. This is the groundwork and cornerstone of its diversification strategy, as it links its social and economic development, which ultimately connects to employment opportunities for young Omanis. This sector promotes accelerated growth much more quickly than other sectors and ensures more avenues for jobs. Other sectors like the tourism industry, health and insurance, banking and finance, agriculture, aviation, railway projects and so on contribute to the economy, but not as significantly as the industrial sector. Oman's mineral industry now also contributes to its GDP, which once used to be dependent only on depleting oil resources. The main reason to convert Oman's economy from oil based to knowledge based was to bring in diversification so as to give its economy a boost in terms of globalization. Oman's mineral resources include chromite, zinc, silicon, limestone and so on, and many global investors are greatly attracted to these, as they are intended to give fruitful results and contribute greatly towards the country's GDP. The mineral sector also contributes towards the national development process, which in turn clears the path for young Omanis in terms of high-earning jobs and national economic success [3].

Another factor which plays a very prominent role in the growth of a country's economy is its infrastructure [3]. It is said that natural beauty lies in the eyes of the beholder; likewise, a country's economy and development are enhanced via its beautification. One of the determinant factors for Oman's sustainable development is its continuous investment in its infrastructure, promising flourishing growth of its economy. Oman's government has been giving special focus to its infrastructure in terms of airports, seaports, education, hospitals, health centers and various other infrastructure projects, which have added another feather to the cap of its economy [3].

Human capital development is the need of the times. Oman's government has developed various training and development programs where young Omanis and other nationals are trained in various skills and competencies to promote employment opportunities in the private sector [3]. This has been created due to a policy enacted by the government called Omanization, which ensures that expatriate workers will be replaced by trained Omani personnel so as to reduce dependency on expatriate manpower and open up new opportunities for nationals [4–8]. Specific quotas have been set by the government in various industries to give more opportunities to nationally trained Omanis rather than foreigners [3, 4–8]. The various benefits the government will see due to this Omanization policy include less public spending on subsidized services like electricity, health and so on that are consumed mainly by expatriates. Second, substituting Omanis for foreign workers would help reduce Oman's payment deficit balance as well because it is directly proportional to workers' remittances. Workers' remittances, which were USD 1.7 billion in 1996, will drop automatically when national Omanis replace the expatriate workforce. This reduction will positively affect Oman's balance of payment deficit, resulting in better economic prospects for Oman [4–8]. Additionally, Omanis taking over for the expatriate workforce would contribute to faster GDP growth potential, as domestic spending would increase due to the multiplier effect [4–8]. Furthermore, under the Omanization policy, the SANAD entrepreneurial development program has been initiated to support young entrepreneurs with minimal cost to start their small businesses, helping them to grow in trade and professions [3, 4–8]. All in all, keeping the previous factors in mind, the Omanization policy is well on its way to successful economic growth if followed in the same way and with the same zeal, with major prioritization of education and training.

The *In-Country Value Development Blue Print Strategy* (ICV) of the Sultanate of Oman 2013–2020 plays a vital role in Oman's economic development vision. This strategy concentrates on retaining all the expenditure within the country to aid in job opportunities, economic development, human capital resource development and establishment of new industries locally to fuel productivity, with a major emphasis on the oil and gas sector [3]. The aim of the ICV is to enhance the value of goods, services and skills in the oil and gas sector so as to stimulate local production, which would in turn decrease the import ratio and offer more opportunities to nationals. The dependency on expatriates would decrease, and nationals would enjoy a lucrative share of the opportunities offered by Oman, thereby increasing their contribution toward the oil and gas sector [3]. These sectors have an ICV mission and strategy to achieve short- and long-term goals. The ICV mission states, "Developing a competitive and sustainable local supply market: goods, services and skills . . . TOGETHER!" and its strategy states, "Leveraging the oil and gas industry collaborative efforts to progressively and effectively develop the Omani supply market and enhance the ICV development environment" [9]. ICV's mission and strategy collectively prove that Oman's national economy would get a boost if competitive and sustainable local goods, services and skills were developed. Additionally, its strategy to use oil and gas resources to their maximum advantage would definitely boost the Omani supply market and present an improved picture of the ICV growth environment. In 2012, there were 22,369 Omanis working in the oil and gas sector, and the workforce Omanis need by 2020 is 72,704 as a result of ICV strategy and part of Oman's Vision 2020 [9]. According to Ministry resources, Accenture Management Consulting – an international consultant agency – has been given the task of documenting a blueprint ICV plan for Oman [10]. This study would help in carrying out a comprehensive analysis of the supply and demand gap of goods, services and skills – the three important elements of ICV's mission – required by 2020 [10].

Small and medium-sized enterprises (SMEs) have played a significant role in stimulating Oman's economy. The Omani government has, in the past few years, placed special emphasis on funding SMEs so that they may compete on international grounds, leading to a better economy per Vision 2020. To accomplish this, an independent body was created, the Public Authority for Small and Medium Enterprises Development (PASMED), which aims at encouraging young entrepreneurs and providing them necessary assistance in terms of technical education, marketing, finance, training and so on, as these enterprises would further help encourage Oman's economic development. More SMEs mean better job creation, as entrepreneurship leads to a sizeable increase in job prospects [3].

Oman has also initiated a rail network which will also contribute to its economy and serve as a router between major ports, industrial areas and free zones within a refined GCC network [3]. Oman's Vision 2020 also includes a port and industrial zone project in one of the newest industrial areas, the Duqm region. This will be a major breakthrough in the history of Oman's economic development, as the port will act as a strong link to unlock potential growth opportunities [3].

Another sector which greatly contributes to Oman's economic development is its tourism sector. This sector fills in the socio-economic development gap and encourages appreciation of the Sultanate's natural cultural heritage and traditional hospitality. Economic transformation is a promising factor of the tourism sector, as it ensures economic diversification, preservation of cultural integrity and protection of the sultanate's environment [3]. The latest statistics state that tourism accounts for 2.4% of Oman's GDP, and it is expected to grow to 3% by 2020 [3]. The Omani government has a whole-hearted wish that Omani nationals play a significant role in all areas of trade and professional employment. For the same reason, training and education are being greatly prioritized and have served as a cornerstone in all the five-year planning of the sultanate. The Ministry of Education is committed to the cause of providing modernized education – while maintaining traditional values – which is prominent in the Sultanate's educational programs designed to compete in the modern world [3].

Taxation is also the icing on the cake for Oman's economy. In 2009, Oman introduced a new tax law which concentrated on the elimination of discrimination in tax rates between foreign branches and Omani companies. Furthermore, it was decided that 12% would be a unified rate for all regardless of whether the branch is local or foreign. This was a strategy initiated by Omani government which further helped the flourishing of Oman's economic development [3]. Another major shift introduced by the new tax law is a changeover from a territorial tax system to a global tax system whereby the tax rate is obligatory on any revenue earned outside Oman's territory, giving a boost to its economy on the whole [3].

Keeping all the previous ingredients in mind, Oman's shift from an oil-based economy to a diversified economy is surely a positive step. Though challenging, its economic and social goals, visions and strategies for 2020 will change the canvas of its economy. Despite the various challenges, Oman is striving for better economic prospects, and its diversity will definitely pay off in the near future.

Qatar's economic development vision

A remarkable social and economic transformation has been achieved by Qatar in less than a generation. The reason behind its spectacular achievement has been capitalization on its rich natural resources. Qatar's National Vision 2030 (QNV 2030), launched in October 2008, articulates a long-term development outcome plan for Qatar's economy. It was developed by His Highness Hamad bin Khalifa Al-Thani [11]. According to him, comprehensive development is the goal for which Qatar is striving in order to provide growth and prosperity for its people [12]. The foundation for QNV 2030 has been laid on Qatar's permanent constitution's guiding principles and revolves around four imperative pillars which are closely interrelated. These significant pillars include human development, social development, economic development and environmental development [11]. Each pillar of QNV 2030 has clearly defined goals and long-term outcomes with clear interconnections with each other. In order to achieve these outcomes and ensure a positive economic impact, one has to pass through challenging hurdles, and therefore Qatar has agreed to balance five important and critical strategies which are of paramount importance if the four important pillars of QNV 2030 are to be achieved and implemented. These include 1) modernizing the economy but preserving traditions simultaneously, 2) clearly balancing the needs of both the current and future generations, 3) as a result of economic growth, strategically managing growth and uncontrolled expansion, 4) managing the size and quality of the expatriate workforce and the chosen path leading to development, and 5) managing social, economic and environmental development [11]. According to a 2008 report, Qatar has been and continues to strive to make detectable progress in polishing human capital development. Lately, out of 179 countries, Qatar has embarked on a new journey from the 57th to 34th position in the United Nations Development Program's (UNDP) Human Development Index between the years 1997 and 2006. Human and social development and preserving environmental development are the most challenging key factors and should harmonize together. In the big picture, they are all interlinked. Sustainable development can have an adverse outcome if economic growth is too high, urban development is too rapid and population growth is high [11]. This means urban development and economic growth are inversely proportional to sustainable development. This inverse relationship can further project a risk to water security achievement, marine environment security and preservation and climate change long-term impact reduction, and, simultaneously, adjustment to the expected consequences of climate change would be at risk, too [11].

In the upcoming sections, we will explore QNV 2030's four pillars in more detail.

First pillar – human development

A very important pillar of QNV 2030 is human development. Qataris have long exploited oil and gas resources, but as part of Vision 2030, they need to shift from only being an oil-based economy to a knowledge-based economy. This international order is extremely competitive and challenging, and for future economic progress, it is essential that the Qatari people develop those skills required for an ideal knowledge-based economy. In order to meet the challenge, the Qatari government is giving prior importance to education and health care. Also, advanced educational institutes and health care systems are being established, and special focus is being given to increasing active participation of Qataris in the labor force. At the same time, steps are being taken to attract expatriates in all fields to increase the workforce. Education plays a vital role in social progress and is considered its basic pillar. State-of-the-art and modernized educational facilities are being planned to be provided to students which would be competitive to those being provided anywhere in the world. This state-of-the-art system will provide citizens with all the training and skills required to reach their full potential and prepare them to reach an unprecedented level of success so that they may quickly adapt to changes in order to reach their long-term goals [12]. Skillful training would definitely lead to innovation, creativity and analytical and high-order thinking skills. This will in turn promote respect for Qatari societal values and at the same time make way for interaction with other nations [12]. Furthermore, human development support requires a research center where quality scientific research and intellectual activity may be carried out, and Qataris aspire to the same.

Likewise, in order to improve health care systems, Qatar aspires to develop an integrated system for health care competitive with world-class standards which will meet the needs of existing and future generations and provide increasingly healthy and long lives for all citizens. Qatar aspires to make these facilities available to its entire population, as its goal is to provide equality to existing and future generations with no element of discrimination [12].

The foreseeable future of Qatar requires the workforce to manage the rapidly diversifying economy. Since the local workforce will not be enough to meet the requirements, Qatar will have to take support from expatriate workers to make up for its shortages. The right mix of skills will be required to achieve a diversified economy; therefore, appropriate incentives need to be offered to expatriate workers. Additionally, ensuring the rights and safety of expatriate workers requires institutional arrangements [12].

The human development pillar, if it adheres to these goals, will enable Qatar to achieve a diversified economy, as skills, expertise, education, health care and safeguarding the rights of expatriates will boost its economy, and skillful, healthy and educated citizens will definitely transform its economy.

Second pillar – social development

Social development is also a very important pillar of QNV 2030. For a prosperous economic transformation, Qatar aspires to develop and advance its social dimensions by giving its citizens enough room to nurture their abilities effectively and flexibly for the requirements of the era. Furthermore, it aspires to preserve strong and coherent families that enjoy a lucrative share of support, care and social protection. As part of social development, women will also be given a chance to assume an important role in all walks of life, especially by participating in economic and political decision-making. Qatari society is a mixture of various values, including justice, benevolence, freedom, equality and high morals all in one package, and it will promote openness towards other cultures, keeping in mind its Arab and Islamic identity. Moreover, it will ensure that all social dimensions are distributed equally among its citizens, as its motive is to balance rights and opportunities equally among current and future generations. Qatar plays an important role in the framework of the Gulf Cooperation Council, and through its social development pillar articulated in QNV 2030, it will aspire to promote its role in the GCC, the Islamic Conference and the Arab League. As a social development goal, Qatar will contribute to attaining internal security and peace and will dedicatedly fulfill its international commitments as a responsible member of the international community economically, culturally and politically [12].

Third pillar – economic development

Economic prosperity and steady improvement in livelihood will be based on a vibrant Qatari economy. Economic development is the third pillar of QNV 2030 and encapsulates each aspect of society. Wise management of exhaustible resources is required to sustain prosperity over a long period of time to ensure that future generations are fully equipped with ample resources to meet their future aspirations. An important part of this wise management is to make sure that optimum utilization of these resources is secured and an equilibrium between reserves and production is created, along with a state-of-the-art balance between economic diversification and non-renewable hydrocarbon resource diminution [12]. Converting these natural assets into financial wealth will open avenues to invest in world-class infrastructure and help in promoting economic development. At the same time, investing in these natural assets will help in building a highly skilled and prolific work force, which will in turn play an imperative role in the development of entrepreneurship and innovation capabilities. All this, if attained, will constitute a major turning point in Qatari's diversified economy and enable it to improve its positioning as the major hub for knowledge and gain a high value for industrial and service activities. All this involves challenges, and Qatar is well prepared to dive in, equipped with its vision and dedication, to achieve its goals [12].

The first challenge facing Qatar's vision to encourage economic development is that the private sector must take steps to play an central role in achieving sustainable development. For this to be carried out, it is essential that entrepreneurs be trained to be skilled so that the private sector may carry out its role effectively and also provide financial and non-financial support to small and medium-sized enterprises. Qatar has already made an effort to build a political and organizational climate that relates to the business sector. In a nutshell, massive steps are further required to enhance competitiveness and attract investment in order to facilitate Qatar's becoming a vibrant and highly borderless international economy.

A second challenge which stands in the path of achieving the full potential of economic development for Qatar is finding a path which will lead to prosperity but at the same time avoid economic imbalances and stresses. This can be better understood by keeping the scenario in mind that if inflation becomes entrenched and different development projects are introduced into the system in the same time, it would become difficult to handle burgeoning demands for public services – where does Qatar stand in this situation? In order to attenuate risks, it is essential that a skillful and farsighted economic management strategy be implemented by effective institutions.

There are other challenges waiting around the corner, but in order to meet all these challenges and achieve a vibrant economic development platform, it is mandatory that Qatar's economic strategy be prepared for the upcoming risks that could limit it in achieving its long-term goal of becoming a hub of a knowledge-based economy. These risks can be curtailed to a great extent if the support of open and flexible markets is involved and at the same time affordable social protection mechanisms and strategic planning of financial reserves are properly outlined.

Fourth pillar – environmental development

Nature plays an important role in beautifying a country's environment. Keeping this in mind, the State of Qatar plans to preserve and protect its unique environment, nurturing it at the same time in the same shape as granted by God. This is important so as to attain comprehensive and manageable development for generations to come. According to Mozah bint Nasser Al-Misnid, the natural environment is a gift to us from God, and if we nurture it, it will nurture us in the long run [12]. This pillar is of increased importance, as Qatar has to streamline to deal with local environmental issues, including diminishing water impact and hydrocarbon resources, the potential impact of global warming on Qatar's water levels and the effects of environmental deprivation and increased pollution. The solution to all this requires evaluating risk hazards and dealing with projected transformation linked to mobilizing capacities as well as coordinating amicable efforts to deal with mitigating risks and upcoming challenges [12].

The achievement of Qatar's National Vision requires a commitment of responsibility from all citizens and the nation as a whole. It will need teamwork from the whole nation, which can only be achieved via everyone's dedication and utmost support. All sectors and society need to join hands to accomplish all the goals and pillars of this vision and to help in transforming the country into a knowledge-based hub so that it can play a significant role in the GCC. This further requires that all institutions and organizations practice capacity building, transparent public services and efficient delivery, vibrant bonding of public and private partnerships and cooperation and, most importantly, inculcation of a vibrant business climate and a significant place for civil society [12].

The previous challenges are affirmed in the QNV, which focuses on creating a balance between them [13]. The vision initiative or national development strategy of any country, especially with reference to the GCC, is directly linked to the topic of reforms. The most important circumstances and conditions in dire need of radical and rapid reform are the previously mentioned challenges for Qatar to deal with so that they may become an integral part of economic transformation [13].

Bahrain's economic development vision

Economic diversification has been the main agenda of economic planners for many decades in the GCC states [14]. At the heart of Bahrain's economic vision lies a mixture of guiding principles which combines sustainability, competitiveness and fairness. Converting these aspirations into realty requires comprehensive strategic planning, which the Bahraini government has articulated in the Bahrain Economic Vision 2030. All these require a strategic conversion of these aspirations into a tangible and coordinated national strategy across all government institutions [15].

According to the Bahrain Economic Vision 2030, the goal of national economic development is to make a shift from an oil-based national economy to a competitive and diversified one based on high technology and a private innovative sector [16]. Economic Vision 2030 strives to enable every Bahraini to lead a secure and rich life to reach their full potential, as this will lead to a prosperous economic transformation [15].

Bahrain's economy has been greatly prospering over the past few decades. Its GDP has had an increase of more than 6% per annum from 2012 to 2016. A thriving financial sector behind this is a stimulant, and a regional economic boom has come from the oil sector [15]. The ultimate aim is to guarantee that every Bahraini household has at least twice its current disposable income by 2030. Economic Vision 2030 intends to accomplish this by providing clear guidelines for Bahrain to become a global contender for all citizens by offering them better education, employment opportunities and higher earning packages, along with a better living standard and lifestyle in a safe and secure living environment [15]. This is only possible if all of Bahraini society, the government, the private sector and every individual join hands together and work tirelessly to make this happen [15].

The current economy of Bahrain is facing a massive shortage of appropriate skills and top-quality employment opportunities. According to Bahrain's vision, this shortage should be replaced by a workforce double in size that of today over the period from 2016 to 2026. Currently, 4,000 Bahrainis with at least a college degree are graduating per year and entering the job market with minimal wages. If the current economic trends continue, the quality and number of jobs available in the market will not be sufficient to meet the upcoming demands of future generations. Over the past few years, an increasing number of low-wage jobs has been created in Bahrain, leading to stagnation of low-market competitive wages in the private sector [15]. On top of all this, for this small number of low-paid jobs in the private sector, Bahrainis are not the ultimate choice for positions, as these require appropriate skills and education to meet the requirements of the job. For the past few years, Bahrain has been striving to address these issues, as these are major chinks in its economic development armor. It has been trying to redistribute oil revenues and offering jobs for citizens in the public sector. This has resulted in an oversized public sector, which will definitely become a constraint in the long run and have a negative impact on Bahrain's economic development, keeping in mind the steady decline in oil reserves [15]. The solution to this problem lies in the courts of the private sector. It's up to them that they cooperate to resolve this imbalance and raise the quality of employment, which will ultimately lead to economic transformation and dynamic enterprises offering attractive job opportunities to diverse and skilled Bahrainis.

In the past few years, there has been a sudden Gulf Cooperation Council boom in the market as the countries have been enjoying a lucrative share of economic growth. The GCC has become an emerging model of finance, industry and tourism, with massive inflows of capital due to the oil-based economy and the high prices of oil for the past few years. Due to the recent volatility in the global economic climate, the graph of this significant growth is expected to continuously rise at fluctuating rates [15]. Having said all this, Bahrain is well positioned to offer its investors a wealth of opportunities, which include an exceedingly favorable business environment, an unwavering and progressive government and an aspiring multicultural society. All these opportunities hold an entire world of benefits for investors, which includes Bahrain being well located at the heart of the GCC and serving as a gateway for Asia, Europe and Africa. Besides other economic incentives, it offers zero taxation for private companies, free movement of capital and fewer indirect taxes for private enterprises and individuals, which is like the icing on the cake. Additionally, the political reforms Bahrain has embraced have built a foundation for a cohesive and inclusive society which is truly supported by ambitious programs inclusive of economic and social change. Bahranis have always been very ambitious in their collective struggle to bring about a thriving future. They are very hospitable and warmly welcome foreigners to their host country and give them space to integrate into their community in the true picture of Islamic tradition, which includes tolerance and hospitality. This has resulted in a diversified population, invigorated economic development and one family spirit living and working together peacefully [15]. Building all these qualities requires compliance and oneness. In Bahrain, decisions are taken at a very accelerated pace, as it is critical to speed up reforms if capitalizing upon regional growth opportunities is the topmost priority **[15]**.

An imperative edge in globalization and ever-growing competition is to change the country's reliance on cheap expatriate labor. As demand increases productivity, innovation needs to be increased, which leads to a shortage of workers, forcing the country to rely on an expatriate workforce. This reliance becomes unsustainable, as emerging global centers of low-cost manufacturing are slowly eroding this long-term economic growth asset. Bahrain now needs to identify new sources of future economic growth. The world economy is increasing at a much accelerated pace, and companies are learning new trends and becoming more productive to compete in the global world and become economic transformation change makers. This leads to more innovation and productivity challenges for Bahrain, and it needs to focus on two main areas: it needs to accelerate its labor productivity. Compared to other countries, its productivity in this area is 17% over a period of 25 years, while other countries have accelerated this area to 21% within the same time span. Another area which requires Bahrain's focus is innovation. Globally, Bahrain's innovation is negligible. Thus, both these areas need Bahrain's special focus, as innovation and productivity are the needs of the time, and without these two tiers, Bahrain's companies will not be able to operate smoothly in the global economy **[15]**. Bahrain's vision is to swiftly transform its economy, acquire the right mix of skills and boost productivity and innovation so as to compete in the real world where economic development and transformation challenges await it **[15]**.

A country's economic vision should be based on a firm ground of factors that determine prosperity either in economy, government or society. The Economic Vision of Bahrain was a very comprehensive one which was the result of collaborative contributions of all Bahrainis from all walks of life. International top-of-the-line practices were also evaluated to see which suited Bahrain's framework. Bahrain's Economic Vision is based on three guiding principles: sustainability, competitiveness and fairness. All these principles are interrelated; therefore, supporting any one of them will have a positive impact on our success in the form of upholding the others **[15]**.

Bahrain's growth over the last two decades has been dependent solely on the public sector. As global economic competition increases and government finances become tighter, it will be difficult for the public sector to cope with the same; therefore, by 2030, it is assumed that the private sector will be driving economic growth in Bahrain independently. Bahrain will be able to use its resources to invest in the future of its people in the form of human capital development through training and education, especially in the applied sciences sector **[15]**. In today's modern economic world, competition around the globe is at its peak, and product life span is decreasing as the global market has become stagnant. In this scenario, steps in innovation and entrepreneurship will ensure Bahrain's economic sustainability in the private sector. Environment and cultural heritage are the two pillars which should not be sacrificed for economic growth, as the well-being of Bahrainis is important for the country. All necessary steps will be taken by Bahrain to safeguard and preserve these two pillars **[15]**.

According to its vision, Bahrain should attain a high level of competitiveness in the global economy. A competitive environment drives increased productivity, resulting in economic growth, profitability and wages. This is only possible if productivity continues to increase in a cycle of improvement which will force businesses to offer good salary packages to the employees of Bahrain. Higher productivity requires highly skilled people to meet the requirements of high positions. Competitive countries across the globe go to great lengths to train and educate their people and hire foreign workers who possess the skills lacking in their local workers. For Bahrain to attain a flourishing economy requires attraction of both local and foreign businesses. At the same time, a good infrastructure, environment and high-quality public services are value-added services which attract investors and promote better economic growth with productivity and competitiveness, and all these should be offered by Bahrain **[15]**.

If fairness needs to be nurtured, there should be fair and transparent transactions being carried out in the public and private sectors. As the name suggests, fairness refers to the fact that all must be seen and treated the same in accordance with international human rights standards and concentrating on the fact that everyone should be given an equal share of rights to education, health facilities and human capital development **[15]**.

Thus, fundamental changes are required to embark on the journey of accelerated national growth. All the aspirations and goals of Bahrain have been outlined previously, and Bahrain will strive to achieve its goals as a part of its Vision 2030. Success is not a one-way street; it will require untiring efforts of all sectors of society as well as individuals to convert Bahrain's vision into a solid reality. Bahrain aspires to master all the challenges to make this endeavor a major success so that current and future generations enjoy the fruits of reforms in the form of increasingly productive and flourishing economic growth **[15]**.

UAE's economic development vision

According to the UAE Economic Vision 2021, the United Arab Emirates aspires to be among the best countries of the world in terms of economic growth and transformation by 2021. Its vision clearly states that it wants to transform its economy into a model where knowledge and innovation are the prime factors driving economic growth. In a nutshell, future developments in UAE will involve various departments which include investments in science, technology and research **[17]**. Apart from all this, the country will concentrate on intellectual property protection and infrastructure development, equipped with world-class assets of communication, information and other service sector development **[16]**.

To achieve this, Emiratis need to achieve the following goals. By 2021, Emiratis will be fully self reliant and shall possess exemplary state-of-the-art skills in carving out their future based on entrepreneurship and responsibility. At the same time, they shall embrace moral values for richer fulfillment of the vision **[18]**. At the heart of every Emirati's aspirations lies insightful awareness of duty toward their nation. This will lead to a profound groundwork of commitment, personal success and prosperity hand in hand with moral responsibility. This will keep them alert to changes and events which will positively impact their country and vision. Their proactive and persistent nature will enable them to rise to and face the challenges the nation's economic growth presents **[18]**.

Closely networked and prosperous families will eventually embrace traditional values, which will be packaged in the shape of continuing women's empowerment, marriage and maintaining very close links between family members to ensure their rightful role in society. The nucleus of Emirati society requires large and unified societies. Marriage is one of its most prominent values, and strong steps will be taken to maintain this vibrant facet of the culture by tying them in a strong and stable bond. Respect for these traditions will give Emiratis an edge and will wholeheartedly support emerging women's empowerment **[18]**. If all these goals are accomplished, women will be able to enjoy all the flavors of life without any hint of discrimination in all spheres of work and society.

A well-knit and vibrant Emirati economic society is a result of strong and active communities and underpins a strong bond of harmony among citizens, encouraging them to share openness with residents. Emiratis are all sailing in the same boat. Good initiatives like charitable work, grassroots-level problem identification and volunteer work instill a notion of social awareness and responsibility. This will help all Emiratis ensure the quality of oneness in an inclusive society **[18]**.

A vibrant culture is the backbone of any country's economy. It is counted as a nation's most sacred and richest heritage. The distinct culture of UAE will remain based on the distinct features of progressive and moderate Islamic values and topped with the rich Arabic language. This will leave an open ground for Emiratis to enjoy their traditions and heritage, along with national identity reinforcement. A vibrant and diversified culture is a crucial ingredient of national pride and social responsibility for UAE, and it will strive to reach a level where there are no bounds for the country to sacrifice economic growth **[18]**.

The UAE federation will take all necessary steps to maintain the legacy of its forefathers so that a wave of balanced development harmonizes throughout the Emirates. This will only be possible via active coordination within the sectors of the government and the amalgamation of national integrated planning and full implementation of the same in all policy areas **[18]**. This will help UAE flourish on the defined grounds of an inclusive society where all Emiratis will enjoy an equal share of opportunities and rewards networked in a growing sense of national unity.

Protecting and safeguarding citizens from various threats and providing them safety is the foremost duty of a nation. UAE, keeping the same in mind, is taking steps along with its government to provide economic resilience and stability to its citizens and give them peace and security along with a sense of empowerment. This will allow all Emiratis to overcome adversity and contribute positively to society [18].

UAE's enhanced international standing will continue to grow as its list of successes comes into the limelight and it highlights itself as a regional and international role model excelling in areas such as diplomacy, development and humanitarian aid, as well as hosting international events.

Holding the reins of fully national human capital development requires maximizing the participation of Emiratis, making space for entrepreneurship, nurturing the skills of home-grown leaders from the public and private sectors and retaining home talent. For industries which require expertise from the global market, UAE will make sure to bring that talent into its own country, as human capital development is a current need. UAE will offer this global inborn talent attractive packages and a place to live so that citizens may learn from them and gain insights and knowledge which will prove fruitful in the long run [18].

UAE has a vision of a diversified and sustainable economy with enough flexibility to adapt to new economic models and capitalize on global economic partnerships to champion long-term prosperity for current and future generations of UAE, especially in the sectors of trade and commerce.

A long, healthy and quality life is a dream of every human being. To safeguard the same, UAE will promote long and healthy lives by providing people with state-of-the-art medical facilities on an equitable ground and creating awareness campaigns to prevent citizens from becoming victims to any dangers. The UAE government will also act as an intermediary and work tirelessly to safeguard the nation against diseases [18].

A first-rate education is a right of every citizen, also on equitable ground. Every citizen will have an equal right to this first-rate education. This will further help them in enhancing their educational attainments and contributing positively to society. This will help UAE to foster their confidence and inner abilities and instill in them a feeling of responsibility [18].

A well rounded lifestyle is a dream and goal of every citizen. UAE is taking steps to ensure a quality lifestyle for its citizens and nurture this standard of life on the grounds of state-of-the-art world-class public infrastructure, government services and a lucrative recreational environment full of peace and prosperity [18]. In a nutshell, UAE will make its reputation as a complete nation as attractive to business and investors as it is an overall well-rounded country to live in.

A well-preserved natural environment is a necessary factor for every citizen, as it promotes esprit de corps and places one in the realm of calmness and prosperity. At the heart of humanity, UAE desires to take steps to shield its environment as a part of its worldwide responsibility. UAE, as the leader of green revolution, wants to ensure that steps are being taken to change the fabric of its economic growth and that future generations inherit an environmentally sustainable world [18].

Kuwait's economic development vision

Kuwait is a founding member of the Gulf Cooperation Council and the Petroleum Exporting Countries Organization. It contains the sixth-largest oil reserves globally, approximately 101.5 billion barrels [19]. Kuwait's 2035 Vision is a network of vision and aspirations it strives to achieve. It is based on tangible strides and clear reforms to build a contemporary economy to empower the private sector so that it may contribute to the national economy [20]. Kuwait aspires to attain an intact and diversified economy which will benefit and empower the private sector, increase the percentage of small and medium-sized enterprises and attract foreign investments. All these are essential for Kuwait to achieve a higher level of diversification for its long-term and well-managed economic growth [20].

According to Kuwait's Vision 2035, there are various sectors which offer colossal opportunities for future economic growth and will enable it to be an exemplary member of the Gulf Economic Cooperation. These include infrastructure; environmental services; industrial oil and gas; downstream chemical manufacturing; education and training; health care; integrated housing projects and urban development; storage and logistic services; banking; financial services and insurance; air, maritime and rail passenger support; tourism; hotels and entertainment; IT and software development; culture; media; and marketing [19]. All these will play an central role in enhancing its economy. The productivity of these sectors is one of the Kuwaiti government's prime objectives for building an economy based on a mixed blend of modernity, sustainability and diversification by 2035 [20]. Kuwait plans to increase its budget for 2035 as compared to the current one since it aspires to shift from solely an oil-based economy to a diversified and knowledge-based economy since oil revenues will be different and limited as compared to other productive sectors, including banking, technology, tourism and services, small and medium-sized enterprises and so on [20]. As stated previously, the private sector of Kuwait will contribute to the national economy; therefore, various specialized bodies and authorities have been established, including Kuwait Authority for Partnership Projects (KAPP), Kuwait Direct Investment Promotion Authority (KDIPA), Capital Markets Authority (CMA) and National Fund for Small and Medium Sized Enterprises. All these authorities will lead to a modernized and diversified economy whose pillars will be based on private sector empowerment, increasing the size of small and medium-sized enterprises and foreign investment attraction [20].

Kuwait has been ranked third for macroeconomic environment among 140 countries according to the World Economic Forum (WEF)'s global competitiveness report in 2015–2016. Additionally, it has been ranked first for government budget balance of GDP [19]. According to a *Kuwait Times* special report, Kuwait's financial and economic reform program seeks to accomplish a number of goals, including selection of projects with high development impact in order to rationalize spending and increase investment efficiency, a developed tax system through increased public revenues and current subsidy review, rationalizing and restructuring **[20]**. Kuwait is cost competitive in terms of water, labor, land and power **[19]**. It is strategically located on the outskirts of the three major markets of KSA, Iraq and Iran, which it faces across the Gulf. Its strategic location allows for extended market access in various directions, including the Commonwealth of Independent States, Turkey, Eastern Asia and Eastern and Central Europe. The entrepreneurial nature of Kuwaiti citizens provides a comfort zone to various business sectors, including aviation design, financial services, telecom, animation art and so on, as, for these leading businesses, Kuwait is like a home which provides overseas entrepreneurial ventures for promoting scalable businesses **[19]**.

Recreational facilities are the need of the time, as co-curricular activities for citizens ensure a better future and well-developed facilities and sports avenues for families and sports lovers. It also offers immigrant facilities and work permit visas, along with a residency visa, which can be acquired via a valid employment offer from a private organization or Kuwaiti government organization. Expatriates get a "No Objection certificate" after the Kuwaiti employer applies for a residency visa on the employees' behalf. A residency visa is issued subject to the time when the expatriate actually enters the Kuwaiti world **[19]**. Kuwait is always on the lookout for ways to give protection and security to its citizens, and there has been a great reduction in crime rates as compared to various Western countries. It does not support any kind of terrorism and violence and makes sure that police protection is on alert, which discourages crime to a great extent **[19]**.

Kuwait has developed five programs which will help it in overcoming the challenges waiting around the corner to hinder the achievement of interrelated goals linked to sustainability and diversification of the economy. These include creating a business-like environment for the private sector; diversification of the production sector; development of a national tourism sector, which is a current need; launching a knowledge base program to promote economic growth; and the financial and economic reform plan. On a bigger scale, all these programs and departments will help Kuwait achieve its long-term goal of economic reform and growth, which is a collaborative vision of the Gulf Cooperation Council **[20]**.

Kingdom of Saudi Arabia's economic development vision

All success stories revolve around a vision, and successful visions are based on strong pillars. Likewise, Saudi Arabia's economic development vision is based on three pillars: 1) to become the heart of the Arabic and Islamic world; 2) the determination to become a global investment powerhouse; and 3) ransforming its unique location into a global hub connecting three major continents: Asia, Europe and Africa.

The vision is based on three themes: a vibrant society, thriving economy and ambitious nation. All these themes combine to promote the three pillars, which will finally lead to a prosperous country and a hub for the best economic growth among all the nations of the Gulf Cooperation Council **[21]**.

The "vibrant society" theme is the most vital to achieve KSA's vision and a strong base for economic prosperity. A vibrant society has three main components: strong roots, fulfilling lives and strong foundations.

The first objective, a *vibrant society with strong roots*, revolves around goals which need to be achieved by 2030. These goals include increasing the capacity for welcoming Umrah visitors from 8 million to 30 million every year and UNESCO registrations of the number of Saudi heritage sites to be more than doubled by 2030. The vision to achieve these goals for a vibrant society with strong roots revolves around the country's commitments, which includes the honor to serve the number of Umrah visitors in the best possible way and, second, to build the largest Islamic museum **[21]**.

The second objective, *vibrant society with fulfilling lives*, first focuses on promoting a better culture and environment. Second, it focuses on providing a healthy and balanced lifestyle, as this is a crucial goal to achieve a sustainable and fulfilling life. Third, it focuses on developing cities with high levels of security and development. Last, it focuses on achieving environmental sustainability which preserves environmental and natural resources to fulfill Islamic, moral and human duties. A vibrant society with fulfilling lives revolves around goals which need to be achieved by 2030. These goals include, first, acquiring a status where three Saudi cities will be recognized among the top-ranked 100 cities of the world. Second, for the cultural and entertainment activities ratio to be doubled, from 2.9% to 6%. Last, to increase the number of individuals exercising once a week from 13% of the population to 40%. To achieve this, the commitments revolve around providing meaningful entertainment for citizens. KSA has a promising commitment that by 2020, it will be equipped with 450 registered clubs and professionally organized amateur clubs that will provide a variety of cultural and entertainment activities **[21]**.

The third objective, *a vibrant society with strong foundations*, focuses on caring for KSA's families and developing children's character from infancy via educational and academic systems. Additionally, it focuses on empowering society with all the basic essentials of life and building a state-of-the-art health care system. A vibrant society with strong foundations revolves around goals which need to be achieved by 2030. These goals include raising the country's position from 26th to 10th in the social capital index and increasing the average life expectancy of the citizens from 74 years currently to 80 years. To achieve this, the commitments revolve first around "*irtiqa*," a prominent role of families in educating their children, and second, corporatization: transferring the responsibilities of health care to public organizations that compete against each other and the public sector **[21]**.

A *thriving economy* theme is the second most vital theme to achieve KSA's vision and to provide opportunities for all its citizens by building a state-of-the-art education system in line with market needs. This would be aligned with the motive to provide economic opportunities for entrepreneurs, large corporations and small enterprises. This will help them unlock promising economic sectors, diversify the economy and make space for job opportunities. The thriving economy theme has four main objectives: rewarding opportunities, investment for long run, being open for business and leveraging its unique position [21].

The first objective, a *thriving economy with rewarding opportunities*, revolves around goals which need to be achieved by 2030. These goals include lowering the rate of unemployment from 11.6% to 7%, increasing SME contribution to the GDP from 20% to 35% and increasing women's empowerment in the workforce from 22% to 30%. To achieve this, the commitments revolve around an education system that contributes to economic growth and a greater role for small and medium-sized enterprises [21].

The second objective, a *thriving economy with investment for the long run*, revolves around some goals which include shifting from the 19th-largest economy in the world to the top 15; localization of oil and gas sectors incrementally from 40% to 75%; and boosting the Public Investment Fund's assets from SAR 600 billion to over 7 trillion. To achieve this, the commitments include localized investment industries, the mining sector contributing to the national economy at its full potential, and a renewable energy market, which is planned to increase threefold by 2030 [21].

The third objective, a *thriving economy open for business*, revolves around goals which include rising from the 25th position to the top 10 countries on the Global Competitiveness Index; to increase foreign direct investment from a GDP of 3.8% to 5.7%; and to increase private sector organization from a GDP of 40% to 65%. To achieve this, the commitments include a restructured and state-of-the-art King Abdullah financial district, a flourishing and vibrant retail sector and an infrastructure which is digitally developed [21].

The fourth objective, a *thriving economy leveraging its unique position*, revolves around a few goals: in the Logistics Performance Index, raising the country's global ranking from 49 to 25, making sure that the Kingdom is a regional leader and to raise the share of non-oil exports in non-oil GDP from 16% to 50% [21].

An ambitious nation theme is the third most vital theme built on a proficient and high-performing government. KSA will make sure that the private sector, citizens and the non-profit sector take ownership of their responsibilities by providing them the right mix of environment and enabling them to take a step towards meeting challenges and seizing opportunities. The ambitious nation theme has two main objectives: an ambitious nation effectively governed and an ambitious nation responsibly enabled [21].

The first objective, *an ambitious nation effectively governed*, revolves around goals which need to be achieved by 2030: to increase non-oil government revenue from SAR 63 billion to SAR 1 trillion, to increase KSA's ranking in the Government Effectiveness Index from 80 to 20 and to raise the E-Government Survey Index ranking from 36 to among the top five nations. To achieve this, the commitments include human capital development through the King Salman program, shared services across government agencies, increasing spending efficiency (QAWAM) and making significant progress in e-government [21].

The second objective, *an ambitious nation responsibly enabled*, revolves around goals which need to be achieved by 2030: to raise household savings from 6% to 10%, to raise the non-profit sector's contribution to the GDP from less than 1% to 5% and to rally 1 million volunteers per year. To achieve this, the commitments include a more impactful and long-lasting non-profit sector, which will provide state-of-the-art high-quality training to staff and promote a culture of volunteering [21].

The Saudi Arabian General Investment Authority has released a list of sectors which, according to it, are the means of investment for Saudi Arabia. These include renewable energy, education, car manufacturing, tourism, health care, housing, ICT, oil and gas, water, electricity, power, mining, agriculture, transport, building materials and engineering [22, 23].

Saudi Arabia will be able to acquire benefits from a colossal investment in education and infrastructure. Better education and infrastructure will lead to the strengthening of the long-term prospects for which GCC countries are striving [22]. According to the official data, the ratio of Saudis working in the private sector rose from 11% in 2011 to 16% in 2016 [22]. There has been a visible and notable change in the employment style of the Kingdom. Saudi nationals are now working as taxi drivers and gym and hotel receptionists. This notable change presents a positive transformation in the employment graph in Saudi Arabia, which is unusual compared with Kuwait or UAE [22]. Saudi women are enjoying a lucrative share of employment in the private sector, from 30,000 in 2005 to 500,000 in 2015. Private-sector organizations generally look upon female graduate job seekers as a valuable domestic resource. Saudi Arabia has the prime consumer market in the Arab world and comparatively high population growth. The consumer market is largely supplied by imported goods rather than concentrating on investment in domestic production. Saudi Arabia also has a state-of-the-art consumer market in the Middle East and North Africa (MENA), the spending of which is dependent on the government and thus indirectly on oil prices. The Kingdom has remarkably become a world leader in petrochemical production. Its production moves up the value chain via renewable energy–based industries, but the main point to keep in mind is that it also depends on oil and gas as a part of a comparative advantage [22]. Non–oil driven sectors need to be revived via investing in them to maintain growth and prosperity beyond the oil era. Renewable energy transformation and development are the prime focus for economic growth. A clear competitive advantage for Saudi Arabia in the non-oil industries is religious tourism, as the Kingdom has a clear competitive edge as custodian of the holy sites of Mecca and Medina. The development of its economic growth is likely to improve if other modest tradable sectors like education, human capital and technology are improved [22].

For the past few years, the Kingdom has been making impressive growth in a number of sectors. The Kingdom has been best in economic, industrial and development advances, with continued improvements in the lifestyle and living standards of the Saudi citizens [24]. The Kingdom's achievement of collaborating within the government and private sector is an added achievement with regard to impressive growth. The private sector has also grown remarkably by participating in increasing activities and improved competitiveness. All economic sectors have flourished as a result of government–private collaboration. In addition, administrative reforms, economic and social stability, government economic policies and institutional development have all helped have a favorable impact on the achievements already accomplished by the Kingdom [24].

Some of the more promising areas for nationalization within the workforce include health care, tourism, retail, mining, high-class education and local services [22].

Vision 2030 aspires for an entertainment economy to be developed in the Kingdom with the intention of doubling household spending on entertainment and culture, making space for 100,000 jobs. The General Entertainment Authority (GEA) has been established by the government and will focus on more cultural and entertainment events. Furthermore, Vision 2030 also promises a profound future for Saudi film directors, some of whom have already received international accreditation [22]. The aspiring aim of attracting more tourists is a boon for the Saudi government. This will ease social restrictions to a great extent [22].

Riyadh is undoubtedly the only capital in the entire GCC where hotels lower their prices on weekends for tourists to enjoy their time to the fullest as residents and expatriates head to other Gulf countries and beyond their own city. This is a very positive step for Saudi Arabia, as it is well on its way to become a hub for tourism, which is one of the goals to which Vision 2030 aspires [22].

Saudi Arabia's National Plan for Science, Technology and Innovation is a part of its development program for economic growth in 2010–2025. This plan brings into the limelight the fact that Saudi Arabia intends to become a pioneer among the GCC countries in the fields of science, technology and innovation by 2020. The Saudi Arabian Business Innovation Research Program has also been set up as an umbrella for all the investment industries to work under so as to become the pioneer of economic growth in all the Gulf Cooperation Council states [25].

Comparative analysis of economic development visions in the Gulf Cooperation Council

The previous literature throws a comprehensive light on the economic development visions of all six states of the Gulf Cooperation Council. In light of this, it is necessary to mention the crux factors which play a pivotal role in the comparative analysis of economic development. The following figure gives a clear picture of the Global Competitiveness Index (GCI) rank of oil-exporting economies in the Middle East, with a special focus on the pillars which are the main ingredients of the economic development visions of the GCC countries.

Although the oil-exporting economies are diversified in their competitiveness, Figure 2.1 points to two commonalities: all the GCC countries' economic

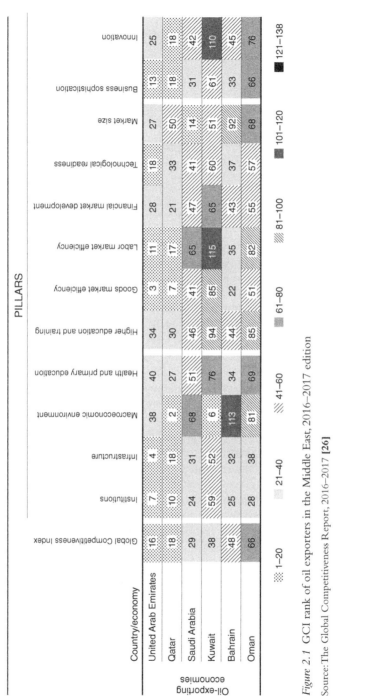

Figure 2.1 GCI rank of oil exporters in the Middle East, 2016–2017 edition

Source: The Global Competitiveness Report, 2016–2017 [26]

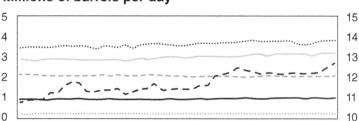

Millions of barrels per day

Figure 2.2 Oil production

Source: International Monetary Fund, Gulf Cooperation Council, October 26, 2016, Riyadh, Saudi Arabia

development visions revolve around a key driving factor, privatization, but most nations remain dominated by the state. In KSA, the state's stake in state-owned enterprises amounts to 19.8% of the GDP; in UAE, it accounts for 21.8% and in Qatar 23.1%. The second commonality observed points to the fact that, as the Fourth Industrial Revolution picks up pace, more focus should be on innovation, health care, primary education and technological advancement. These should go hand in hand with a diversified economy but away from the energy sector [26].

Figure 2.2 gives a clear picture that oil production in some GCC countries reached a record-breaking point in July 2016, where Saudi Arabia, UAE and Kuwait reached an extreme range of 0.5 mb/d higher than 2015 [27].

GCC oil-exporting economies are aspiring to foster growth development in a much more challenging environment. Macroeconomic stability in these countries has improved to a great extent because of recent reforms and lower oil prices [28]. Despite this fact, the growth economic factor remains fragile and weak, tending to be 3.5% in 2016 as compared to 4.5%, projected to be the rank in 2017. In this challenging environment, it has become crucial to step up reform momentum, creating more room to spend on infrastructure, health care and education, as well as targeted social assistance, making more space for economic development [28].

Figure 2.3 focuses on the employment of GCC nationals. Labor market policies need special attention in the GCC region because businesses consistently treat less educated labor and restrictive labor regulations as their biggest hurdle and enemy. This is the biggest challenge for GCC countries and has kept the private sector from increasing its national workforce at a crucial time when

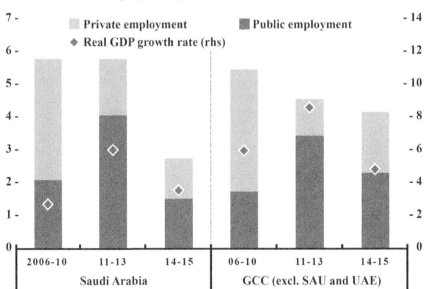

Figure 2.3 Employment of GCC nationals

Source: International Monetary Fund, Regional Economic Outlook, October 26, 2016, Middle East and Central Asia

the public sector itself has been employing nationals at a very slow pace and percentage, leading to a decrease in the growth of nationals employed overall (Figure 2.3) **[28]**. If steps are taken to narrow the gap between the wages of the public and private sectors, the end result would be an attraction toward the private sector for nationals.

Renewable energy market analysis and transition

The transition toward renewable energy is a green signal for GCC countries for better economic growth and to fashion a critical role in the global transition **[29]**. The Gulf countries are all set to drive smoothly on the road of capitalizing on solar resources for power generation and water desalination due to the advent of the lowest solar prices globally. If the GCC region achieves the renewable energy targets the national and subnational governments have established for them, the region will be more likely to cut its annual water use by 16% and save up to 400 million barrels of oil, along with creating approximately 210,000 jobs and decreasing its per capita carbon footprint by 8% in 2030 **[29]**.

GCC countries can be sure of their long-term social and economic prosperity through a clean energy future if they take advantage of their country's leadership in the energy sector and continue to embrace their region's abundance of renewable energy resources. One-fifth of the world gas reserves belongs to the GCC region, along with almost one-third of the crude oil reserves. The socio-economic development gap has been narrowed to a great extent in the past few decades in the GCC region driven by oil and gas revenues and by growth and aspiring policies which have enabled all six states to reach a stage where they may be proudly included in some of the countries with the highest urbanization rates and state-of-the-art living standards **[29]**.

The previous figure (Figure 2.4) projects a clear picture of sustainable energy plans and targets in the Gulf Cooperation Council. The aspirations for a more sustainable energy future have led several GCC countries to announce their renewable energy and energy efficiency targets to conserve natural resources, improve energy efficiency and deploy renewable technologies. If these renewable energy targets and plans are achieved, it is estimated that close to 140,000 direct jobs every year could be created. By 2030 alone, it is estimated that almost 210,000 jobs could be created in renewable energy **[29]**.

The GCC countries have been blessed with hydrocarbon resources that have injected a new energy into the heart of the development and economic growth sector in the past few decades. This in turn can lead to providing employment for future generations with sustainability.

The various ministries involved in energy-related planning and decision-making in the GCC include Ministry of Oil/Energy, Ministry of Electricity and Water, Ministry of Environmental Affairs and Ministry of Foreign Affairs. All these ministries are required due to the strategic nature of energy sector planning (Figure 2.5) **[29]**.

In Saudi Arabia, K.A.CARE was established to give a boost to the renewable energy sector of the country. Recent developments in policy and institutional framework suggest that renewable energy project development may be initiated in the near future. Renewable energy development projects in remote areas have been initiated and led by Saudi Aramco **[29]**.

Institutions for research and innovation serve as the backbone for the entire sustainable energy strategy. These institutions contribute to the expert development of local centers to inform and advice industrial diversification and policy building. R&D and workforce training will play an important role in strengthening the fabric of the value chain and in turn will facilitate project deployment. The key examples which serve the same purpose include the Kuwait Institute for Scientific and Research (KISR), Sultan Qaboos University in Oman, Qatar Foundation, K.A.CARE and the King Abdullah Petroleum Studies and Research Center in Saudi Arabia **[29]**.

The installed renewable energy capacity in the GCC countries is dominated by a handful of centralized solar projects, namely Solar PV and CSP, which constitute around 85% of the existing capacity and more than 80% of the project pipeline (Figure 2.6) **[29]**.

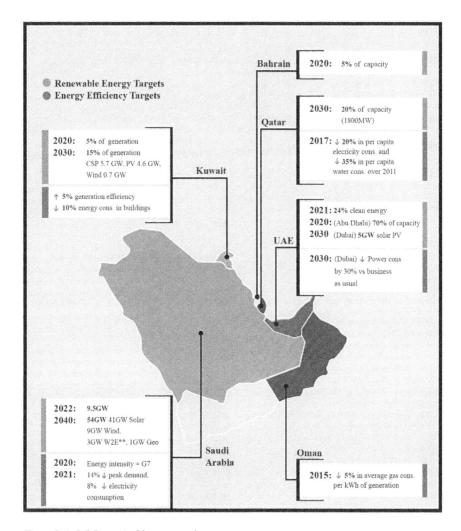

Figure 2.4 GCC sustainable energy plans

Source: Renewable Energy Market Analysis, GCC Region, International Renewable Energy Agency [29], based on Lahn et al., 2013; RCREEE, 2015a and others

Investments in renewable energy in the GCC took a spontaneous jump in 2011 with USD 800 million worth of investment in UAE's one CSP plant, which became operational in 2013. The same investment activity dropped in 2012. However, investments in new projects are on the rise (Figure 2.7), taking into account cost effectiveness improvements. By 2015, Kuwait reached the highest peak among GCC renewable energy investments (Figure 2.8) [29].

Country	Oil & Gas	Electricity and Water
Bahrain	National Oil and Gas Authority (NOGA)	Electricity and Water Authority (EWA)
Kuwait	Supreme Petroleum Council (SPC), Ministry of Petroleum	Ministry of Electricity and Water
Oman	Ministry of Oil and Gas (MOG)	Ministry of Electricity and Water
Qatar	Ministry of Energy and Industry (MEI)	Qatar General Electricity and Water Corporation (Kahramaa)
Saudi Arabia	Ministry of Petroleum and Mineral resources (MOPM)	Ministry of Water and Electricity
UAE	Ministry of Energy	Ministry of Energy
UAE, Abu Dhabi	Supreme Petroleum Council, Executive Affairs Authority	Abu Dhabi Water and Electricity Authority (ADWEA)
UAE, Dubai	Dubai Supreme Council of Energy	Dubai Electricity and Water Authority (DEWA), Dubai Supreme Council of Energy

Figure 2.5 Institutions involved in policy making and planning in the GCC energy sectors

Source: Renewable Energy Market Analysis, GCC Region, International Renewable Energy Agency [29]

Countries/ Capacity (MW)	2011 Total RE*	2012 Total RE*	2013 Total RE*	2014 Total RE*	Wind	PV	CSP	Biomass and Waste
Bahrain	0.6	0.6	0.6	0.6	0.5	0.1	0	0
Kuwait	0.1	0.1	0.2	0.2	0	1	0	0
Oman**	0	0	0	0.7	0	0.7	0	0
Qatar	25	28.2	28.2	28.2	0	3.2	0	25
Saudi Arabia	0	19	25	25	0	25	0	0
UAE, Abu Dhabi	19.5	20	134.9	134.9	0.9	33	100	1
Total	45.2	67.9	188.9	190.4	1.4	63	100	26

Figure 2.6 Installed renewable energy capacity in the GCC countries, as of 2014

Source: IRENA Renewable Energy Statistics; REN21 et al., 2013; RCREEE, 2015b [29]

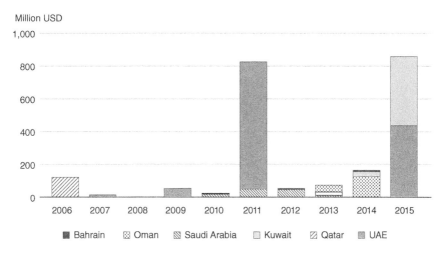

Million USD

Figure 2.7 Renewable energy projects in the GCC

Source: Ferroukhi et al. (2013a, with updates) **[29]**

Employment by country analysis through IRENA clearly indicates that if the region's renewable energy plans are achieved, the end result would be approximately 140,000 direct jobs every year on an average scale. This will furthermore extend to 207,000 by 2030. A major portion of this will be encapsulated by UAE and Saudi Arabia, as renewable energy resources offer considerable potential for white-collar and large-scale job creation (Figure 2.9).

Tailor-made renewable energy in the GCC region revolves around a policy mix that will support energy transition. The focus of the policy mix should be on institutional development, capacity building, programs and policies which can further enhance the capabilities of local companies, skill development through education and training in order to support the expansion of renewable energy sector, protective measures to support the development of local industries so that deployment may be supported while fulfilling broader socio-economic goals, strengthening of domestic capabilities and boosting the development of local industries so as to help maximize the benefits of renewable deployment, support for R&D activities in the sector to boost technology adaptation and an investment-friendly environment to attract the private sector. All these policies will combine to promote renewable energy transition in the GCC region and at the same time will reap multiple benefits across the region **[29]**.

National economic strategies of the GCC countries are clearly compared in a nutshell in Figure 2.10.

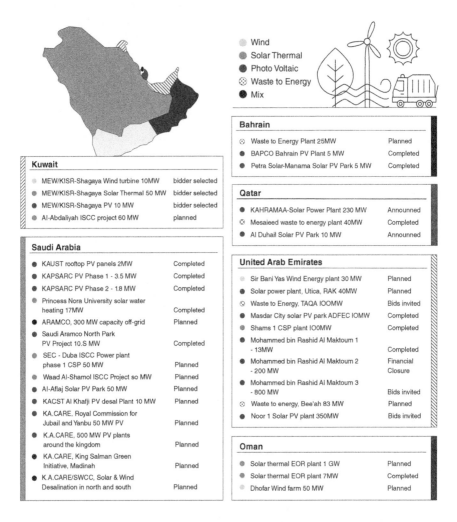

Wind
Solar Thermal
Photo Voltaic
Waste to Energy
Mix

Bahrain

Waste to Energy Plant 25MW	Planned
BAPCO Bahrain PV Plant 5 MW	Completed
Petra Solar-Manama Solar PV Park 5 MW	Completed

Kuwait

MEW/KISR-Shagaya Wind turbine 10MW	bidder selected
MEW/KISR-Shagaya Solar Thermal 50 MW	bidder selected
MEW/KISR-Shagaya PV 10 MW	bidder selected
Al-Abdaliyah ISCC project 60 MW	planned

Qatar

KAHRAMAA-Solar Power Plant 230 MW	Announced
Mesaieed waste to energy plant 40MW	Completed
Al Duhail Solar PV Park 10 MW	Announced

Saudi Arabia

KAUST rooftop PV panels 2MW	Completed
KAPSARC PV Phase 1 - 3.5 MW	Completed
KAPSARC PV Phase 2 - 1.8 MW	Completed
Princess Nora University solar water heating 17MW	Completed
ARAMCO, 300 MW capacity off-grid	Planned
Saudi Aramco North Park PV Project 10.5 MW	Completed
SEC - Duba ISCC Power plant phase 1 CSP 50 MW	Planned
Waad Al-Shamol ISCC Project so MW	Planned
Al-Aflaj Solar PV Park 50 MW	Planned
KACST Al Khafji PV desal Plant 10 MW	Planned
KA.CARE, Royal Commission for Jubail and Yanbu 50 MW PV	Planned
K.A.CARE, 500 MW PV plants around the kingdom	Planned
KA.CARE, King Salman Green Initiative, Madinah	Planned
K.A.CARE/SWCC, Solar & Wind Desalination in north and south	Planned

United Arab Emirates

Sir Bani Yas Wind Energy plant 30 MW	Planned
Solar power plant, Utica, RAK 40MW	Planned
Waste to Energy, TAQA 100MW	Bids invited
Masdar City solar PV park ADFEC 10MW	Completed
Shams 1 CSP plant 100MW	Completed
Mohammed bin Rashid Al Maktoum 1 - 13MW	Completed
Mohammed bin Rashid Al Maktoum 2 - 200 MW	Financial Closure
Mohammed bin Rashid Al Maktoum 3 - 800 MW	Bids invited
Waste to energy, Bee'ah 83 MW	Planned
Noor 1 Solar PV plant 350MW	Bids invited

Oman

Solar thermal EOR plant 1 GW	Planned
Solar thermal EOR plant 7MW	Completed
Dhofar Wind farm 50 MW	Planned

Figure 2.8 GCC renewable energy investments from 2006 to 2015 (millions USD)

Source: BNEF data with additions from IRENA based on interaction with GCC experts including Alhajraf (2015) **[29]**

The progress of women in GCC countries: the road to empowerment

Positive reforms in the Gulf countries have led to a journey of empowerment for women where they are being heard much more clearly than before. The road toward empowerment is slow and challenging, but the route which leads to the progress of women is being worked on much faster than before so that

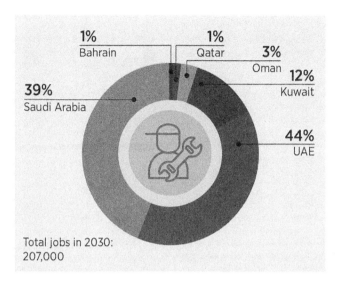

Figure 2.9 Breakdown of direct jobs in the renewable energy sector in the region by country in 2030 (%)

Source: Renewable Energy Market Analysis, GCC Region, International Renewable Energy Agency [29]

the journey may be a smooth one [30]. All these have led to an exemplary level of motivation, determination and aspirations from all the women who dream of becoming an eminent part of society and are striving to participate in the economic growth of their country. Today, women in the GCC region are having a profound impact on society by being an integral part of all major careers from all walks of life. This has enabled them to move beyond the confinements of home and family and gear up for a journey to achievements and confidence [30].

The majority of women in the GCC are literate and are at the forefront of academic reforms, with major advancements in the education sector. In the GCC, the adult literacy rate in the 15-plus age group stands at 84%, with a major and better-educated talent pool of women than men in most GCC countries [31]. Of all the graduates in 2009, 60% were women from Kuwait, Qatar and UAE (Figure 2.11). Distinguished names who have played a major role in politics and business in the GCC countries include H.E. Sheikha Lubna bint Khalid bin Sultan, Al Qasimi, Lubna Olayan and Lama Al Sulaiman [31]. On the other hand, female participation in the GCC countries' labor market is very low, which needs to improve, as it is essential for the economic growth of any country. The world average female participation in the labor market constitutes about 51.7%, out of which the GCC female labor force accounts for 26.9%. If socio-cultural norms and customs are rectified in most GCC

Bahrain's *Economic Vision* 2030 calls for a 'shift from an economy built on oil wealth to a productive, globally competitive economy, shaped by the government and driven by a pioneering private sector'. Much emphasis is on attracting foreign direct investment to create jobs. By 2030, the strategy envisions financial services as the main pillar of the economy together with oil and gas, complemented by tourism, business services, manufacturing and logistics.

Kuwait's *Vision Plan* 2035 and current *5-Year Development Plan* focus on economic diversification and aim to position the country as a regional trade and financial hub. The plan focuses on infrastructure investment, including transportation, a new port, and the development of the business hub 'Silk City' in Subiyah.

Oman's *Vision 2020* and successive *5 Year Development Plans* aim for further diversification from the oil sector and development of human resources and infrastructure. Its *In-country* Value Strategy increases spending to benefit business growth and human-resource development. Tourism is seen as a key economic sector for growth and employment creation for nationals. More than half the budget of the past development plan went toward improved airports and roads.

Qatar's *National Vision 2030* and *National Development Strategy (2011 – 2016)* foresee a dominant role for hydrocarbons in the future economy but also provide a gradual and managed diversification strategy with greater involvement of the private sector. National institutions are developing strategies for investments in transport infrastructure, housing, and industrial activities to prepare for the FIFA World Cup in 2022.

The **Saudi Arabian** *Long Term Strategy 2025* emphasises the challenges of the growing youth unemployment among nationals and of boosting income in the country. Goals include reducing government reliance on oil revenues from 72% of total exports to 37% between 2004 and 2024 and doubling national income in this time period. The associated *Ninth Development Plan* aims for increased participation by the private sector in the economy.

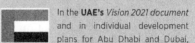

In the **UAE's** *Vision 2021 document* and in individual development plans for Abu Dhabi and Dubai, continued economic diversification is emphasised with a focus on growing sectors of tourism, aviation, and financial services. The country is positioning itself as regional hub of research and innovation and sustainable energy. The Dubai Expo 2020 is expected to attract more than 25 million visits and have a positive impact on tourism, travel and real estate.

Figure 2.10 National economic strategies of the GCC countries

Source: Hvidt, 2013 **[29]**

countries, the female labor market will flourish. Out of 10.2 million literate women in the working age group of 15-plus, only 3.3 million are employed, while the other 6.9 million are unemployed. This pool of talented women needs to be tapped and utilized if the economic growth of the GCC countries

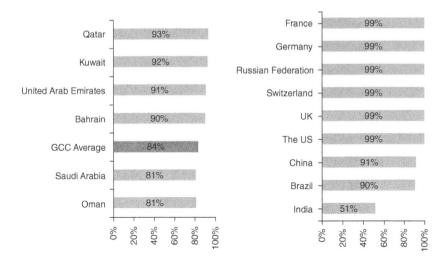

Figure 2.11 Adult literacy rate among women in the GCC vis-à-vis developed and emerging countries

Source: Global Gender Gap Report 2011, The World Bank, Al Masah Capital Research **[31]**

is not to suffer a massive loss **[31]** (Figure 2.12, Figure 2.13). Thus, regional governments are taking concrete steps to address this issue, and Saudi Arabia was prepared to take material action by issuing a royal decree in 2011 which allowed for 52,000 jobs at government schools for talented and educated men and women. Out of this, a major chunk of 75%, or 39,000 jobs, were reserved for women, which opened new avenues for the Kingdom's economic growth and prosperity **[31]**.

With an eye to academic reform, Saudi Arabia released another decree in September 2011 to put into practice a framework for creating more job opportunities for women in the education sector. UAE followed in these footsteps and launched a five-year plan for women to enjoy a lucrative share of becoming future leaders and to enhance the role of women. Qatar and Kuwait also have business forums set up for women which aim to see business women step up, rise and contribute toward the economic growth of their countries **[31]**. 2015 saw a new transition in the history of Saudi Arabia, which initiated a new chapter in economic growth and women's empowerment when King Abdullah released a new pronouncement which permitted women to vote and stand in municipal elections.

The number of working women in the GCC has grown to approximately 1.5 million in the span of 2001–2010 (Figure 2.14) **[31]**.

GCC governments have heavily invested in education, which has enabled significant progress toward achieving the United Nations Millennium Development Goal of universal primary education, as it is the need of the time. The

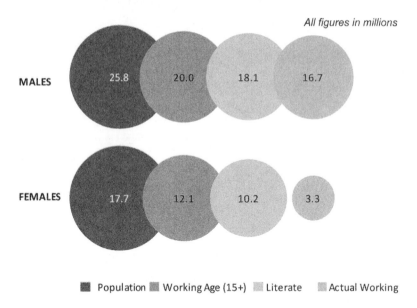

Figure 2.12 Women's capability is underutilized in the GCC region

Source: The World Bank, Al Masah Capital Research **[31]**

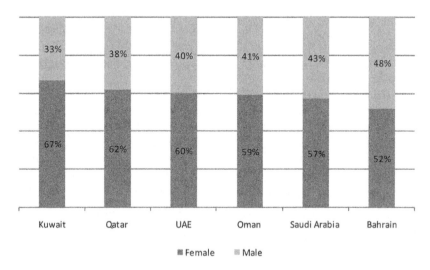

Figure 2.13 Percentage of female graduates outnumbers male graduates in the GCC

Source: Booz & Company, Global Education Digest 2011, Kingdom of Bahrain MoE **[31]**

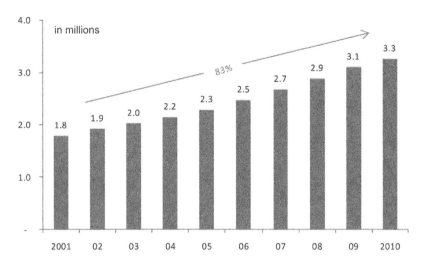

Figure 2.14 Female labor force in the GCC, 2001–2010
Source: The World Bank, Al Masah Capital Research **[31]**

progress they have made is admirable, keeping in mind gender equality achievement in school students and providing financial assistance to female students in all areas and diversified stages of education **[30]**. According to UNESCO statistics, in 2009, the ratio of girls at the official age of primary school education reached a high level of 97% in Bahrain, 87% in Kuwait, 77% in Oman, 93% in Qatar, 85% in Saudi Arabia and 89% in UAE **[30]**. Young women have outnumbered men via their large number of enrolments and participation in higher education **[30]**, but their participation as technical workers, professional legislators, senior officials and managers is still low (Figure 2.15) **[31]**.

Education is one of the greatest weapons for empowering women and a catalyst for social and cultural change. Saudi Arabia, as the largest economy of the GCC, has taken many positive steps to bring about academic reforms, especially for females in the Kingdom **[31]**. The Kingdom has sanctioned SAR 168.6 billion for the construction of schools, buildings, various technical and vocational institutions and colleges along with overseas scholarships, which is a very strong initiative for the progress of women, leading to empowerment and academic reforms **[31]**.

According to an INSEAD article **[32]**, women's wealth in the GCC countries came into existence a few decades ago. Back then, it was something of a catastrophic situation, as the women had no clue where to invest due to low literacy rates and a lack of education. But today, the situation is different. Women in GCC countries and in the world hold a massive share of wealth (Figure 2.16). Today, a female Arab investor is much more informed, literate

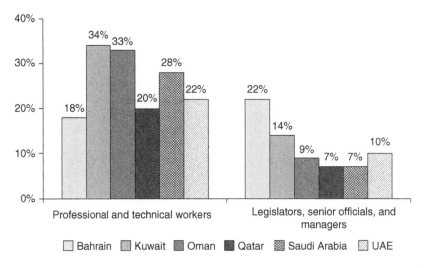

Figure 2.15 Females as legislators and technical workers (as % of the total)
Source: Global Gender Gap Report 2011 **[31]**

Rank		AUM held by women, as % of total assets	AUm (USD Tn)
1	North America	33%	9.00
2	Australia/New Zealand	31%	0.50
3	Asia (ex Japan)	29%	2.80
4	Western Europe	26%	5.30
5	Middle East	22%	0.50
6	Russia	21%	0.10
7	Eastern Europe (ex Russia)	19%	0.04
8	Latin America	18%	0.40
9	Japan	14%	1.50
10	Africa	11%	0.04

Figure 2.16 Assets under management (AUM) controlled by women worldwide
Source: BCG Global Wealth Market Sizing Database, 2010 **[31]**

and tech savvy and knows how to smartly turn the tables of investment and speak openly about money without any shyness or reluctance. This in turn has opened more doors for opportunities for Arab women to talk about investment and financial issues to safeguard their future. This, in a nutshell, is a strong step toward a smooth journey of progress and women's empowerment **[31]**.

Thus, state-of-the-art positive changes and development have had a profound impact on the status of GCC women for the past few decades. The best progression in the region has been women's education and their significant presence in the labor market **[30]**. A new educational and academic reform strategy is required for young women, with equal opportunities in the GCC region, including massive changes in the structural school system, which in turn will respond to the demands and priorities of a dynamic society with major emphasis on economic growth. A modern society needs women to be extensively educated and empowered, as they tend to play a major role in transforming the economy of a country, and they are the most valuable potential resource and asset in development. Additionally, women will exuberantly participate in the economic transition of a country from an oil-based economy to a knowledge-based economy, and investment in women will definitely yield good results today as well as in the future **[30]**.

Conclusion

To adjust to the twenty-first century, and to diversify their economies and create skilled occupations for their nationals, the Arab Gulf states are developing human capital and pushing toward information- and knowledge-based economic growth. Some GCC states have constructed their dreams in light of an information- and development-based economy; others are executing plans and projects to drive their economies toward this objective. The vision declarations and development plans of the Arab Gulf states make particular references to learning, knowledge and innovation-based monetary improvements. The Arab Gulf states are at different phases of broadening their economies, with the Saudi Arabia and UAE considered the most branched-out economies among the GCC states.

Sustainability is possibly the biggest concept in discussion over the past years. Countries are pouring resources into discovering where they stand in sustainability. This chapter set out to inspect the supportability of the substance of Saudi Arabia's Vision 2030 in the setting of the Sustainable Society Index (SSI). From the discussion of KSA's economic development vision, unmistakably, maintainability is a crucial idea crossing the natural, monetary and social parts of society. This is sensibly reflected in the SSI measures, making it an appropriate benchmark for evaluation of the supportability substance of Vision 2030 and the National Transformation Plan 2020.

This chapter is an endeavor to look at the substance of Saudi Arabia's Vision 2030 to examine its effectiveness given the objectives of manageability. The degree of accomplishment of the vital objectives, however, firmly rests on the accomplishment of the key goals, projects and intercessions. A pivotal advance to affirm the accomplishment of supportability in Vision 2030 is to complete exhaustive and intermittent evaluations of how well the key execution pointers in the 2020 National Transformation Program have been accomplished in view of the data and targets.

References

1 Muhammad Khurram Khan, T. Al-Saud, Alkhathlan, H. and Derham, H. (2014). New reforms of research, innovation and entrepreneurship in the GCC countries. *Innovation: Management, Policy & Practice* 16(2), 174–176. ISBN:978-1-921980-07-7.

2 Al-Khouri, Ali M. (2014). Digital identity: Transforming GCC economies. *Innovation: Management, Policy & Practice* 16(2), 184–194.

3 Oman 2020 Vision by Alfred Strolla, managing partner, Oman, Sudan and Yemen, Deloitte Middle East and Phaninder Peri, senior manager, Tax, Deloitte Middle East Deloitte.

4 www.mei.edu/content/omanization-policy-and-international-migration-oman

5 Directorate General of Labor Affairs. (1995). *Omanization Directory in the Private Sector* (1st ed.).

6 Gokhale, N. (2004). *Localization of Labor and International Migration: A Case Study of Sultanate of Oman*. Mumbai: International Institute for Population Sciences.

7 International Organization for Migration. (2003). *World Migration Report 2003*. International Organization for Migration (IOM), United Nations.

8 Ministry of National Economy, Govt. of Oman. (2001). *Sixth Five Year Development Plan – Basic Components and Main Indicators of the Plan 2001–2005*.

9 Irshad Al Lawati CEO of Oman Society for Petroleum Services OPAL, Secretary of the ICV Committee. Retrieved from www.incountryvalueoman.net/getattachment/f3f1a8a0-7a5e-4605-bbe7-d44331395e9e/ICV-Development-Blueprint-Strategy.

10 http://timesofoman.com/article/22436/Business/In-country-value-strategy-for-Omans-oil-and-gas-sector-soon

11 Qatar National Vision 2030. (2009). *Advancing Sustainable Development. Qatar's Second National Human Development Report*, General Secretariat for Development Planning, July.

12 Qatar National Vision 2030.

13 Al-Kuwārī, A.K. (2012). The visions and strategies of the GCC countries from the perspective of reforms: The case of Qatar. *Contemporary Arab Affairs* 5(1), 86–106. doi:10.1080/17550912.2011.647417.

14 Economic Stability in the GCC Countries Nayef Al Musehel and Ziyad Alfawzan, March 2017/KS-2017-DP03.

15 From Regional Pioneer to Global Contender – Our Vision – The Economic Vision 2030 for Bahrain.

16 Shkvarya, L.V. and Frolova, E.D. (2017). Transformations in socio-economic development of the gulf group states. *Ekonomikaregiona* [Economy of Region] 13(2), 570–578.

17 Science, Technology and Innovation Through Entrepreneurship Education in the United Arab Emirates (UAE), 9 December 2016.

18 Vision 2021, United Arab Emirates.

19 *Investing in Kuwait: A Guide for Investment Opportunities in Kuwait* (1st ed.).

20 *Kuwait Times-Special Report*, Tuesday, 25 April 2017.

21 Vision 2030, Kingdom of Saudi Arabia.

22 Research Paper—Jane Kinninmont—Middle East and North Africa Programme, July 2017. Vision 2030 and Saudi Arabia's social contract-austerity and transformation.

23 Saudi Arabian General Investment Authority website. https://sagia.gov.sa/

24 Kingdom of Saudi Arabia, Ministry of Economy & Planning. *The Eighth Development Plan 1425–1430 H 2005–2009*.

25 Shkvarya, L.V. and Frolova, E.D. (2017). Transformations in socio-economic development of the Gulf group states. *Ekonomikaregiona* [Economy of Region], 13(2), 570–578.

26 World Economic Forum. *The Global Competitiveness Report 2016–2017.*
27 International Monetary Fund. Gulf Cooperation Council, 26 October 2016, Riyadh Saudi Arabia.
28 International Monetary Fund. Regional Economic Outlook, 26 October 2016, Middle East and Central Asia.
29 International Renewable Energy Agency. *Renewable Energy Market Analysis, GCC Region.*
30 www.arabnews.com/progression-women-gcc-countries-road-empowerment
31 Al Masah Capital Limited. *GCC Women: Challenging the Status Quo.*
32 INSEAD Knowledge. *Arab Oil Money: Empowering Women.* October 2011.

3 Saudi entrepreneurship case studies and analysis

Muhammad Babar Khan and Sadia Iqbal

Introduction

This chapter presents a full survey of associated literature to describe the diverse aspects that power has and show how Saudi entrepreneurship is a basic and significant factor that plays a fundamental role in the growth of a country's wealth and its transition. The study depicts a focused full picture of the elements which allow for a transitional relation between entrepreneurship and modernization. It is a concise statement about how to improve entrepreneurial capability, including the outlook of an entrepreneur. It further presents a full picture of the elements and explains that entrepreneurs are a basic resource meant to be treasured for the economic growth of a country. Last but not least, this chapter covers the challenges faced by entrepreneurs. Entrepreneurs are essential ingredients for Saudi Arabian transformation on the basis of competitiveness, and furthermore, they lay the foundation for economic development and services. Saudi entrepreneurs have started to prove themselves a connected part of the Saudi economy. The accomplishments of Saudi entrepreneurs outlined here are based on sustained efforts to upgrade the Saudi business environment and to meet entrepreneurs' specific needs.

A knowledge-based technology is essential for improving economic expansion in the populace. Saudi Arabian graduates from schools, colleges and universities are seeking jobs, as it is not possible for them all to acquire jobs in the public and private sectors. Therefore, entrepreneurship is the medium for tackling the problems of unemployment. Entrepreneurship leads to various societal benefits, including innovation, solving unemployment issues and furthermore facilitating new consumer demands. This chapter explains the dynamics of entrepreneurship and how Saudi Arabia is striving to make entrepreneurship a basic pillar of its society. This research stresses the long-lasting impact of entrepreneurship on the unemployment rate in the Kingdom of Saudi Arabia and provides a complete case study to enhance the role of entrepreneurship as an integral part of its economy and transformation.

Literature review

Entrepreneurs are essential components of a country's economy. Entrepreneurial ventures aim to uplift the economy and form a solid base for capital, diversity and competition **[1–5, 6]**. Efficient business registrations serve as an intermediary for entrepreneurial activities to reach high achievement in all aspects **[6, 7]**. In the coming years, Saudi Arabia's top priority is to create job opportunities for its youth so that the size of this population and its innovation and energy may be utilized at home only, or else this talent may be lost to better opportunities abroad so as to increase economic activity **[8]**. According to the World Economic Forum, Saudi Arabia needs to create 75 million jobs by 2020, which will be a major jump of over 40 percent more jobs as compared to 2011. This in turn will lead to a better business environment in which entrepreneurs may initiate new business ventures and companies, be a source of economic growth, spread innovation and spur economic activity **[8]**. This requires that policy makers and business leaders be vigilant enough to identify and recognize what motivates people to start businesses. Furthermore, they should possess a sense of community so that the components of a healthy entrepreneurial ecosystem are well balanced and focused and loopholes in the Middle East and North Africa (MENA) region are well identified. The economic lack or immaturity in the MENA region may be found in entrepreneurial culture, regulatory frameworks, infrastructure, finance for small and medium-sized enterprises and formal entrepreneurship education **[8]**. In the words of Emile Cubeisy, managing director, Interactive Ventures Holding Company, Jordan, and a young global leader, "As an Arab entrepreneur, there has never been a more opportune moment to start a venture. Now is also the best time to fail."

Corporate entrepreneurs are motivated by a lucrative share of profits, but personally, they are driven by one or a combination of three intrinsic factors, namely lifestyle or passion, social good and fortune. Similarly, entrepreneurs are driven by one or by a combination of three extrinsic factors, namely innovation, opportunity and necessity **[8, 22]**.

It is an established fact that a society, to fully enjoy benefits, needs to ensure the existing working force is being provided with ample jobs and opportunities so that they may participate in economic growth. The MENA region is already facing challenges to balance unemployment rates, a basic stumbling block in the region's economic development, which are in double digits in most MENA countries, with a major decline in Yemen, at 35 percent **[8]**. If job opportunities are not created in these regions, the accelerating rate of unemployment may lead the regions to lose their youth to emigration, as it is a sign of danger when a massive number of young citizens lack opportunities **[8]**. In all this, entrepreneurship is the most important key to accelerate job creation in the region. Entrepreneurship will not only force start-ups to employ people but will also lead to significant benefits for society as a whole. Once start-ups mature into small and medium-sized enterprises, they may become leading contributors to employment and gross domestic product (GDP) **[8]** (Figure 3.1, data as of 2008).

The scholarly literature has a plethora of case studies available on entrepreneurship. Whether intrinsic or extrinsic factors are involved in entrepreneurial success, entrepreneurs contribute significantly to the global economy **[6, 14, 15]**.

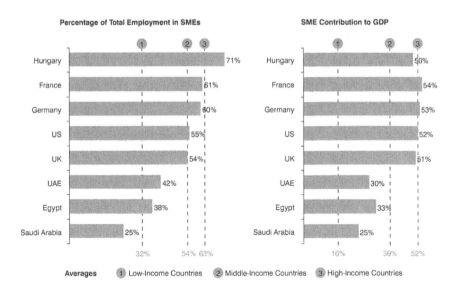

Figure 3.1 SME contribution to economies

Source: European Commission SME Performance Review; U.S. Department of Statistics; OECD; UNECE; World Bank; Zawya

In various countries, the success and failure of entrepreneurial ventures are dependent upon regulations **[9, 10, 19]**. The other factors which contribute to the triumphs and failures of new businesses includes entrepreneur motivation and ability to fight challenges **[20, 16, 17, 24]**. Governments and entrepreneurs share the same vision of aspiring to better economic growth of individuals and society as a whole **[18, 25]**.

When economic development and entrepreneurship have a U-shaped relation, rapid growth in service industries will be triggered due to low transaction costs and entry barriers **[5, 11, 12, 13]**. Saudi Arabia is predominantly a consumption country beyond hydrocarbons, but Saudi officials are continuing to make efforts to attract foreign multinational companies in order to make way for local industries to be established by them. This will enable Saudis to be less dependent on foreign products and open up new avenues for employment. Saudi Arabian authorities, while setting up economic policies, should make entrepreneurs an integral part of them, which will lead to less dependency on foreign products and open up a smooth pathway for local industries to be established, resulting in fruitful economic development and growth **[6, 21]**. Higher Saudi entrepreneurship will circumvent unemployment and make room for local industries. All in all, success lies in the court of Saudi Arabia's authorities and how strategically they plan to make their citizens participate in fruitful economic growth with the rise in entrepreneurship **[6]**.

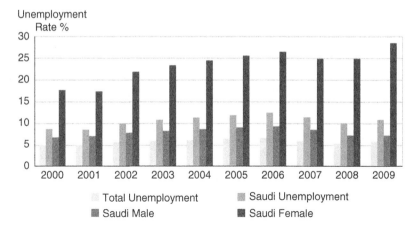

Figure 3.2 Unemployment rate in Saudi Arabia (2000–2009)

Source: Saudi Arabian Monetary Agency (SAMA), 2011 **[32]**

The Saudi economy is rapidly on the rise, but at the same time, the challenges which await it include poverty and unemployment **[23, 26]**. Despite surplus capital and opportunities, entrepreneurship in Saudi Arabia is still lacking **[27, 28]** as shown in Figure 3.2. The basic barrier to entrepreneurship in Saudi Arabia lies in gender disparities **[29, 31]**. Only educated women venture into entrepreneurship, while other women are discouraged, and, on the other hand, there are many male entrepreneurs, whether from the educated or non-educated class. Women are expected to work harder and put in more effort to excel in the field of emerging entrepreneurship markets as compared to their male counterparts **[29, 31]**.

Entrepreneurship as a solution to unemployment in Saudi Arabia

According to Central Department of Statistics and Information data, 2009 marks the highest unemployment rate in Saudi Arabia: 463,009. This rate decreased from 2006–2008 but again fluctuated, with a massive increase in 2009 with an 8 percent increase from 2008 onwards **[32]**.

Furthermore, Figure 3.3 depicts a clear picture of the unemployment rate of male and female Saudi residents and non-residents. It is clear from the figure that the unemployment rate of non-residents is the lowest rate in Saudi Arabia **[30, 32]**.

The World Bank, in its annual Ease of Doing Business Report, recognized the Kingdom of Saudi Arabia as among the world's top reformers. According to the report, Saudi Arabia improved its rank from 159 in 2007 to 38 in 2008,

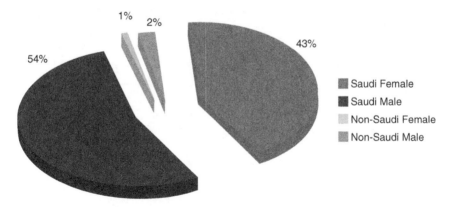

Figure 3.3 Shares of Saudi unemployment in 2009
Source: Saudi Arabian Monetary Agency (SAMA), 2011 **[32]**

which gave it a boost for doing business with ease due to recent reforms and developments **[33]**. The World Bank report represents a new journey for Saudi Arabia by ranking it as the best place for doing business (entrepreneurship) out of the Middle Eastern and Arab countries. In 2006, King Abdullah stated that he wanted to see Saudi Arabia among the top ten countries of the world doing business by 2010, and no Middle Eastern country should have better investment prospects than Saudi Arabia by 2007. Keeping the same in mind, a wave of motivation struck Saudi Arabia, and a 10-by-10 initiative was created whose main focus was to include Saudi Arabia among the ten best and most competitive economies of the world **[32]**. The World Bank ratings ranked Saudi Arabia as 12th out of 183 countries, placing it among the world's largest leading reformers. Table 3.1 presents a complete picture of Saudi Arabia's latest Word Bank rankings for doing business **[32]**.

Success and failure go hand in hand. No success can be guaranteed; therefore, despite all, Saudi entrepreneurship still faces challenges and difficulties related to employment and job opportunities. The Global Economic Monitor (GEM) marks Saudi Arabia as having the lowest Total Entrepreneurial Activity (TEA) rate among the factor-driven economies of the world at 4.7 percent, which rose to 9.4 percent in 2010, marking it as the third-lowest factor-driven economy according to TEA **[34]**.

Current efforts to support entrepreneurship in Saudi Arabia

According to an SME and Entrepreneurship Support Services in Saudi Arabia Stakeholder Mapping report by Saudi Arabia for General Investment Authority (SAGIA), existing efforts to support entrepreneurship include financing,

Table 3.1 Doing business ranking indicators of Saudi Arabia (2011–2012)

Indicator	Saudi Arabia 2012	Saudi Arabia 2012	Best Performance 2012
Starting a Business	14	10	New Zealand
Dealing with Construction Permits	6	4	Hong Kong
Getting Electricity	17	18	Iceland
Registering Property	1	1	New Zealand
Getting Credit	45	48	United Kingdom
Protecting Investors	16	17	New Zealand
Paying Taxes	10	10	Canada
Trading Across Borders	18	18	Singapore
Enforcing Contracts	138	138	Luxembourg
Resolving Insolvency	69	73	Japan

Source: The World Bank, 2012

awareness and incubation [35]. These parent efforts further branch out into child efforts for better contributions to making Saudi Arabia a land of opportunities.

Financing includes various funding programs which facilitate young entrepreneurs in funding their start-ups and maintaining their sustainability for better participation in economic growth. These help in accelerating entrepreneurship in KSA. This also includes various government entities related to business and the economic sector in Saudi Arabia.

Saudi Industrial Development Fund – Kafalah program

The Saudi Industrial Development Fund (SIDF) is a government-based financial institution established in 1974 with the goal of financing and supporting private industrial sector development. It was developed with the vision of providing medium- and long-term loans so that new factories may be set up and existing ones may be upgraded, expanded and modernized accordingly. SIDF is already involved in providing consultancy services to local industrial projects in various walks of life. The Kingdom's industrial development is massively supported by SIDF's finance and support of industrial investments. Figure 3.4 depicts a clear picture of support by SIDF to the current efforts of entrepreneurship in Saudi Arabia [35].

The Public Investment Fund

The Saudi Arabia Public Investment Fund (PIF) was established in 1971 with the vision of providing financial support to projects of strategic significance to the national economy. The PIF has many credits attached to its name, including managing and supporting a number of companies which are a base for innovation, diversification and non–oil sector development in KSA. Currently, the PIF has a diversified portfolio which includes approximately 200 investments, out of which 20 are listed on the Saudi Stock Exchange. March 2015

Figure 3.4 SIDF project financing categories

Source: Industrial Investors Guide – Saudi Arabia; Land of Opportunities **[35]**

marked a major transformation for the PIF as its role shifted from the Ministry of Finance to the Council of Economic and Development Affairs (CEDA), which further led to a new board establishment chaired by Prince Mohammad Bin Salman Al Saud. The PIF is now on a new journey where positive changes and new strategies await it to make its role stronger than before. Additionally, the PIF plays an imperative role in the Kingdom's economy and therefore needs to be perfectly aligned with Saudi Arabia's Vision 2030 **[35]**.

Saudi Technology Development and Investments Company

Saudi Technology Development and Investment Company (TAQNIA) is a multi-strategy technology development and investment company which falls under the umbrella of Saudi Arabia's Public Investment Fund. TAQNIA was established in 2011 with the goal of accelerating the diversification of the Kingdom's economy through innovation and knowledge-based industries leading to value-added job transformation. It also plays a central role in partnering with industry leaders, venture capital and academia so as to add maximum strategic value to the Kingdom while being on the road to attractive return on investment TAQNIA targets three major investment sectors: industrial, investment and service, which are the key areas to promote Saudi Arabia's economy and make way for a smooth transition to a knowledge-based economy [35].

Centennial Fund

The Centennial Fund is an independent, non-profit foundation with the vision of supporting youth projects and encouraging young people to become successful business owners. It was established in 1425 AH and was named Centennial because it emerged when the Kingdom of Saudi Arabia was celebrating 100 years after it was taken over by King Abdul Aziz. The Centennial Fund was initially established to fund youth projects at a time when there was a sheer lack of programs to decrease unemployment and encourage youth to start small and medium-sized enterprises and at the same time help them participate in supporting the local economy of the country. The Centennial Fund aspired to achieve some value-added goals which included supporting and developing innovation in business and expansion of lucrative chances for projects to achieve rapid growth through training, mentoring and funding. This will enable the local economy to grow and help to create new job opportunities [35].

Prince Sultan bin Abdul Aziz Fund: nurturing women entrepreneurs

The Prince Sultan Bin Abdul Aziz Fund to support small women's enterprises came into existence in 2007 in Dammam. This fund was initiated by Prince Mohammed bin Fahd bin Abdul Aziz. The aim of this fund is to support aspiring women entrepreneurs with technical as well as financial support. The fund has supported 32 projects in a span of two years. There is no age criteria for women to apply for the fund. A review board has been set up which reviews the business proposals submitted by aspiring entrepreneurs and businesswomen as a partial requirement for fund approval. The finalists who qualify are then expected to go through a 10-day training program called "Intilakati" which represents a new journey and is considered the first step towards successful entrepreneurship. After training, the finalists are expected to submit a complete business plan and feasibility study to a group of competitive sponsors. As a part of grooming, the finalists are also taught human development skills like human resources, development, finance, accounts, marketing, cash management and so on, which are important skills for building a venture or start-up. Under the umbrella of the Prince Sultan Bin Abdul Aziz Fund, a center by the name of Prince Mohammed bin Fahd Leaders Preparation Center was established in 2009, realizing the importance of leadership skills to be inculcated in young Saudi girls, and this center strives to teach these skills within the age span of 6 to 25. Its aim is to prepare the young generation to lead a better tomorrow [36].

Siraj Capital: building future entrepreneurs

Building market leaders for any economy is the need of the time. Siraj Capital, sensing this need, aspires to provide support to the entrepreneurs of Saudi Arabia and MENA. For Siraj Capital to fund these entrepreneurs, the basic key elements which should be inculcated in entrepreneurs include determination, vision and an ambition to build future market leaders. Siraj Capital has been built on the belief that these entrepreneurs are the backbone of the economy and hold the greatest potential for job creation in Saudi Arabia. It was founded in 2005, and since its inception, Siraj Capital's private equity business has been focusing on providing enlightened business solutions, primarily to the Saudi Arabian market. Its main focus is on the White Box approach rather than the traditional Black Box approach, with investment involved in the projects. Siraj Capital's vision is not only to identify opportunities and invest in them, but it also aspires to help the CEOs of the companies it is incubating to achieve their business goals. Its incubating process follows a two-day strategic training session with the respective companies and makes a list of assignments to be conducted by each member of Siraj development team, which then conducts follow-ups year-round to make sure that the tasks are being accomplished and the respective project is on the road to success. Apart from all this, Siraj Capital has become one of the key players in the Islamic finance industry as well. Siraj Capital has been one of the pioneers in sensing a potential in Sukuk offerings and has also been involved in the structuring of a Sukuk offering for Western projects [35].

Arab Fund for Economic and Social Development

The Arab Fund for Economic and Social Development (AFESD) is a fund which is based in Kuwait and strives to support economic and social development projects in the Arab countries, including Saudi Arabia. It finances public and private projects and provides grants and expert advice, giving an edge to economic growth. It is a joint Arab action with all the Arab countries as its members and seeks to meet the economic and development needs of all its members and also ensure that projects are feasible and transparent. Being an Arab institution, the Arab Fund plays a special role in providing solutions for Arab issues and concerns. It also plays a key role in economic and social development projects like health care, drinking water, education, rural development and social welfare, leading to a reduction in poverty. It has also played an eminent role in supporting Arab countries in dealing with the effects of war and natural disasters [35, 37].

Bab Rizq Jameel

Bab Rizq Jameel (BRJ) is one of the most important private-sector programs which aspires to assist young Saudi entrepreneurs to lead their own enterprises. It was established in 2007 in Jeddah and has been working under the umbrella of the Abdul Latif Jameel Community services program. In 2009, BRJ financed 5,110 small ventures and projects and, as a result, 41,284 jobs were created for young men and women. Out of these 5,110 projects financed by BRJ were beauty salon ventures, wedding planning projects, laundries, bakeries, cell phone companies and computers distribution projects. During the past two years, BRJ has expanded to 18 branches throughout the Kingdom. BRJ offers diversified programs, including direct employment, employment training, SME financing, taxi and truck ownership and work from home and franchise programs. The Islamic Development Bank Group (IDB) signed a memorandum of understanding with BRJ recently for private enterprise growth promotion, job creation stimulation and sharing of funding expertise so as to support entrepreneurship in the Kingdom. BRJ is working towards changing the landscape of SMEs by supporting more durable small projects in the Kingdom [36].

Arab Monetary Fund

The Arab Monetary Fund, located in the heart of United Arab Emirates, aspires to provide assistance to Arab financial market development and provides advice to member states on the investment of resources through the Arab Trade Financing Program (ATFP). ATFP is a multi-Arab financial institution which aspires to promote Arab trade and to expand the competitive edge of Arab exporters and importers. ATFP came into existence in 1989 with 53 shareholders, including the Arab Monetary Fund and public and private financial institutions including joint Arab-foreign financial and banking institutions [35, 38].

Inter-Arab Investment Guarantee Corporation

The Inter-Arab Investment Guarantee Corporation came into existence with the purpose of promoting foreign direct investment (FDI) via political risk insurance to Arab and non-Arab investors and lenders. It also strives to provide political and commercial risk insurance to Arab exporters in order to enhance the Kingdom's exports [35].

Local financing options

Leading Arab investment banks, such as Samba Bank, SABB and Al Rajhi, consider Saudi Arabia their motherland. All of these are included in the list of the largest 1,000 banks in the world. The second half of the twentieth century marked a new chapter in which many foreign banks chose to do their business in Saudi Arabia from a Gulf Cooperation Council hub as a result of several policies. Thirteen foreign banks received licenses to operate in Saudi Arabia through the Saudi Arabia Monetary Agency [35].

Prince Mohammed bin Salman bin Abdul Aziz Foundation

The Prince Mohammed bin Salman bin Abdul Aziz Foundation (MiSK) is a nonprofit organization whose main focus is to nurture learning and leadership in Saudi Arabia's youth. Its nurturing revolves around three key fields, education, media and culture. Learning is the need of the time, and this is the basic ingredient a country needs to nourish its economy. Through a diversified variety of incubators, the MiSK Foundation is trying to play an eminent role in developing intellectual capital and unlocking the inner potential of all Saudi people. The MiSK Foundation believes in three guiding principles: commitment, impact and integrity. As a part of Saudi Arabia's Vision 2030, MiSK has taken it as its foremost duty to use its team, expertise and resources to achieve the Vision 2030 goals to the fullest **[39, 40]**.

MiSK Foundation initiatives

The MiSK Global Forum is a flagship platform of the MiSK Foundation which spearheads an annual gathering every year. It was established in 2016 and its main focus is on "Meeting the Challenge of Change." The MiSK Global Forum intends to gather young leaders, the world's sharpest and most innovative talent, creators and thinkers, on the same platform so that the participants may explore, participate and experiment with ideas and trends emerging in the knowledge economy **[39–42]**.

Global Grand Challenges is a collaboration between the MiSK Foundation and the Bill & Melinda Gates Foundation. The Bill & Melinda Gates Foundation funds global health and diversified development programs for the world's underprivileged people. In the upcoming three years, the MiSK Global Forum, via its Grand Challenges, aspires to launch new challenges every six months. According to the Grand Challenges, 100 innovators across the world will be offered a grant of USD 100,000 for their ingenious ideas to convert them into practical and concrete concepts. The upcoming challenges will focus on two main themes: Education and Global Citizenship. The Education theme will help bring in new and innovative ideas and solutions to transform the education system and give empowerment to youth to gain success in transforming Saudi Arabia's oil-based economy into a knowledge-based economy. The Global Citizenship theme will help the MiSK Global Forum to gather innovative and bright ideas so that young people may attain global goals for sustainable development of the economy **[43]**. Grand Challenges revolve around three goals: empower, activate and inspire. All these goals aim to develop human capital development and give many avenues to youth. Today is a fast-paced time, and we are living in a technological world which is changing faster and transforming the way we live and contribute to our communities. Through these Grand Challenges, everyone will be able to harness this change together and build a better world full of opportunities for tomorrow. If the winners of the Grand Challenges are able to prove themselves in transforming their ideas into concrete plans and proper solutions, the ground will be open for them to apply for more funding [43]. Indeed, this is an awesome platform for economic transformation and provides a chance for people globally to showcase their talent and participate in the economic growth of Saudi Arabia. The Global Challenge Forum invites everyone to change the world, so are we up to the challenge?

MiSK Schools is another initiative by the MiSK Foundation which focuses on a creative environment, holistic learning, inquiry-based learning, project-based learning and open communication. MiSK Schools focus on imparting a world-class education based on the International Baccalaureate (IB) Program. They are based in the heart of Saudi Arabia, and their aim is to nurture young Saudis' cognitive, social and academic skills and prepare them for a global economic life and as custodians of the Kingdom's future. The end result is that MiSK students turn out to be great thinkers, leaders and innovators as MiSK aspires to prepare students to face everyday challenges [44].

Riyadh Virtual Schools is also an initiative by the MiSK Foundation, along with other board members, to provide an opportunity to overseas students to study national projects from grades 1–12. Students enrolled in this program receive immediate feedback through a learning management system [45].

Recently the MiSK Foundation launched three new strategic ventures in Riyadh to boost innovation, training and investment. These ventures are aimed to build the skills, knowledge and capability for economic growth within the tech sector of Saudi Arabia. MiSK Academy, MiSK Technovation and MiSK Booster have been launched to empower, inspire and nurture young Saudi men and women to recognize their inner potential and talent as a part of the economic transformation of the country. The 2017 two-day MiSK Global Forum was followed by these three venture announcements. MiSK Academy will open new doors for international training in Saudi Arabia, keeping in mind the ever-emerging need for skills in today's digital world. The Academy aims to train 5,000 leaders, developers and designers from all walks of life, including app development, artificial intelligence, gaming, virtual reality and animation. MiSK Technovation aims to support young talent by incubating new and creative ideas and converting talent and ideas into tangible business initiatives. Through the Technovation ventures, MiSK aims to build a digital community full of digital experts across diversified fields, including artificial intelligence, programming, cyber security, cloud computing and fields including the internet. Its state-of-the-art focus is on new domestic app development and giving a lucrative chance to women to increase their number in the sector. MiSK Booster is based on components which include venture capital of about USD 50 million to invest in start-ups, which will open new doors for versatile digital solutions and services and give a boost to the Kingdom's Vision 2030. This will help in creating a community that will enable mentorship among Saudi peers and open new avenues for entrepreneurship in Saudi Arabia [46].

Government entities in Saudi Arabia related to business and the economy include:

1   Saudi Arabia for General Investment Authority
2   Saudi Food and Drug Authority
3   Logistic, Re-export and Bonded Zones
4   Saudi Fund for Development
5   Saudi Export Program
6   Saudi Workforce Development Funding **[35]**

Awareness includes various programs which help young entrepreneurs to participate in various entrepreneurship recognition programs for their start-ups and maintain sustainability for better participation in economic growth.

Saudi Fast Growth 100

Saudi Fast Growth 100 is a new program designed to promote entrepreneurship and create awareness among the masses about the benefits of start-up projects. This awareness program is based on innovation and ranks the best revenue generation and fastest-growing companies in the Kingdom. More than 70 percent of Saudi Fast Growth 100 CEOs are serial entrepreneurs whose businesses reflect their true dedication and sincerity. Their competitiveness is the best ingredient which keeps them rolling, and their revenue doubles in size at an average rate of 43 percent annually, which is nearly ten times the rate of the Kingdom's private sector. According to the Saudi Arabian General Investment Authority, Saudi Arabia is competitive enough to compete among the best nations of the world, and in order to accomplish its ambition, Saudi Arabia needs to nurture emerging companies, as they are the backbone and oxygen of the economy **[36]**.

Prince Salman bin Abdul Aziz – Young Entrepreneur Awards

The aim of these awards is to build tomorrow's leaders. These awards were initiated by Prince Salman bin Abdul Aziz in order to instill a new entrepreneurial spirit among the young men and women who are the future generation leaders of Saudi Arabia. The youth of the Kingdom are considered the fuel of civilization, and therefore these awards recognize the eminent role the young generation plays in the Kingdom's economy. These awards are given in six categories for outstanding entrepreneurs: leadership, agriculture, technical, trade, service and industry. The parameters for these awards include 1) the entrant must be a Saudi national between the ages of 18 and 40; 2) he or she should have established a business or project proving to have contributed to society in some way in one of the previous six categories; and 3) the company should possess at least a one-year track record in the same area. Any new start-ups or projects that meet these criteria are eligible to participate in these awards. Apart from the previous six categories, these awards also include the best government award and best private sector organization award, as well as the best leading businessperson award for someone who has provided exceptional support and guidance to young entrepreneurs. 2010 saw a new motivational spin as the Centennial Fund was awarded the best government award, National Commercial Bank (NCB) received the best private organization award and Mohammed Abdul Latif Jameel was declared the best businessman of the year. These awards also arrange seminars and workshops for entrepreneurs so as to participate in human capital development [36].

Injaz-Saudi program

The Injaz-Saudi program is an awareness program which basically concentrates on educating young minds at an early age, teaching them what innovation and competitiveness are all about and how to initiate small business projects. This program partners with various private companies so as to take advantage of their expertise and inculcate the same in young minds to boost them for better economic growth for the country [36, 47].

MIT Arab business plan competition

The Massachusetts Institute of Technology (MIT) Arab business plan competition is one of the most recent initiatives taken to award young entrepreneurs in the Kingdom via partnering with Abdul Latif Jameel Foundation community service programs (ALJCSP). In 2009, this competition promoted a feeling of community and brought together 17 countries on the same platform, including North African, Gulf and Levant countries, along with Saudi Arabia, and these were represented by six business teams. This competition had 1,200 participants, and among them, three Saudi teams were shortlisted out of nine semifinalists and finalists. MIT aspires to promote entrepreneurship and establish it as the cornerstone of the Arab mindset. This yearly competition recognizes entrepreneurs in three diversified tracks: start-up track, idea track and social entrepreneurship track. The winning entrepreneur of this competition is awarded more than USD 160,000 as the winning prize and wins additional benefits which include training, mentoring, networking opportunities, media exposure and so on [36, 48]. The MIT business plan competition will definitely break the shackles of unemployment and motivate young citizens to take a strong initiative for economic growth and knowledge-based transformation of the Kingdom of Saudi Arabia.

Incubation, which is a ground for innovation, includes various university incubators which aim to accelerate the national base of science and technology to foster innovation and sustainable economic growth.

King Abdullah University for Science and Technology

King Abdullah University for Science and Technology (KAUST) is a globally renowned graduate research university which aims to foster and nurture the entrepreneurship skills of young entrepreneurs and give them a boost over others. KAUST strives to make a massive contribution to society by supporting scientific and technological projects and enabling Saudi Arabia to attain increased economic growth and transformation [35, 49]. The university's Innovative Industrial Collaboration Program (KICP) aims to foster and nurture strong ties with local, global and regional businesses that have the same vision of strengthening entrepreneurship in the country and establishing a very strong bond between economic growth and academic research [36].

Badir program technology incubator

Badir is a technology-based incubator program initiated by King Abdul Aziz City for Science and Technology (KACST) in 2007. The word "Badir" means "to initiate." Badir is a national program which strives to support and accelerate emerging technology-based projects and businesses in the Kingdom. Badir has the aim of fostering, advancing and supporting innovation, technology and entrepreneurship in whatever projects and ventures the country plans to advance. Its significant support includes services like business service consultancy, secretarial and administrative support, office space and many other services which target converting technological ideas into promising and revenue-generating projects so as to promote better economic growth of the country [35, 50].

Badir for Biotechnology was launched in 2010 as the first Saudi bio business incubator. It provides support for the creation, growth and development of new projects in the field of biotechnology. It is known to provide state-of-the-art business services and unique facilities to help businesses reach their full potential and growth. It aspires to be recognized as the leading global biotechnology incubator. Badir for Biotechnology is ready to incubate businesses falling into four major technology sectors: 1) health care and pharmaceuticals, 2) live science, 3) food and agriculture and 4) environment. Its incubation-related programs include 1) the Technology Entrepreneurship Awareness Program and 2) pre-incubation programs. All these programs are available for both men and women without any discrimination. Badir for Biotechnology strives to create value-added employment opportunities along with a vibrant environment for the Saudi biotechnology sector [50].

Badir for Biotechnology incubator projects include 1) Innovative Technologies Development (ITD), 2) Mesned Clinical Research Organization (MCRO), 3) UFC Biotech, 4) Diabetes Science International Foundation, 5) Endodontic Obturator, 6) Dr. Zone, 7) ACE Biotech, 8) Saudi Research Consultants LLC, 9) The Stability Lab, 10) MEDLICIOUS, 11) Organic Standards, 12) Scientific Diamond Laboratory, 13) Bioanalytical Research Laboratory (BRL), 14) Tilad,

15) Viam-BSA, 16) Faizgen, 17) RTD, 18) Sudair Pharma, 19) EQUAME and 20) Dcare **[50]**.

The Badir Incubator for Information and Communication Technology was established at the end of 2008 in order to help the Kingdom's information and communication technology sector flourish. It was the first technology incubator in the Kingdom and was established by Badir in affiliation with KACST. Its scope of work includes smart phone applications, multimedia, infrastructure of information and communication technology, software and solutions and computer and communication devices. The Badir Incubator for Information and Communication Technology aspires to become the Kingdom's global incubator to support creativity and development and promote the information and technology sector of the Kingdom.

Badir Incubator for Information and Communication Technology projects are as follows: 1) ShopMate, 2) Dhad, 3) NOGA, 4) Competitive Technology, 5) Wade7, 6) AlMaured, 7) esign, 8) Enwani, 9) MyGrapefruit, 10) Saudi Match, 11) Saudi Guides, 12) VOTEME, 13) Naqaa, 14) IExist, 15) Omlaty, 16) ZEEZ, 17) Games For Fun, 18) POS, 19) Marnpos, 20) Wlimtk, 21) SEMA-NOOR, 22) Za7maa, 23) INFINITY, 24) BUZNIKIN GAMES, 25) Audustry, 26) Plus Gamer, 27) Mekshat, 28) Trieval, 29) Easell, 30) Navirize, 31) Saudi Gamer, 32) Foodics, 33) Mrsool, 34) Marntech, 35) Feeedz, 36) The Third ID, 37) MyCN, 38) Modern IT, 39) Tadarrb, 40) Slnee, 41) Smart Menu, 42) Dusfan, 43) Qiola, 44) Shora, 45) Mango Jazan, 46) Shater, 47) Haweee, 48) 6abeeb.com, 49) Qaym.com, 50) Hrakat, 51) Telfaz, 52) Competitive Technologies, 53) Isterlab, 54) MUWATHIQ, 55) Raj International, 56) ASPNS, 57) Dutizer, 58) Seera Store, 59) Waqood, 60) Application Vieen, 61) Ebtikarat DEV, 62) Riyadh School Guide, 63) Mod Cloud, 64) TeeeShare, 65) Tidy School, 66) Practech LLC, 67) Wade7, 68) ENSAT, 69) Morni, 70) Magsafi, 71) Shaleeh net, 72) Way of Fitness, 73) Qoyod, 74) Quant, 75) HerafApp, 76) Tahkeem, 77) MasjidVoice, 78) Jebli Delivery and 79) Hroof **[51]**.

This science and technology incubator further aims to provide free residency services to its clients with significant other services which include offices for men and women, basic office equipment, telecommunication services, seminars, videoconferencing and conference room facilities, maintenance and cleaning services, an open office area, a library, an LCD screen facility, self-service machines for snacks and so on **[51]**.

The Badir Advanced Manufacturing Technology incubator program was established by the Badir for Information and Communication Technology incubator in May 2010. Organizations or projects that wish to adapt advanced industrial technology as a part of entrepreneurship are supported by this incubator program. The incubator's scope of work includes innovation and development of advanced industrial equipment, production of advanced industrial materials and new and innovative products. Its services include administrative and commercial services, a product life center and training services. It has various projects attached to its name, which include 1) Electric lift, 2) Nota, 3) Mathayel al-jubail Factory for safety equipment, 4) Smart Building Systems,

5) Automation, 6) LED Technology, 7) Jwain, 8) Yatooq, 9) smart control, 10) Pressure tank, 11) Control System, 12) Fire Retardant Cables, 13) Laroma, 14) Air Cooler, 15) Smart Pillow, 16) ALSAQYAH, 17) The Electromagnetic float, 18) Complex Electronix, 19) self-extinguishing, 20) Air Filters, 21) Feed pick machine, 22) Autistic Children, 23) Engine Monitoring Devices, 24) Roving Caravan, 25) Developed Umbrella, 26) Sand Cleaning Device, 27) CNC and 28) Magnetic sweeper apparatus for airport runways [52].

The Badir Technology Incubator in Taif was established on August 13, 2015. In order to meet the objectives of the program and provide ample support for entrepreneurship and technology, it has joined with local entities like Taif Chamber of Commerce and Industry and Taif University. Its scope of work includes information and communication technology, advanced manufacturing and biotechnology. The projects attached to its name and supported under its umbrella include 1) Wardat, 2) Rashed Factory, 3) Wayfinder and 4) Notah [53].

Programs established under the wing of Badir include technology groups, technology enterprise funding units, incubator support service departments and the Saudi Business Incubator Network and Entrepreneurship program [50].

Riyadh Techno Valley

Riyadh Techno Valley (RTV) is one of King Saud University's contributions to building partnerships. The purpose of this valley is to attract local and global investment in technological research. The valley aspires to further support dynamic research activity within the university and the Kingdom and plans to harness innovation in order to enable existing economic institutions within the Kingdom. Its vision is to transfer or generate advanced technology so as to facilitate Saudi Arabia in its transformation into a knowledge-based economy [35, 54].

Dhahran Technology Valley

Dhahran Technology Valley (DTV) was a major project initiated by King Fahd University of Petroleum and Minerals (KFUPM) in 2006. DTV provides support services like development, marketing and production for academic research and within the premises of a business environment. Its key purpose is to provide top-of-the-line infrastructure for industrial resources and development to flourish in the Kingdom. The faculty at KFUPM has been hired to match the top-of-the-line faculty at international universities like those in Singapore, Hong Kong, New York, Silicon Valley and so on [35, 55]. KFUPM values include integrity, innovation, fairness, transparency, passion, inclusiveness, care, discipline and so on. KFUPM aims to be unique and to make a difference in whatever steps it takes and to concentrate on human capital development to enable its graduates to stand out from the crowd. It also aims to engage stakeholders in ventures focused on contributing to the prosperity and intellectual level of the community [35, 55].

Saudi success stories

According to SME and Entrepreneurship Support Services in Saudi Arabia, there are many success stories attached to its name. Various sectors have had fruitful results, and the emerging projects and their entrepreneurs in the respective sectors have undoubtedly played an eminent role in accelerating the economic growth and development of the Kingdom. The following will discuss the highlights of these ventures.

Brains Contracting Ltd. Co. belongs to the construction/engineering sector. It was launched in 2002. It was initially launched with 40,000 SR, grossed up to more than 20 million SR in 2009 and is now recognized as one of the premier maintenance companies in the Eastern Province. Brains expanded its maintenance services in the oil and gas sector when it formed MCE Gulf in 2007 as a joint venture with Germany. Brains was ranked eighth out of the top ten companies on the Saudi Fast growth 100 list, announced in 2010. The chairman of Brains now has two companies under his wing and two more in the pipeline. He is now working on mentoring young entrepreneurs through the Chamber of Commerce, as he believes that it is the foremost duty of every citizen to guide young minds on the right track so that the Kingdom may prosper [36, 56].

Midrar Development Company belongs to the development management sector. This company may be a new introduction to the market, but it has 100 years of experience under its belt. It was established in 2007 in Jeddah. This company takes pride in being a house of experts, with staff from various walks of life, including real estate, architecture, facility management firms and so on. Its goal is to provide state-of-the-art real estate management and consulting services to entrepreneurs and the real estate development market of Saudi Arabia. Midrar is believed to have been the first company in the Kingdom to offer development management services. Midrar itself was incubated by Siraj Capital and had two contracts from the start of incubation and reached a staff of 25 in the first year. Its growth rate accelerated to about 280 percent by the end of the second year. Recently it was ranked fourth in Saudi Fast Growth services in both development management and facility management services [36, 57].

Bayan Gardens School (BGS) belongs to the education sector. It was established in 1999 in Saudi Arabia. Bayan Gardens School is the brainchild of director Yasmeen Husain and her entrepreneurial family. The need for such a quality bilingual school was felt when she saw people starving for a good-quality school, especially a good English curriculum. BGS focuses on both a state-of-the-art English and Arabic curriculum, with special attention to international staff, which, according to Husain, is difficult to hire, as it takes time for them to adjust to Saudi Arabia's culture from overseas. Bayan Gardens School is in the process of implementing a new innovative project by the name of TREP$ which aspires to train children from grades 4 to 8 to become entrepreneurs and teach them everything they need to start their own business according to their wishes. Innovation, creativity and success are linked to quality education, and this is the primary thing which will lead the country to a level where its economic growth will have no limits. Keeping this in mind, Saudi Arabia is giving more importance to school education and putting in efforts to improve the landscape of education in the Kingdom, as it believes whatever it invests in these children, they will repay back in significant amounts to the country in the coming years **[36, 58]**.

EDUCON Educational Services also belongs to the education sector. It was established in 2005. It is an educational consulting service that arranges English-language programs, recognizes potential, plans for foreign university degree programs and provides facilities for young students aged 8 to 16 for summer camp placements. It is headquartered in Jeddah, with one branch in London, and plans to spread its wings in Saudi Arabia by 2010. Al-Harith Al-Qureshi, who launched EDUCON, had a vision of giving students in Saudi Arabia and MENA the support he was unable to have while studying abroad. Since 2005, EDUCON has provided assistance to 1,800 students from Saudi Arabia, Libya, Iraq, UAE and Yemen. The EDUCON website was launched in 2006 and since then has been receiving 25,000 hits a month. There were a lot of challenges EDUCON had to face; one of the biggest was to find a solution for those who were totally undecided in their fields, and another was to appear competitive and popular in the market, as in the beginning, only a few colleges and universities would sign up with it. The EDUCON working staff in Jeddah is 100 percent Saudi and can perfectly relate to the needs of its student clientele, as they themselves are young. EDUCON was ranked fifth on the Saudi Fast Growth 100 list in 2010, among the fastest growing start-up companies **[36, 59]**.

Lomar: thobe [re]defined belongs to the fashion and textiles sector. It is a Saudi-based fashion brand which specializes in [re]defined thobes, which is an ankle-length garment with long sleeves worn by men in the Arabian Gulf region. This venture reached revenue of around 18 million SR in 2009. Today it has four stores, two in Jeddah, one in Riyadh and one in Al-Khobar, and its brand is well established throughout Saudi Arabia. Lomar is expected to become a franchise locally and another franchise overseas by 2012. The Lomar CEO has worked untiringly to reach to this level. Lomar has now become a coveted brand throughout Saudi Arabia, and for the past three years, KAUST graduates have been wearing Lomar thobes at their graduation. Lomar's vision is based on innovation, and Lomar's CEO is aspiring to change the landscape of fashion design. It is a Siraj Capital–incubated portfolio company and has been recognized as one of the fastest growing start-up companies **[36, 60]**.

Amwal Financial Consultants belongs to the financial services sector. It was founded in 2005 and aspires to create more entrepreneurs rather than employees because the Kingdom is in dire need of them. Fahad A. Al Kassim, its founder and CEO, mentors young entrepreneurs and also encourages employees to become entrepreneurs because he believes that one should plunge into something one loves as the key which will lead one to ultimate success. Amwal was ranked one of the fastest-growing start-up companies in 2009 and 2010 in the Saudi Fast Growth 100 winners **[36, 61]**.

Dentalia Clinics belongs to the health care and dental services sector. It was founded in 2005 by King Abdul Aziz University graduates. This clinic was constructed from scratch with the funding of its five partners. Dentalia is the first fully digital clinic built in Jeddah with the state-of-the-art European equipment. What makes it so different is its own water plant, and its water disinfection is carried out through ultra-water lighting. The beauty of this project that it recycles 100 percent of its trash. Its personalized touch and extraordinary care and services make it stand out from other similar clinics in the Kingdom. Dentalia was proud to be on the Saudi Fast Growth Companies list in 2010 **[36, 62]**.

H.E.A.L. – Healthcare Environment Advisory and Logistics Inc. is a health care company and was founded in 2010. This project focuses on three main sectors: health care, environment and hospitality. The H.E.A.L. team specializes in helping its clients establish health care– and hospitality-related projects that adhere to international standards. H.E.A.L. aspires to guide its clients in the right direction if they want to initiate or expand a current health care facility in Saudi Arabia. The client is given a clear direction from brainstorming to construction, leading to implementation of a final full-scale operational project. Green principles are the need of the time, and by integrating them as part of its daily dealings, H.E.A.L. can generate approximately 40 percent savings in the planning and design stages for its clients, along with a high performance rate. H.E.A.L. is striving for positive change in the Kingdom **[36, 63]**.

Hodema Consulting Services is in hospitality consulting services. It was founded in 2004 and provides business mentoring to entrepreneurs. It partnered with Siraj Capital in 2008, which accelerated its business entry in the Kingdom. Hodema Consulting Services aspires to identify new opportunities in untapped sectors so as to maximize development and investment returns. Hodema is a promising young company which is committed to forming lasting and long-term relationships with its clients. It is headquartered in Beirut and has branches in Jeddah, Riyadh and Damascus, with tripling revenue generation annually since 2007 **[36, 64]**.

ALMARWA.net belongs to the IT/e-commerce/technology provider sector. It was officially registered as a company in 2007. Almarwa.net is an information technology service and e-commerce solution company whose focus is to produce the most determined, highly educated and independent-minded Saudi businesswomen of the new generation. Almarwa.net was founded by Marwa Al Saleh, who always aspired to be an entrepreneur. She faced a lot of challenges while establishing Almarwa.net; balancing finances, making a business plan and human resource hiring were all new to her. She got a lot of support from the Eastern Province Chamber of Commerce, which gave her a signature piece of advice on how to go about hiring people and how to handle administrative start-up details. Less than four years later, Almarwa is on the road to success, with six female employees and more than 50 loyal clients, including the Eastern Province Commerce and many small and medium-sized enterprises. 2008 marked a new chapter for Al Saleh's company when it was recognized as the most promising IT service provider in the Eastern Pprovince, and two years later, Saudi Fast Growth 100 companies ranked it third on the watch list. As a businesswoman who followed a difficult path to pursue her dreams, Al Salehnow mentors young females who join as her employees, as she wants to them to believe that they are the next entrepreneurs in line **[36, 65]**.

Alcantara group was founded in 1997 and is one of Saudi Arabia's leading systems integration and solutions providers. Its vision was to bring Western technology to Saudi Arabia and provide it with the same platform as the West. It bridges the technology gap and handles everything for companies to relieve them from unnecessary stress. Over the past decade, Alcantara group has become the parent company for a diverse range of technology providers. 2003 saw a new achievement for Alcantara group in the form of becoming the largest Enterprise Resource Planning (ERP) implementer in the Kingdom. Alcantara faced many challenges, as it was being launched at a time when there was a scarcity of net facilities, and bankruptcy saw its doors close several times, but Alcantara returned stronger every time, and its success is clear proof of its strength. At one time, the term "ERP" was unknown, but now Alcantara has made it an essential ingredient of everyone's daily life. Technology is always a difficult sector to sell in a developing country; it takes a lot of determination and spending quality time and budget on educating consumers and making space for it in quality terms. This is what Alcantara has been striving for. In 2009, it was recognized as one of the top ten fastest-growing companies on the Saudi Fast Growth 100 list, and in 2006, Nexus Arabia – a joint venture between Alcantara and Nexus AG – was recognized as one of the largest health information system deals in the Kingdom's history. Alcantara is proud that it has contributed to society in such a way. Suleimani is also of the opinion that Saudi Fast Growth 100 is one of the most prestigious awards for Saudi Arabia, as it gives every large or small entrepreneur a chance to be recognized and provides a platform for networking with other fast-growth companies at the same time, which is an extra benefit **[36, 66]**.

Al Yaqoub Attorneys & Legal Advisors (AYALA) belongs to the legal services sector. It was founded in 2005 as a Riyadh law-based firm in association with Lovells, an international firm with 28 offices spread out globally. The managing partner of Al Yaqoub Attorneys & Legal Advisors, Montasir Al Mohammad, studied law when it was considered taboo among Saudi university students. His intuition was that familiarity with law and a Saudi with legal expertise would definitely bridge the gap between Western law and Shariah in Saudi Arabia. His intuition proved right, and in less than five years, AYALA has established itself as the leading law firm in Saudi Arabia. AYALA specializes in real estate and litigation services, including multi-purpose services such as investment, corporate, finance, construction and intellectual property. Its clients include the holding company of the Kingdom. AYALA, after experiencing success, has now opened an office in Jeddah in association with Lovells. Lovells has added another feather to the management cap of AYALA, as international firms require qualified local Saudi personnel to practice in the Kingdom. Soon, AYALA will be contributing to a great extent to the economic growth of Saudi Arabia while providing top-of-the-line legal services **[36, 67]**.

3eesho – Nurturing My Life belongs to the lifestyle services sector. It launched its beta version in January 2010. 3eesho was established with the purpose of providing state-of-the-art lifestyle services and developing better skills for society. 3eesho started on the path of entrepreneurship when it was recognized by the MIT Arab business plan competition in 2008–2009 as one of the semifinalist business teams out of 1,200 participants. It is a web-based portal application which works as a dashboard in order to monitor, measure and change one's habits, which leads to a better lifestyle. Users log their habits to monitor the level of impact on their lifestyle and also compare them with other groups. It is a social network with three main components: My Wallet, My Lifestyle and My Health. Rafah Al Khatib, the CEO of 3eesho, had a vision to create a network which would enable people to network with others using constructive topics like a nurturing life and better lifestyle habits to discuss, along with diet challenges and financial planning. The mechanism of this creative venture works in such a way that data entered as daily eating habits is recorded and analyzed in the form of graphs in the My Lifestyle section. Health and nutrition were the two topics Al Khatib had in mind while 3eesho was in the planning phase. She worked for a leading portal prior to establishing 3eesho and wanted something unique which would contribute to society and the economic growth of the Kingdom as a whole. To curtail obesity, which has now evolved into a global problem, especially in the GCC countries where Kuwait and Saudi Arabia rank the highest, 3eesho stepped in and helped change people's obese lifestyle to a great extent and enabled them to lead better lives. 3eesho has enabled Arab society to curb its unhealthy eating habits using technology and has contributed to society to a great extent with the goal in mind that every change starts with the individual **[36, 68]**.

IBS: Innovative Business Solutions is a Jeddah-based company which was founded in 2005 as a one-man show. The founder and CEO of IBS and his family sacrificed to establish and mature IBS and bring it to a market level. IBS is devoted to providing strategy and management consultancy, information services, start-up expertise, project management and analysis support for IT in Saudi Arabia and Gulf countries. It has been ranked in the Saudi Fast Growth 100 leading start-up list two years in a row. IBS is on the road to becoming the most appreciated consultants in the Kingdom. It embarked on a new journey within five years of its establishment with dramatic success of more than 123 percent and an average revenue of more than SR 5–10 million annually. Osama Natto – the founder and CEO of IBS – claims that running a small business is not a piece of cake and requires sheer hard work. He aspires to get IBS tasks like printing, courier service and so on done by small companies so that the pool of economic growth can accelerate, giving a chance to others to grow in the same pool and beyond, as it is very important for every entrepreneur to support and believe in the potential of other entrepreneurs. Natto aspires to make a difference in society and participate in the economic growth of the country and therefore gives lectures at the Jeddah Chamber of Commerce and Effat University and inspires others to build businesses **[36, 69]**.

Trans-Arabian Creative Communications (TRACCS) belongs to the PR/advertising sector and was established in 1997. It is one of the largest public relations networks in the Middle East and North Africa. A big success of TRACCS is that 50 percent of its staff is female, and five of its managing directors are women – a true women's empowerment success story. TRACCS initially stepped out to become a local public relations company and moved on to a much broader path to become a regional enterprise controlling 10 percent of the market and branches from northwest Africa to the Arabian Gulf. TRACCS's managing partner, Sarah A. Al Ayed, is one of Saudi Arabia's most successful businesswomen and is also a founding member of the first Saudi Arabian Businesswomen's committee. TRACCS started its journey from a shared office space, and within three months, it was well on the road to independence with its own headquarters. It quickly found fame as the market leaders to become one of the first local public relations agencies in Saudi Arabia. 1999 and 2000 saw another chapter of achievement in the history of TRACCS when it received the runner-up award in the Coca-Cola Middle East Agency annual awards. In 2005, TRACCS began a new chapter in the form of the Arab Conferences Company (ACC) to boost its communications platform. ACC conducts a yearly public relations conference in Jeddah which is an open platform for all PR practitioners globally. Additionally, TRACCS has broadened its links by contributing to a Strategic Communications Outreach Program on the outskirts of Riyadh's Prince Sultan University. The first corporate social responsibility conference in Kuwait was sponsored and organized by TRACCS in 2005. Al Ayed says that entrepreneurship is the need of the time and SMEs are the heart of any country's economic growth **[36, 70]**.

3points Advertising Agency was established in 1998 by three co-founders. The establishment of 3points Advertising Agency enabled these three co-founders to become market leaders of the mushrooming local advertising sector. Marwan Qutub, Eissa Bougary and Loai Naseem decided to launch this venture when they sensed the local advertising market of Saudi Arabia was extremely underdeveloped and was ruled mainly by non-Saudis. They set a new trend in Saudi Arabia, as 3points Advertising Agency was the first of its kind to be Saudi owned and Saudi run. The Jeddah-based company is growing and spreading its wings in Dubai and Riyadh. Its first print campaign for a local consulting firm became the talk of the town and resulted in attracting an army of new clients. By 2003, it was well on the way to attracting a colossal number of corporate clients, including Rabea Tea and Al Sawani. According to the 3points CEO, Saudi Arabia is an emerging economy, and sectors like telecommunications, aviation and new economic cities being developed offer a massive space for advertising, with a major and fruitful impact on the Kingdom's economy. The foundation for public service announcements (PSAs) was laid down by 3points, as it has always aspired to give back to society via PSAs. Apart from 3points, other ventures under the belt of its CEO, along with one of its other co-founders, include a sister concern in 2006 named Gluetube which specializes in web design and digital marketing. The same year saw another revolution when Under the Carpet, a film production company on the outskirts of Dubai Media City, followed Gluetube. Saudi Arabia is a land of opportunities, and as long as its markets keep expanding, people will continue to showcase their potential. 3points has changed the landscape of the advertising world in Saudi Arabia. The founders have become mentors and role models for many agencies and individuals who want to become entrepreneurs in the days to come [36, 71].

Secutronic belongs to the security solutions providers sector. It was established in 2003 and is a network of 200 entrepreneurs working together with a no-boss concept, which has contributed to its success because this thinking creates a positive environment which benefits the entire organization, including clients and stakeholders. Secutronic aspires to change the shape of business thinking by using the talent of its staff in the right place, as it believes that if employee talent is rightly used, it will help a business reach its full potential. The CEO and co-founder of Secutronic equates employee satisfaction with successful customer retention and a successful enterprise. Customer retention is of prime importance, and the company's expansion rate of 2,500 percent in a span of five years, including its annual average revenue of SR 10 to 50 million, is clear proof of this belief. Additionally, along with customer retention, employee retention is of great importance, and a 95 percent retention rate among its 200 employees is impressive. Out of these, 35 percent are from Saudi Arabia, while the rest are multinational. Secutronic is headquartered in Jeddah and has branch offices in Riyadh and Dammam. It provides state-of-the-art security services which include virtual control rooms, security management and other security-based services. The company's goal is to become a transparent, entrenched success story among client organizations. 2009 marked a new success story for Secutronic when it was nominated as the number-one Saudi Fast Growth 100 winner. This nomination has made its clients more confident that they are investing in the right place, their team is happy that their hard work has paid off and stockholders are proud to be number one [36, 72].

Jeddah United Sports Company belongs to the sports sector and came into existence in 2006. Lina Almaeena – director of JUSC – had a vision of shaping the future of women's sports in Saudi Arabia. JUSC aims to be the first local training and event management sports company for young men and women to include a sports program for girls aged 4 to 17. Women's basketball divisions and men's soccer and basketball divisions are run under the umbrella of JUSC. As a part of its corporate social responsibility program, JUSC considers it an inherent part of its philosophy to train disabled women in basketball and also offers sports programs for underprivileged youth. Almaeena aspires to endorse sports and a prosperous, healthy lifestyle for women and youth within the context of Saudi Arabia's culture and tradition. It was her desire to promote sports in Saudi Arabia, as there was scarcity of sports federations and proper training programs. She set off to launch JUSC along with her husband so as to change the field of sports awareness and training in Saudi Arabia. JUSC has an edge, as it has organized innumerable basketball tournaments which revolve around diverse and unique themes like anti-smoking, father and son relationships and so on. It also spearheaded the first women's street basketball tournament in 2007, followed by two basketball clinics with ex-Women's National Basketball Association (WNBA) players. JUSC was the first to be endorsed by Nike and Pepsi in the Middle East and also the first Saudi Arabian women's basketball league. Khobar United is another venture launched by the JUSC team and Haji Husein Alireza & Co. This venture is the first women's sports organization in Al Khobar and was launched as a result of inspiration from JUSC and its ground-breaking success. JUSC had a vision to inspire the sports sector and make an impact on society, and Khobar United is clear proof of the impact it has had on the economic growth and development of Saudi Arabia. It has indeed proved itself a trendsetter in the sports sector [36, 73].

Intercontinental Travel Company (ITC) belongs to the travel sector and was established in 2005. No success story is a bed of roses, and same is true for ITC. This project was revived by Khalid Alfadl in 2005 after its failure with a debt of around SR 500,000. He believed in challenges and rolled up his sleeves to plunge into a venture against everyone's advice, as he trusted his gut instincts and his passion. His instincts proved him right, and he was able to pull ITC back from the brink. ITC embarked on a new journey to success and now has two more branches in the north and east of Jeddah, which led to revenue generation. With new branches came more staff, offering more employment opportunities to the unemployed. In 2006, it was able to establish two more branches. Alfadl was successful in pulling ITC out of debt via sheer hard work, investing in his own capital and aggressively marketing ITC's website for online bookings, which led to the company's expansion. His plan to bring in more VIP client accounts proved the icing on the cake. ITC's excellent service earned the company several awards, including the Superior Lufthansa City Center Award by Lufthansa Airlines in 2007 and 2008 and the Lifetime Achievement Award by Emirates Airlines in 2008, and it was ranked among the fastest-growing companies on the Saudi Fast Growth 100 list, coming in 14th on the list in 2009 and 6th in 2010. Alfadl is proud that he owns a company that was once in debt but now on the road to success. It is, indeed, a proud moment for Saudi Arabia and its economic growth [36, 74].

ACWA Power International belongs to the water, energy and power sector. It was established in 2004 with the unique goal of establishing itself as a full-capacity developer, owner and operator of an independent seawater desalination and power generation plant. When Saudi Arabia's government made the decision to privatize the water supply and power generation sector, ACWA Power Development was the first company to respond to this call in 2004. Power at that time was one of the major infrastructures which required much improvement and modernization, and ACWA aims to be the lead developer. It has a global team from diverse fields and 25 different nationalities. To date, there are five mega-projects attached to the success story of ACWA: Rabigh

Independent Water Stream and Power Project (IWSPP), Shuaibah Independent Water Power Project (IWPP), Shuaibah Expansion Independent Water Project (IWP), MarafiqJubail IWPP and Shuqaiq IWPP. Additionally, two more lucrative projects were constructed by ACWA, which are self-supporting desalination plants. Their capabilities include 25,000 cubic meters of water daily, and once they are fully operational, the end result will be 6,000 megawatts of power along with 2.24 million m³/day of desalinated water. ACWA further aspires to expand regionally and ultimately become a global player in phase II. It is currently ranked the third-largest IWPP regionally with an approximate value of USD 1.6 million. The Saudi Fast Growth 100 ranked it third on the 2009 start-up list. These recognitions are inspiring for entrepreneurs and give a further boost to the economic growth and development of Saudi Arabia, along with putting it on the map [36, 75].

Al Sale Eastern Company Ltd. belongs to the weighing system and scrap processing sector. It was established in 1976 and depicts a true picture of women's empowerment in Saudi Arabia. Shiekha Nadia Al-Dossary is an iconic lady whose will knows no bounds. Prior to joining Al Sale Eastern in 1996 as a manager and investor, she worked for five years as a trainer and then as a general manager for Avon Cosmetics in Saudi Arabia, as she wanted to gain an expert edge to lead Al Sale Eastern. Avon Cosmetics taught her to be ambitious and enabled her to take over as a general manager for Al Sale Eastern when her husband, the founder of Al Sale Eastern, met with an accident that left him in a coma for two months, followed by several years of recovery. When she took over as the general manager, she was the only woman among 128 employees. It was a bold leap, as the scrap business involves a lot money exchanged on a daily basis. Her management injected a new spirit into Al Sale Eastern, and it thrived. Within five years, the company was on the road to profit of up to 500 percent. Her spearheaded improvements launched a new journey for the company, and she proved to be the first to implement European environmental and safety controls for the collection of scrap metals. She wants her company to go completely green and contribute to making the environment radioactive free. 2008 started a new chapter of success for Al Sale Eastern when it was declared a leader in GCC and Saudi Arabian industry. The same year, the company installed the first giant shredder in the history of the Kingdom, capable of shredding and dismantling anything from cars to computers, and it keeps a close eye on environmental issues. The company controls more than 65 percent of the market in Saudi Arabia and is also a major exporter to the Far East. Corporate social responsibility is an important aspect Al Dossary puts special focus on. She wants Saudi youth to be entrepreneurs instead of employees, and to this end, her company launched the National Micro Yard Program so that youth may co-own a scrap yard. Additionally, the company provides necessary training, initial capital and necessary equipment for micro-yards. Al-Dossary has won several awards for her innovativeness, uniqueness and accomplishments as an entrepreneur. In 2006 and 2007, *Arab News* ranked her the top businesswoman of the year. The same year, *Financial Times* chose her as one of the top

25 influential women in the Middle East. She is a true picture of success and a truly inspirational women's empowerment story in Saudi Arabia **[36, 76]**.

Conclusion

This chapter brings into the limelight the potential which distinguishes the citizens of Saudi Arabia. It further breaks stereotypes and focuses on the fact that great entrepreneurial ideas can emerge from anyone in the industry, and a great entrepreneur is not necessarily a man. Women can play an equal role in being great entrepreneurs. Many success stories covered in this chapter depict a clear picture of true women's empowerment in Saudi Arabia. The existing efforts to support entrepreneurship, like various funding programs, awareness and entrepreneurship ventures, recognition programs and various incubators illustrate in depth the significant role these play in putting Saudi Arabia on the map and further demonstrating it is a land of opportunities. Though Saudi Arabia is a kingdom, its Vision 2030 is on the road to transformation with massive support for entrepreneurs and ample chances for youth to explore their entrepreneurial ideas. Under the current prevailing system in Saudi Arabia, tenacity, persistence and building relationships with government bodies is mandatory so that the burdensome regulatory process may be navigated. Saudi Arabia is on the road to success to become the number-one choice for international business, being a land of abundant liquidity and opportunities. This chapter will truly help entrepreneurs all over the world explore massive platforms for their ventures and funding at the same time. Furthermore, the economy all over the world will flourish, as knowledge is currency for a country and a transition towards a knowledge-based economy is a current global need.

References

1 Block, J.H., Thurik, R., and Zhou, H. (2013). What turns knowledge into innovative products? The role of entrepreneurship and knowledge spillovers. *Journal of Evolutionary Economics* 23, 693–718.

2 Galindo, M.Á. and Méndez, M.T. (2014). Entrepreneurship, economic growth, and innovation: Are feedback effects at work? *Journal of Business Research* 67, 825–829.

3 Lee, K., Kim, B.Y., Park, Y.Y., and Sanidas, E. (2013). Big businesses and economic growth: Identifying a binding constraint for growth with country panel analysis. *Journal of Comparative Economics* 41, 561–582.

4 Qian, H. and Acs, Z.J. (2013). An absorptive capacity theory of knowledge spill over entrepreneurship. *Small Business Economics* 40, 185–197.

5 Xiaoyu, Y. and Xiangming, T. (2015). An inverted U-shape relationship between entrepreneurial failure experiences and new product development performance: The multiple mediating effects of entrepreneurial orientation. *Journal of Entrepreneurship & Organization Management* 5, 1.

6 Spencer, F.M. (2016). Success strategies Saudi entrepreneurs used to navigate through regulations in Jeddah. *J. Entrepren. Organiz. Manag.* 5, 199. doi:10.4172/2169-026X.1000199.

7 Dye, B.G. (2014). Gatekeepers of entrepreneurial activity: Formal institutions and the entrepreneurial ecology.

8 World Economic Forum. *Accelerating Entrepreneurship in the Arab World*. The Forum of Young Global Leaders and published on 22nd of October 2011.

9 Abu-Sharkh, A. and Alshubaili, W. (2013). *Saudi Arabia at a Glance*. The Forum of Young Global Leaders.

10 Autio, E., Kenney, M., Mustar, P., Siegel, D., and Wright, M. (2014). Entrepreneurial innovation: The importance of context. *Research Policy* 43, 1097–1108.

11 Cassell, M.A. and Blake, R.J. (2012). Analysis of Hofstede's 5-D model: The implications of conducting business in Saudi Arabia. *International Journal of Management & Information Systems* 16, 151–160.

12 Wales, W.J., Shirokova, G., Sokolova, L., and Stein, C. (2016). Entrepreneurial orientation in the emerging Russian regulatory context: The criticality of interpersonal relationships. *European Journal of International Management* 10, 359–382.

13 Smallbone, D. and Welter, F. (2012). Entrepreneurship and institutional change in transition economies: The commonwealth of independent states, Central and Eastern Europe and China compared. *Entrepreneurship & Regional Development* 24, 215–233.

14 Arregle, J.L., Batjargal, B., Hitt, M.A., Webb, J.W., and Miller, T. (2013). Family ties in entrepreneurs' social networks and new venture growth. *Entrepreneurship Theory and Practice* 3, 313–344.

15 Branstetter, L., Lima, F., Taylor, L.J., and Venâncio, A. (2013). Do entry regulations deter entrepreneurship and job creation? Evidence from recent reforms in Portugal. *Economic Journal* 124, 805–832.

16 Gamble, J.E., Lorenz, M.P., Turnipseed, D.L., and Weaver, K.M. (2013). Determinants of business climate perceptions in small and medium-sized enterprises: Does managerial ownership matter? *Small Business Institute Journal* 9, 18.

17 Geels, F.W. (2013). The impact of the financial–economic crisis on sustainability transitions: Financial investment, governance and public discourse. *Environmental Innovation and Societal Transitions* 6, 67–95.

18 Munemo, J. (2014). Business start-up regulations and the complementarity between foreign and domestic investment. *Review of World Economics* 150, 745–761.

19 Sutter, D. and Beaulier, S. (2013). Entrepreneurship and the link between economic freedom and growth. *American Journal of Entrepreneurship* 6, 1–11.

20 Genberg, H., Martinez, A., and Salemi, M. (2014). *The IMF/WEO Forecast Process*. Washington, DC: Independent Evaluation Office of the International Monetary Fund.

21 Alrashidi, Y.A. (2013). Exporting motivations and Saudi SMEs: An exploratory study. *World Journal of Social Sciences* 3, 204–219.

22 Robinson, A.T. and Grayson, J. (2014). How perceptions of the global economic slowdown impact and local risks adversely affect perceived opportunities and subsequent start-up activities. *Business & Management Research* 3, 75.

23 Alharbi, J. and Singh, S. (2013). Knowledge transfer, controls, and performance of MNE subsidiaries in the Kingdom of Saudi Arabia. *Foresight* 15, 294–306.

24 Weber, S., Oser, F., Achtenhagen, F., Fretschner, M., and Trost, S. (eds.). (2014). *Becoming an Entrepreneur-Epilog*. Sense Publishers.

25 Simón-Moya, V., Revuelto-Taboada, L., Guerrero, R.F. (2014). Institutional and economic drivers of entrepreneurship: An international perspective. *Journal of Business Research* 67, 715–721.

26 Berger, E.S.C. and Kuckertz, A. (2016). Female entrepreneurship in startup ecosystems worldwide. *Journal of Business Research* 69(11), 5163–5168.

27 Zamberi, A.S. (2012). Micro, small and medium-sized enterprises development in the Kingdom of Saudi Arabia: Problems and constraints. *World Journal of Entrepreneurship, Management and Sustainable Development* 8, 217–232.

28 Mohamed, Y. and Mnguu, Y.O. (2014). Fiscal and monetary policies: Challenges for small and medium enterprises SMEs development in Tanzania. *International Journal of Social Sciences and Entrepreneurship* 1, 305–320.

29 Berger, E.S.C. and Kuckertz, A. (2016). Female entrepreneurship in startup ecosystems worldwide. *Journal of Business Research* 69(11), 5163–5168.

30 Goyal, P. and Yadav, V. (2014). To be or not to be a woman entrepreneur in a developing country. *Psychosociological Issues in Human Resource Management* 2, 68–78.

31 Thébaud, S. and Sharkey, A.J. (2016). Unequal hard times: The influence of the great recession on gender bias in entrepreneurial financing. *Sociological Science* 3, 1–31.

32 Bokhari, A.A.H., Alothmany N.S., Magbool S.S. (2012). *Entrepreneurship and Unemployment in The Kingdom of Saudi Arabia.* Conference: The Saudi Economy Conference: Challenges and Opportunities.

33 Belayachi, K. and Haidar, J. (2008). *Saudi Arabia: Competitiveness from Innovation, Not Inheritance, Celebrating Reform.* Retrieved 2 January 2012, from www.doing business.org/reports/case-studies/2008/starting-a-business-insaudi-arabia.

34 Bosma, N. and Levie, J. (2010). *Global Entrepreneurship Monitor 2009 Executive Report.* Global Report, Babson.

35 Entrepreneurship and competitiveness: Implications for Saudi Arabia. Industrial Investors Guide-Saudi Arabia; Land of Opportunities. www.tcf.org.sa

36 US-Arab Tradeline. (Spring 2010). A publication of the National U.S. Arab-Chamber of Commerce. XVIII(1).

37 www.arabfund.org

38 www.atfp.org.ae/

39 https://misk.org.sa/en/

40 www.arabnews.com/node/1153241/saudi-arabia

41 www.arabnews.com/tags/misk-foundation

42 http://miskglobalforum.com/

43 http://miskgrandchallenges.org/

44 www.miskschools.edu.sa

45 www.riyadhschools.edu.sa

46 http://sustg.com/three-new-ventures-by-misk-to-empower-and-inspire-saudi-youth-launched/

47 www.cjameel.org/en/initiatives/education-and-training/injaz-saudi-arabia

48 www.mitarabcompetition.com

49 www.kaust.edu.sa

50 https://badir.com.sa/en

51 https://badir.com.sa/en/incubator/information-and-communication-technology-incubator

52 https://badir.com.sa/en/incubator/advanced-manufacturing-technology-incubator

53 https://badir.com.sa/en/incubator/taif-incubator

54 www.ksu.edu.sa

55 www.kfupm.edu.sa

56 www.mcegulf.com

57 www.midrarksa.com

58 www.bayaan.com

59 www.educon.com.sa

60 www.lomarthobe.com

61 www.amwal.com.sa

62 www.dentaliaclinics.com

63 www.heal-me.us

64 www.hodema.net
65 www.almarwa.net.sa
66 www.alcantara-group.com
67 www.alyaqoub.com
68 www.3eesho.com
69 www.ibsolutions.com.sa
70 www.traccs.net
71 www.3points-ad.com
72 www.secutronic.com.sa
73 www.jeddahunited.com
74 www.itc-lcc.com
75 www.acwapi.com
76 www.alsale.com

4 Knowledge-based economy in Saudi Arabia and Vision 2030

The journey so far

Mohammad Nurunnabi

Introduction

> Saudi Arabia's Vision 2030. . . . It is an ambitious yet achievable blueprint, which expresses our long-term goals and expectations and reflects our country's strengths and capabilities. All success stories start with a vision, and successful visions are based on strong pillars. . . . Our Vision is a strong, thriving, and stable Saudi Arabia that provides opportunity for all.
>
> (His Royal Highness Crown Prince and Chairman of the
> Council of Economic and Development Affairs,
> Mohammad bin Salman bin Abdulaziz Al-Saud)

The Saudi economy is deeply dependent on the oil industry. Saudi Arabia is one of the world's largest producers and exporters of oil. Saudi Arabia's Vision 2030 aims to innovate and diversify the economy through economic, educational and related reforms (Nurunnabi, 2017). The key objective is to create rapid economic growth and job creation, especially in the private sector (Arab News, 2016). This agenda will meet the high aspirations of its very young population, which is more than 50 percent of the Saudi population (Global Policy Watch, 2016).

The term "knowledge-based economy" has been used in various ways (e.g. knowledge economy, knowledge society, information economy, digital economy, knowledge-based society etc.) in literature (Organisation for Economic Cooperation and Development [OECD], 1996; Stiglitz, 1999; Strożek, 2014). For instance, the OECD (1996, p. 9) states that

> Knowledge, as embodied in human beings (as "human capital") and in technology, has always been central to economic development. . . . Indeed, it is estimated that more than 50 per cent of Gross Domestic Product (GDP) in the major OECD economies is now knowledge-based.

In this chapter, knowledge-based economy refers to education and research and innovation.

This chapter is organized into five sections: The second section provides related government policies in higher education in Saudi Arabia. The third section discusses innovation and education in Saudi Arabia. The fourth section evaluates Vision 2030 and contributions to education and research. In doing so, the National Transformation Program 2020 is also discussed. The last section contains conclusions and a policy agenda.

National policies in higher education in Saudi Arabia

The Ministry of Economy and Planning (MoEP) (2013) in its report titled *National Strategy for Transformation into Knowledge Society*, detailed microeconomic policies. Various issues were addressed. In this chapter, I will explore two policies in particular: 1) education and human resources (HR) and 2) science, technology and innovation (S&T).

Education and human resources policies

The MoEP (2013, p. 23) reports that there were some challenges such as poor academic performance of students, a shortage of competent teachers and weak competition among schools and universities. Of education and training services, life-long learning (LLL) was also below the level of intended efficiency. Low labor productivity and a high unemployment rate among the youth (male and female) were also found. Indeed, technical and vocational training (TVET) is essential for the youth and the aged labor force. Table 4.1 shows a brief summary of the core policies on higher education.

Table 4.1 Summary of core policies on higher education

Policy type	Higher education
Maintain/harness/improve existing policies	• Enhance research capacity and quality. • Strengthen internationalization. • Enhance the role of independent quality assurance and academic accreditation agencies. • Restructure internal governance for greater leadership of rectors. • Improve college entrance exams.
New policies	• Funding of competitive research which enhances knowledge and achieves higher national objectives. • Brain-Saudi 21 project. • Invite leading global private universities to operate in the Kingdom. • Approve a system of teaching and research assistants.
Reform agenda policies	• Provide merit- and performance-based grants. • Develop a governance system in universities. • Enhance the decentralization system and competiveness in universities.

Source: Ministry of Economy and Planning (2013, pp. 25–26)

Science, technology and innovation policies

The MoEP (2013) stressed the importance of science, technology and innovation in becoming a knowledge-based economy. It reported that although notable progress was made, the science, technology and innovation base was still below the intended level. Therefore, capacity building is needed in this regard. Investments were directed to establish venture capital companies, with the aim of improving the National Innovation System (NIS) and a "soft" policy for ensuring efficiency of R&D activities was prioritized. Some policies were created in this regard (see Table 4.2). Table 4.3 presents some notable achievements of education and human resources and science, technology and innovation based on prior policies.

Additionally, some policy initiatives were taken in the 8th and 9th Development Plans for a knowledge-based economy.

8th Development Plan (2005–2009)

This development plan focused on fundamental developments towards a knowledge-based economy. The plan included the implementation of the first five-year plan of the National Science, Technology and Innovation Policy; adopting the National ICT Plan, the National Industrial Strategy, and the Strategy and Plan for Giftedness, Creativity and Supporting Innovation; establishing the Knowledge Economic City in Medina and the Technology Zone of the Saudi Organization for Industrial Estate and Technology Zones in Dammam; establishment of King Abdullah Economic City; a preparation of a new strategy for higher education (AFAQ); and advancing Saudization.

9th Development Plan (2010–2014)

This development plan focuses on education, in particular knowledge generation and utilization of knowledge in various economic and social sectors. This plan aims to enhance the comparative advantages of the Saudi economy, add to it new competitive advantages, diversify it and increase its productivity and competitiveness, as well as creating appropriate employment opportunities for citizens.

The MoEP (2013) provided three stages for the transformation into a knowledge-based economy, which require major structural changes:

- Stage (1): 1433–1435 (2012–2014): Reinforcing the Ongoing Policy Initiative Aimed at Knowledge Capacity Building
- Stage (2): 1436–1446/47 (2015–2025): Accelerating the Change Momentum and Undertaking Major Structural Reforms
- Stage (3): 1447–1451/52 (2026–2030): Consolidation of the Transformation Process

Relatedly, King Abdul Aziz City for Science and Technology (KACST),[1] an independent scientific organization, started the implementation of the first

Table 4.2 Summary of key policies on science, technology and innovation

Policy type	Capacity building	Networking and cooperation	Commercialization
Maintain/ harness/ improve	• Giving the highest priority to promoting creativity and nurturing talent from childhood to create a generation of innovators and entrepreneurs. • Continuous investment. • Improve management of S&T and innovation activities and their performance. • Establish more technology incubators.	• Maintain technology transfer efforts of universities. • Improve intellectual property rights (IPR) regulation to facilitate spin-off of R&D outputs. • Prepare a long-term strategy for technology valleys and cooperative research centers (King Abdulaziz City for Science and Technology – KACST).	• Better coordination of diverse initiatives (especially industrial clusters and economic cities). • Explore new business opportunities for Saudi Technology Development and Investment Company (TAQNIA) program and other related programs using comparative advantages of the Kingdom (KACST).
New policies	• Establish innovation centers and clubs for general education students. • Establish a new research institute for industrial technology development.		• Launch a national program for industrial technology development. • Provide more funding for industrial technology development activities.
Reform agenda policies	• Reform S&T education system (quality assurance, industrial linkages). • Enhance R&D efficiency through some institutional reforms.	• Establish Saudi-customized framework for technology transfer.	• Contribute to industrial diversification through support of advanced industrial R&D.

Source: Ministry of Economy and Planning (2013, p. 27)

National Plan for Science, Technology, and Innovation (Maarifah 1) in 2007. By the end of the first plan in 2014, the plan had achieved its main objective of creating infrastructure and being top ranked in science, technology and innovation in the region. KACST prepared the second National Plan for Science, Technology, and Innovation (Maarifah 2), which will end in 2020. The Maarifah 2 plan was restructured during the National Transformation Program 2020 (NTP, 2020) and was aligned with the objectives of Vision 2030. As a result,

Table 4.3 Notable achievements and underlying policy initiatives in 2013

	Achievements	Policy initiatives
Education and human resources	• Rapid expansion of the entire education sector, especially higher education.	• Tatweer[1] • Approval of the Future University Education Plan of the Kingdom (AFAQ) "Horizon" Plan • Launching of KAUST • Overseas study programs • MAWHIBA (King Abdulaziz & His Companions Foundation for Giftedness and Creativity) programs[2]
Science, technology and innovation	• Considerable increase in government R&D. • Rapid increase in scientific publications and patents.[3]	• Several substantive National Science, Technology and Innovation (STI) initiatives under the National Science, Technology and Innovation Plan (NSTIP) –capacity building – networking and cooperation – commercialization.

Source: Ministry of Economy and Planning (2013, p. 27)

1 King Abdullah's program for education development (Tatweer) was launched with the aim of address-ing issues at all levels of education: quality of education; teacher training; curriculum development to focus on science, technology and mathematics; expansion of skill-development activities, particularly analytical thinking and hands-on skills; initiative; innovation; entrepreneurship; languages; and future and emerging sciences.
2 With the aim of providing sponsorship of talent and creativity and supporting research and innovation, King Abdul-Aziz and his Companions Foundation for Giftedness and Creativity, "Mawhiba," adopted a strategy to foster giftedness and creativity and support innovation. The vision of Mawhiba envisages that the Kingdom will "be a creative society with a critical mass of gifted and talented young leaders highly educated and well-trained to support the building of the knowledge based economy and the sustained growth and prosperity of the Kingdom."
3 Between 1996 and 2006, the number of scientific papers published by researchers in Saudi Arabia was 26,854. Saudi Arabia ranked second among Arab nations and 48th worldwide.

KACST-approved initiatives in the NTP replaced the Maarifah 2 (King Abdul Aziz City for Science and Technology, 2016, p. 32).

Innovation and education

This section reports the present status of innovation and education and research in Saudi Arabia.

Innovation

King Abdul Aziz City for Science and Technology (2016, p. 17) recently reported that the number of submitted patent applications in 2015 dropped by

45% compared to that of 2014. Saudi Arabia has been a signatory to the World Intellectual Property Organization (WIPO) Convention since 1982. Saudi Arabia enacted national trademark law in 1984, followed by national patent and copyright laws in 1989. KACST is the supervisory body responsible for the enforcement of the patent law, while the Ministry of Commerce acts as the supervisory body for trademark law in Saudi Arabia. The Ministry of Information acts as the supervisory body for all intellectual property rights in Saudi Arabia. According to the MoEP and King Abdul Aziz City for Science and Technology (2015, p. 57):

> In the past few years academic institutions in the Kingdom have witnessed substantial activity in the field of research and development, resulting in the registration of hundreds of patents with local and international patent offices, such as the Saudi Arabian Patent Office (SAPO), the European Patent Office (EPO), the World Intellectual Property Organization (WIPO), the Chinese Bureau of Intellectual Property (SIPO), and the US Patent and Trademark Office (USPTO) – the most recognized worldwide.

The report also stated that the application for a patent from the European Patent Office and the U.S. Patent Office and others all count as a single invention. Patents by academic institutions fall into main research categories according to a rating system followed by the Derwent World Patent Index. The universities in Saudi Arabia also contribute to patents in the fields of medicine and health, water technology, mathematics and physics technology, environmental technology, energy technology, biotechnology and construction technology.

Saudi Arabia ranked 41st and was the second-highest ranked in the GCC in terms of Global Innovation Index 2016 (GII) (see Figure 4.1) (Dutta et al., 2016). Saudi Arabia's drop in the ranking was due to low scores for Innovation Input and Innovation Output. Saudi Arabia–based SABIC was listed in the top five Middle Eastern companies in the global south.

On the other hand, Figure 4.2 shows that the number of Saudi patents was very low from 1964 (1) to 2009 (22). Notably, the number of patents increased significantly from 2011 to 2015, rising gradually from 61 in 2011 to 360 in 2015 (US Patent and Trademark Office, 2016).

Education and research

Research is a central part of all academic systems. Altbach (2013, p. 316). The MoEP (2013, p. 63) earlier highlighted that "research and development capacities are still relatively low and there are few postgraduate programs. Furthermore, the number of intermediary institutions linking higher education with industries is still limited and below the aspired level." According to the MoEP and King Abdul Aziz City for Science and Technology (2015, p. 51), research activity in Saudi Arabia is mainly the responsibility of universities and research centers. There are approximately 143 research centers in Saudi Arabia in both the public and private sectors. However, the government sector or public sector

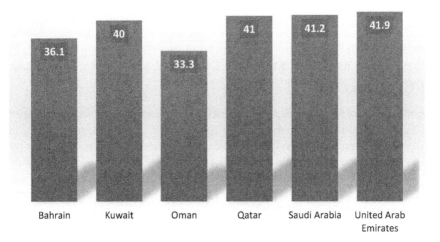

Figure 4.1 Overall score of the GCCs in Global Innovation Index (GII) 2016

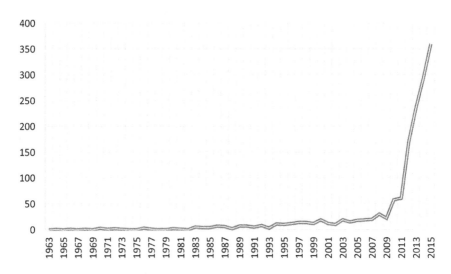

Figure 4.2 Number of patents in Saudi Arabia from 1963 to 2015

Source: U.S. Patent and Trademark Office (2016)

dominated the share of these centers, particularly universities, which combined 89 research centers and 1,167 laboratories. The rest of the research centers are distributed in ministries and other government agencies, as well as the private sector.

The number of research publications was around 1,000 papers per year in the 1980s. The number increased to 1,686 research papers in 2008, following the implementation of the National Science, Technology and Innovation Plan. The number of research papers reached 7,000 papers in 2012, meaning a sevenfold increase in eight years.

The number of research papers published by universities between 2008 and 2012 reached a total of 28,810. King Saud University topped the publications with 7,912 published papers, followed by King Abdul Aziz University with 3,199 published papers, King Fahd University of Petroleum and Minerals with 2,460 published papers and King Faisal Specialist Hospital and Research Centre with 1,474 published papers. The increasing trend was because of the inception of Maarifah 1 in 2008. Notably, the number of published papers tripled for the period 2008 to 2014.

The number of scientific papers dropped in 2015 for the first time since 2008 (King Abdul Aziz City for Science and Technology, 2016, p. 17). This is primarily because of the closure of financial support for the research projects in Maarifah 1 in the last two years.

Table 4.4 presents the Scimago Journal & Country Rank (SJR) in the Middle East from 1996 to 2016. Saudi Arabia ranked fifth in terms of number of

Table 4.4 Scimago Journal & Country Rank (SJR) 1996–2016 in the Middle East

Rank	Country	Documents	Citable documents	Citations	Self-citations	Citations per document	H index
1	Turkey	485,366	453,565	4,414,662	1,039,323	9.1	339
2	Iran	388,672	377,098	2,770,074	1,019,641	7.13	234
3	Israel	320,716	297,182	6,960,963	903,593	21.7	584
4	Egypt	157,835	152,954	1,331,681	262,291	8.44	213
5	Saudi Arabia	133,396	127,612	1,144,870	187,175	8.58	241
6	United Arab Emirates	37,528	34,927	299,155	31,286	7.97	153
7	Jordan	31,552	30,556	259,134	31,390	8.21	130
8	Lebanon	23,968	21,952	248,043	23,697	10.35	157
9	Kuwait	20,252	19,366	197,566	21,507	9.76	123
10	Qatar	17,512	16,313	125,113	15,521	7.14	105
11	Oman	14,804	13,733	118,547	13,787	8.01	105
12	Iraq	14,745	14,098	64,199	9,365	4.35	71
13	Syrian Arab Republic	6,333	6,026	68,933	6,745	10.88	89
14	Bahrain	5,212	4,732	36,028	2,778	6.91	61
15	Palestine	5,133	4,821	44,032	5,222	8.58	69
16	Yemen	3,184	3,088	26,393	2,747	8.29	58

Source: www.scimagojr.com/countryrank.php?region=Middle%20East

publications, with 133,396 papers. The total citations were 1,144,870, and the self-citations were only 1.40%. The citations per paper was 8.58. In terms of citations per paper, Saudi Arabia ranked fourth in the Middle East, while in terms of H index, Saudi Arabia ranked third in the Middle East.

Tables 4.5a and 4.5b show the ranking of Saudi universities from 2009 to 2016. Seventeen universities were globally ranked in 2016 and 2015, while there were only four universities ranked in 2009 (all four were ranked 700 and above). The following five universities were ranked in the top six universities

Table 4.5a Country rank, global rank and Saudi universities (2013–2016)

2016			2015		
Country rank	Global rank	University	Country rank	Global rank	University
1	369	King Saud University	1	414	King Saud University
2	430	King Abdulaziz University	2	481	King Abdulaziz University
3	457	King Abdullah University of Science and Technology	3	489	King Abdullah University of Science and Technology
4	563	King Fahd University of Petroleum and Minerals	4	539	King Fahd University of Petroleum and Minerals
5	597	Alfaisal University	5	594	Alfaisal University
6	605	King Saud bin Abdulaziz University for Health Sciences	6	603	Najran University
7	622	Jazan University	7	616	King Saud bin Abdulaziz University for Health Sciences
8	622	Najran University	8	631	Imam Muhammad ibn Saud Islamic University
9	637	Tabuk University	9	631	Qassim University
10	646	Taif University	10	632	Jazan University
11	653	King Khalid University	11	637	Tabuk University
12	656	Imam Muhammad ibn Saud Islamic University	12	641	Taif University
13	659	King Faisal University	13	646	King Faisal University
14	660	Taibah University	14	648	Taibah University
15	663	Qassim University	15	653	King Khalid University
16	664	Umm Al-Qura University	16	664	University of Hail
17	671	University of Hail	17	667	Umm Al-Qura University
2014			**2013**		
1	466	King Saud University	1	539	King Saud University
2	511	King Abdullah University of Science and Technology	2	563	King Abdullah University of Science and Technology

2016			2015		
Country rank	Global rank	University	Country rank	Global rank	University
3	548	King Fahd University of Petroleum and Minerals	3	586	King Fahd University of Petroleum and Minerals
4	554	King Abdulaziz University	4	617	King Abdulaziz University
5	607	Tabuk University	5	667	King Saud bin Abdulaziz University for Health Sciences
6	619	Imam Muhammad ibn Saud Islamic University	6	670	Taif University
7	632	Alfaisal University	7	676	Jazan University
8	636	King Saud bin Abdulaziz University for Health Sciences	8	684	Qassim University
9	643	Jazan University	9	693	King Faisal University
10	647	Taif University	10	696	Taibah University
11	650	Qassim University	11	701	King Khalid University
12	657	King Faisal University	12	707	Umm Al-Qura University
13	664	Taibah University			
14	666	King Khalid University			
15	680	Umm Al-Qura University			

Table 4.5b Country rank, global rank and Saudi universities (2009–2012)

2012			2011		
Country rank	Global rank	University	Country rank	Global rank	University
1	583	King Abdullah University of Science and Technology	1	679	King Fahd University of Petroleum and Minerals
2	629	King Saud University	2	698	King Abdulaziz University
3	631	King Fahd University of Petroleum and Minerals	3	705	King Saud University
4	659	King Abdulaziz University	4	765	King Khalid University
5	688	Taif University	5	804	King Faisal University
6	745	King Khalid University			
7	753	King Faisal University			
8	769	Umm Al-Qura University			

2010			2009		
1	710	King Fahd University of Petroleum and Minerals	1	702	King Fahd University of Petroleum and Minerals
2	742	King Abdulaziz University	2	756	King Saud University
3	744	King Saud University	3	769	King Abdulaziz University
4	806	King Khalid University	4	852	King Faisal University
5	839	King Faisal University			

Source: www.scimagojr.com/

globally. Alfaisal University was the only private university ranked globally from Saudi Arabia from 2014–2016. This indicates that research productivity is dominated by public and government universities.

- King Saud University (369)
- King Abdulaziz University (430)
- King Abdullah University of Science and Technology (457)
- King Fahd University of Petroleum and Minerals (563)
- Alfaisal University (597)

In addition to universities, research centers and institutions in Saudi Arabia are engaged in research publications (see Table 4.6). For instance, there were only two centers ranked globally in 2009, but this increased to six centers in 2016. Four of the six centers are medical related (King Faisal Specialist Hospital and Research Centre, King Khalid University Hospital, King Abdulaziz Medical City and King Khaled Eye Specialist Hospital). The other two centers were King Abdulaziz City for Science and Technology and Saudi Arabian Oil Company.

Table 4.6 Country rank, global rank and Saudi research institutes/centers (2009–2016)

Country rank	Global rank	2016	Sector
1	620	King Faisal Specialist Hospital and Research Centre	Health
2	621	King Khalid University Hospital	Health
3	653	King Abdulaziz City for Science and Technology	Government
4	655	King Abdulaziz Medical City	Health
5	658	Saudi Arabian Oil Company	Private
6	664	King Khaled Eye Specialist Hospital	Health
Country rank	Global rank	2015	Sector
1	592	King Faisal Specialist Hospital and Research Centre	Health
2	600	King Abdulaziz City for Science and Technology	Government
3	643	King Khalid University Hospital	Health
4	652	King Abdulaziz Medical City	Health
5	659	King Khaled Eye Specialist Hospital	Health
6	663	Saudi Arabian Oil Company	Private
Country rank	Global rank	2014	Sector
1	611	King Faisal Specialist Hospital and Research Centre	Health
2	624	King Abdulaziz City for Science and Technology	Government
3	649	King Khalid University Hospital	Health
4	662	Saudi Arabian Oil Company	Private

Country rank	Global rank	2013	Sector
1	628	King Faisal Specialist Hospital and Research Centre	Health
2	630	King Abdulaziz City for Science and Technology	Government
3	689	King Khalid University Hospital	Health
4	689	Saudi Arabian Oil Company	Private
5	692	King Abdulaziz Medical City	Health

Country rank	Global rank	2012	Sector
1	659	King Faisal Specialist Hospital and Research Centre	Health
2	682	King Abdulaziz City for Science and Technology	Government
3	717	Saudi Arabian Oil Company	Private
4	751	King Khalid University Hospital	Health

Country rank	Global rank	2011	Sector
1	695	King Faisal Specialist Hospital and Research Centre	Health
2	774	Saudi Arabian Oil Company	Private
3	799	King Khalid University Hospital	Health

Country rank	Global rank	2010	Sector
1	722	King Faisal Specialist Hospital and Research Centre	Health
2	805	Saudi Arabian Oil Company	Private
3	832	King Khalid University Hospital	Health

Country rank	Global rank	2009	Sector
1	729	King Faisal Specialist Hospital and Research Centre	Health
2	809	Saudi Arabian Oil Company	Private

Source: www.scimagojr.com/

An overall research overview in Saudi Arabia is presented in Figure 4.3. The research output contributes 12.16% in the region and 0.72% in the world. It is worth mentioning that the percentage of international collaborative papers has increased from 27.27% in 1996 to 76.46% in 2016. With regard to research output by subject area in Saudi Arabia from 1996 to 2016, Figure 4.4 shows that the following major fields contributed more in 2016.

- Medicine (4,291)
- Engineering (4,008)
- Chemistry (3,281)
- Computer science (2,682)
- Biochemistry genetics and molecular biology (2,485)

Figure 4.3 Research overview in Saudi Arabia (1996–2016)

Source: www.scimagojr.com/

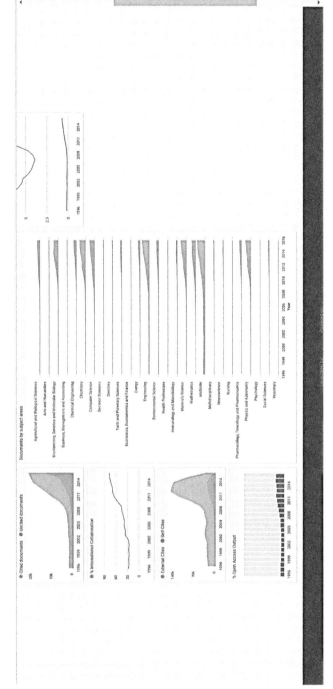

Figure 4.4 Research by subject area in Saudi Arabia (1996–2016)

Source: www.scimagojr.com/

- Mathematics
- Materials science
- Chemical engineering
- Agricultural and biological sciences
- Physics and astronomy

However, the following are still growing but had very limited research from 1996 to 2016:

- Arts and humanities
- Business management and accounting
- Economics
- Social sciences

Saudi Arabia's Vision 2030

Saudi Arabia's Vision 2030 is focused upon three themes:

1   A vibrant society
2   A thriving econom
3   An ambitious nation

In terms of the second theme, Vision 2030 highlights a thriving economy which "provides opportunities for all by building an education system aligned with market needs and creating economic opportunities for the entrepreneur, the small enterprise as well as the large corporation" (Vision 2030, p. 13). In this regard, two areas are shown:

Learning for working

We will continue investing in education and training so that our young men and women are equipped for the jobs of the future. We want Saudi children, wherever they live, to enjoy higher quality, multi-faceted education. We will invest particularly in developing early childhood education, refining our national curriculum and training our teachers and educational leaders. We will also redouble efforts to ensure that the outcomes of our education system are in line with market needs. We have launched the National Labor Gateway (TAQAT), and we plan to establish sector councils that will precisely determine the skills and knowledge required by each socio-economic sector. We will also expand vocational training in order to drive forward economic development. Our scholarship opportunities will be steered towards prestigious international universities and be awarded in the fields that serve our national priorities. We will also focus on innovation in advanced technologies and entrepreneurship.

(Vision 2030, p. 36)

An education that contributes to economic growth

We will close the gap between the outputs of higher education and the requirements of the job market. We will also help our students make careful career decisions, while at the same time training them and facilitating their transition between different educational pathways. In the year 2030, we aim to have at least five Saudi universities among the top 200 universities in international rankings. We shall help our students achieve results above international averages in global education indicators.

To this end, we will prepare a modern curriculum focused on rigorous standards in literacy, numeracy, skills and character development. We will track progress and publish a sophisticated range of education outcomes, showing year-on-year improvements. We will work closely with the private sector to ensure higher education outcomes are in line with the requirements of job market. We will invest in strategic partnerships with apprenticeship providers, new skills councils from industry, and large private companies. We will also work towards developing the job specifications of every education field.

(Vision 2030, p. 40)

In addition, Vision 2030 emphasizes the youth population. This is because more than half of the Saudi population is under the age of 25. The skills of youth could be developed and properly deployed through entrepreneurship and enterprise opportunities. On the other hand, more than 50 percent of university graduates are female. To strengthen for the future and contribute to the development of society and economy, Saudi women could be in the job market.

In order to accomplish Saudi Arabia's Vision 2030 and to identify the challenges through the appropriate mechanisms for follow-up and performance evaluation, the National Transformation Program (NTP) 2020 was launched in 2016. The NTP 2020 has specific strategic objectives that are based on Vision 2030 and addresses performance accordance with specific targets. The program was launched across 24 government bodies, including the ministries represented in the Council of Economics and Development Affairs and a number of public entities associated mainly with the strategic objectives of Saudi Arabia's Vision 2030. Figure 4.5 shows the Operating Model National Transformation Program. Accordingly, 543 initiatives were announced. The overall program cost for the government is around £54 billion, and 40% of funding is expected to come from the private sector.

With regard to higher education, King Abdulaziz City for Science and Technology proposed 30 initiatives within the National Transformation Program 2020 in science, technology and innovation (see Figure 4.6). All 30 initiatives were under three segments: research support, technology transfer and localization and innovation. For research support initiatives, KACST provides funds for basic research (theoretical research). In addition, KACST has a program called the Product Development Program to Establish Local Suppliers. This program

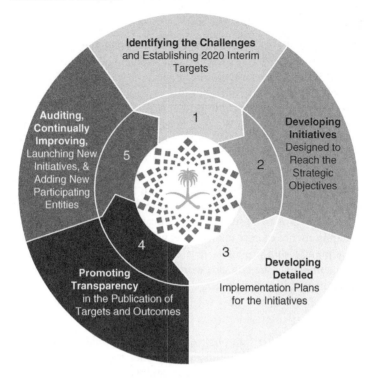

Figure 4.5 Operating model, National Transformation Program

Source: National Transformation Program (2020, p. 13)

supports joint projects between the research and private sectors to establish high-quality small and medium-sized enterprises (SMEs) that will develop products that contribute to maximizing local content and commercial and economic benefits. Over the last seven years, the program invested approximately 7 billion Saudi Riyals (USD 1.87 billion) in R&D.

Conclusion and policy agenda

The findings of this chapter involve the development of research and innovation in Saudi Arabia over the last two decades. Prior to the announcement of Vision 2030, Khorsheed (2015, p. 149) argues that "despite some attempts at economic diversification, the Saudi economy remains heavily dependent on oil and petroleum-related industries including petrochemicals and petroleum refining." Saudi Arabia's Vision 2030 will therefore reinforce growth, stability and development in higher education institutions. The findings reveal that research output is increasing every year and the number of participating institutions is growing.

		Key Performance Indicators	Measurement Unit	Targeted 2020
Research Support	1	Number of published peer-reviewed research papers from scientific institution in the Kingdom	Research (annual)	20,000
	2	Number of patents issued by the Kingdom	Patent (accumulative)	5,000
Technology Transfer and Localization	3	Number of localized and developed technologies in targeted sectors	Technology (accumulative)	125
	4	Number of establishments needed to develop local content	Establishment (accumulative)	17
	5	Number of technical experts who have been skilled	Expert (accumulative)	350
Innovation	6	Number of tech-companies emerging from incubators	Company (accumulative)	600
	7	Number of jobs being generated by start-up companies in incubators	Job (accumulative)	3,600
	8	Number of tech-companies emerging from universities through the Innovative Companies Program	Company (accumulative)	800
	9	Number of jobs being generated by start-up companies in universities	Job (accumulative)	4000
	10	Number of companies that were served or have their capabilities enhanced	Company (accumulative)	400
	11	Number of consulting projects in the targeted sectors that have been submitted	Project (accumulative)	200
	12	Customer satisfaction for consulting services provided	Percentage (%)	80

Figure 4.6 KACST's strategic objectives in the National Transformation Program 2020 (King Abdulaziz City for Science and Technology 2016, p. 35)

As mentioned, the National Transformation Program 2020 has specific objectives to accomplish Vision 2030. The Ministry of Economy and Planning and King Abdul Aziz City for Science and Technology (2015, p. 51) stated, "Although the number of scientific papers has not increased, the Kingdom maintained an increase in the quality of the published papers." Nevertheless, there are some challenges ahead to fulfill Saudi Arabia's Vision 2030 regarding research in the higher education sector. In particular, the quality of research should be monitored and benchmarked. Institutional support is needed in terms of producing quality research.

1   An awareness campaign is needed for all higher education institutions in order to achieve the following:

- Number of published peer-reviewed research papers from scientific institutions in the Kingdom (20,000; annually).
- Number of patents issued by the Kingdom (5,000; accumulative).

2   A clear mechanism is needed to follow progress on that. In other words, a progression monitoring entity should be specified.
3   A target benchmark is needed for each higher education institution based on the number of active research faculties.
4   The research capacity of universities and public laboratories compared to developed countries should be enhanced.
5   The private sector's contribution to research should be increased.
6   Private universities should be more supported for research and creating research labs.

Note

1 King Abdulaziz City for Science and Technology (KACST) is an independent scientific organization administratively reporting to the prime minister and based in Riyadh. KACST supports and encourages scientific research for applied purposes, coordinates the activities of institutions and centers of scientific research in line with the requirements of development in the Kingdom and cooperates with other institutions to identify national priorities and policies in the fields of science and technology in order to build a technological scientific base for development in the fields of agriculture, industry, mining and others.

References

Altbach, P.G. (2013). Advancing the national and global knowledge economy: The role of research universities in developing countries. *Studies in Higher Education* 38(3), 316–330.
Arab News. (2016). Saudi Vision 2030 promotes knowledge-based economy. 22 June 2016. Retrieved 15 July 2017, from www.arabnews.com/node/943041/economy.
Dutta, S., Lanvin, B., and Wunsch-Vincent, S. (eds.). (2016). *Global Innovation Index 2016.* Cornell University, INSEAD, and the World Intellectual Property Organization. Retrieved 27 September 2016, from www.globalinnovationindex.org/gii-2016-report.
Global Policy Watch. (2016). Saudi Arabia's Vision 2030—Ambitions to modernize and diversify the economy. 6 June 2016. Retrieved 22 July 2017, from www.globalpolicywatch.

com/2016/06/saudi-arabias-vision-2030-ambitions-to-modernize-and-diversify-the-economy/.

Khorsheed, M.S. (2015). Saudi Arabia: From oil kingdom to knowledge-based economy. *Middle East Policy* 22(3), 147–157.

King Abdulaziz City for Science and Technology (KACST). (2016). *Annual Report 2016*. Retrieved 5 November 2017, from www.kacst.edu.sa/eng/about/AnnualReports/Annual%20Report%202016En.pdf.

Ministry of Economy and Planning (MoEP). (2013). *National Strategy for Transformation into Knowledge Society*. Saudi Arabia.

Ministry of Economy and Planning (MoEP) and King Abdul Aziz City for Science and Technology (KACST). (2015). *Transition to a Knowledge Society in Saudi Arabia*. Saudi Arabia: Minister of Economy and Planning, KACST, Madar Research and Development, Dubai Internet City. Retrieved from http://publications.kacst.edu.sa/SystemFiles/Books_Pdf/PDF_635518951661650873.pdf

National Transformation Program 2020. (2016). *Kingdom of Saudi Arabia*. Retrieved 7 August 2016, from http://vision2030.gov.sa/sites/default/files/NTP_En.pdf.

Nurunnabi, M. (2017). Transformation from an oil-based economy to a knowledge-based economy in Saudi Arabia: The direction of Saudi Vision 2030. *Journal of the Knowledge Economy* 8(2), 536–564.

Organisation for Economic Co-operation and Development (OECD). (1996). *The Knowledge-Based Economy*. General Distribution OECD/GD(96)102. Paris: OECD. Retrieved 15 August 2016, from www.oecd.org/sti/sci-tech/1913021.pdf.

Stiglitz, J.E. (1999). *Public Policy for a Knowledge Economy*. London: Department for Trade and Industry and Centre for Economic Policy Research.

Strożek, P. (2014). A spatial analysis of the knowledge-based economy in Poland. *Comparative Economic Research* 17(4), 221–236.

US Patent and Trademark Office. (2016). *U.S. Patent Statistics Chart Calendar Years 1963–2015*. Retrieved 17 December 2017, from www.uspto.gov/web/offices/ac/ido/oeip/taf/us_stat.htm.

Vision 2030. (2016). Kingdom of Saudi Arabia. Retrieved 13 June 2017, from http://vision2030.gov.sa/en.

5   Research and development in Saudi Arabia

Ibrahim Babelli

Introduction

Traditionally, specialized units or centers belonging to state agencies, universities, companies and non-government organizations (NGOs) conduct R&D activities. More recently, conducting research, and to a certain extent, development, have acquired new tactics leveraging connectedness and the sourcing of creativity utilizing virtual platforms.

Collaborative networks in a decentralized environment, particularly for commercially driven R&D, have been gaining momentum recently. This novo-research method is producing better results because of flexibility and cost reduction. R&D is spreading across the globe for faster development and unique innovations, but the key remaining requirement is a mix of quality delivery and timeliness.

Companies are decentralizing their R&D units across the globe to extract time and diversity benefits. Saudi Aramco operates eleven research centers and technology offices worldwide, of which three are located in Saudi Arabia, three in Europe, three in the United States and two in Asia [1]. Saudi Basic Industries Corporation (SABIC) reported in 2013 that it would launch four new state-of-the-art technology and innovation facilities, two in Saudi Arabia and one each in India and China, bringing the total number of its research facilities around the world to eighteen [2]. SABIC reports that it entered into strategic agreements with nineteen global research institutions, in addition to supporting research at Saudi universities [3].

What is research and development?

The phrase "research and development," according to the Organization for Economic Co-operation and Development (OECD), refers to "creative work undertaken on a systematic basis in order to increase the stock of knowledge, including knowledge of man, culture and society, and the use of this stock of knowledge to devise new applications" [4].

Research, by itself, can be defined as a search with an open mind, using systematic investigation, for knowledge [5]. In my opinion, there are, generally speaking, four types of research:

1   Basic research, which is work undertaken primarily to acquire new knowledge without any particular application in view
2   Exploratory research, which structures and identifies new problems
3   Mission-driven (applied) research, which develops solutions to problems
4   Skill development research, which aims at improving the skill of researchers even if no tangible result is sought after

New product design and development is more often than not a crucial factor in the survival of a company [4] and the long-term prosperity and sustainability of nations. In a global industrial landscape that is changing fast, firms must continually revise their design and range of products, countries must vigilantly upgrade their capacity to conduct research and develop solutions and products and researchers must − at least − cope with an ever-changing ecosystem of doing research, while the most successful ones will lead this change. This is absolutely necessary due to fierce competition and the evolving ecosystem.

Product development, which can be described as the transformation of a market opportunity into a product available for sale, covers the complete process of bringing a new tangible (something physical that one can touch) or intangible (like a service, process or experience) product to the market. Product development requires a steady inflow of research ideas, coupled with an understanding of customer needs and wants, the competitive environment and the nature of the market [6].

Rigorous research is conducted using well-defined steps, the so-called "Scientific Method" [7], which applies to both basic and applied research. The following steps may serve to illustrate how:

1   Observing and then linking what is being observed to already existing knowledge about a relevant area or establishing the importance of a new area
2   Establishing a hypothesis where a designation of a relationship between two or more variables is testable
3   Setting up a conceptual definition
4   Detailing the operational definition that would create a set of measurable variables
5   Gathering data using well-defined tools/instruments that are valid and reliable
6   Carrying out data analysis for the purpose of drawing preliminary conclusions
7   Converting the data into usable forms, such as tables, figures and pictures

8   Subjecting the original hypothesis to rigorous testing aided with compiled data
9   Arriving at a final conclusion and reiterating if necessary

Some of the most famous research models stem from the World War II era and the subsequent spillover into various U.S. universities and regions. Recently, however, and largely due to the advent of connectivity, new research models have taken firm hold. These include, but are not limited to, the following **[8]**:

1   Open science: Open online collaboration using freely available data and tools
2   Prize competitions: High-risk, high-reward research by independent external teams with payment on meeting technology performance measures
3   Student team contests: Sponsored design contests for university teams to develop new technologies
4   Percent innovation time and "Hack Days": Percent of time allowed each week and organized internal events for staff to work on personal projects that advance the mission
5   Blue-sky research: Funding set aside for exploration of new ideas by staff or partners, based on internal competitions
6   Open innovation: Buying and licensing IP externally and collaborative IP development with external partners
7   R&D venture capital investment: Funding early-stage technology companies with breakthrough solutions to bring adapted technologies to the market
8   Collaborative research contracts: Directed mission-critical applied research through partnership
9   Expert advisory contracts: Technical advice on specific topics from individual experts

As with research, product development can follow certain well-trodden paths. The concept adopted by IDEO, a successful design and consulting firm, is one of the most researched processes in regard to new product development and is a five-step procedure. These steps are listed in chronological order:

1   Understand and observe the market, the client, the technology and the limitations of the problem
2   Synthesize the information collected at the first step
3   Visualize new customers using the product
4   Prototype, evaluate and improve the concept
5   Implementation of design changes which are associated with more technologically advanced procedures and therefore this step will require more time **[6]**

Another famous model for product development is the Booz, Allen and Hamilton (BAH) Model, published in 1982, with its seven steps:

1   New product strategy
2   Idea generation
3   Screening and evaluation
4   Business analysis
5   Development
6   Testing
7   Commercialization **[6]**

Next came the stage-gate model developed in the 1980s as a new tool for managing new product development processes. This model gained wide acceptance, as 88% of U.S. businesses employ a stage-gate system to manage new products from idea to launch. In return, the companies that adopt this system are reported to receive benefits such as improved teamwork, shorter cycle time, improved success rates, earlier detection of failure, a better launch and even shorter cycle times – reduced by about 30% **[6, 9]**. However, over the last few years, the lean startup movement has grown in popularity, challenging many of the assumptions inherent in the stage-gate model **[6]**.

The evolving contribution of startups to R&D and technology development is most evident from the example of Big Pharma corporations that have reduced their R&D substantially and diverted their investment toward chasing startups in the second or third stage of clinical trials. What Big Pharma found in startups is a combination of agility, innovation and significant reduction in cost. Companies such as Procter & Gamble, Johnson & Johnson, Unilever and others are also chasing startups for disruptions **[10]**.

Without an R&D program, a country or a firm must rely on strategic alliances, acquisitions and networks to tap into the innovations of others. While outsourcing some components of research is common, product development is not. If a company, or a country for that matter, does not internalize product development, then research by itself will not yield dividends, even if this research is world class.

R&D spending and country performance

"More than 60 countries in the world annually perform more than a billion dollars each of R&D and their numbers are growing" **[11]**. "And most countries find themselves in fiercely competitive positions for creating new technologies, processes and products to grow their economies" **[11]**. A typical distribution of R&D funding dedicates 33% to salaries and 33% to materials and capital spending. Only 6% is dedicated to outsourcing **[11]**.

Product development remains the largest recipient of funding across the board: two-thirds of U.S. federal funding goes to development, and it is predominantly carried out in-house, with little outsourcing [12]. The Department of Defense in the United States spends 80% of its R&D budget on technology development [11], and the overwhelming majority thereof is spent in country. Looking at all U.S. R&D spending, 64% goes to development, with the industry, federal government, academia and non-profits being responsible for 87%, 8%, 15% and 2%, respectively, of the development budget [11].

World spending on R&D, when government funding contributed more than private sector funding, fluctuated in response to the global health of the economy. Only recently, when the share of the government and private sector firmly reversed, did R&D spending stabilize and witness continued increase, as can be seen in Figure 5.1 [13]. The world leaders in gross domestic spending on R&D, as a percentage of the GDP, are shown in Figure 5.2 for the year 2015 [14].

By way of comparison, Saudi Arabia's R&D spending is shown subsequently [13]. The key milestone achieved that resulted in the 2009–2010 jump in expenditure was the establishment of the King Abdullah University for Science and Technology, whose endowment (among the top ten globally) enabled it to positively impact R&D input and output in Saudi Arabia [15].

Saudi Arabia moved from 44th in 2013 to 39th in 2015 in terms of gross domestic spending on R&D as a percentage of GDP, for reference see figure 5.3[11, 13].

Funding agencies prefer to categorize research as either basic or applied, and most prefer spending money on the latter, particularly corporate funding of research. The United States has always been in the forefront of spending on basic research, at the rate of one-sixth of total R&D funding in 2015, which amounts to roughly USD 83 billion, only 50% of which comes from the

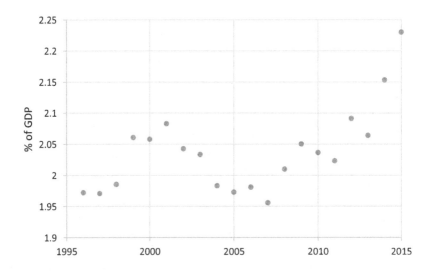

Figure 5.1 World research and development expenditure (% of GDP)

federal government **[16]**. Recently, with 17% of its R&D spending going to basic research, South Korea became the top global spender on basic research in terms of percentage of GDP, amounting to roughly USD 10 billion in 2016 **[12]**.

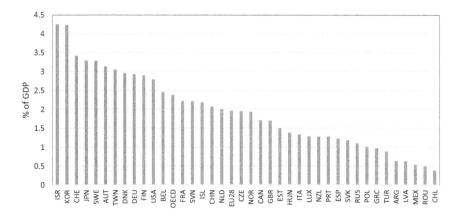

Figure 5.2 OECD countries' gross domestic spending on R&D★

★ "Gross domestic spending on R&D is defined as the total expenditure (current and capital) on R&D carried out by all resident companies, research institutes, university and government laboratories, etc., in a country. It includes R&D funded from abroad, but excludes domestic funds for R&D performed outside the domestic economy" **[14]**.

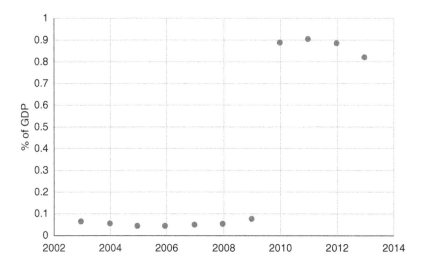

Figure 5.3 Saudi Arabia's research and development expenditure★ (% of GDP) **[11]**

★ The percentage of GDP spent on R&D in Saudi Arabia differs according to who is reporting. This is from the World Bank. In the 2017 edition of the Global R&D Funding Forecast, the Saudi R&D expenditure for year 2015 amounts to 0.4% of the GDP **[11]**.

Another way of looking at countries' performance in R&D is through innovation. On the Global Innovation Index for the year 2017, Saudi Arabia's rank is 55, whereas Switzerland, Sweden, the Netherlands, the United States and the United Kingdom are the world's most innovative countries [17].

In terms of quality of research, Saudi Arabia's rank is 30th among nations conducting high-quality research, as reported by *Nature*, where the top five leaders are the United States, China, Germany, the United Kingdom and Japan [18].

And with respect to R&D by corporations, *Strategy&* reported in the 2017 Global Innovation 1000 Study an analysis of spending at the world's 1,000 largest publicly listed corporate R&D spenders. The only Saudi company reported was SABIC, ranked 247, with R&D expenditure amounting to 1.5% of its total revenue in 2016 [19].

In the United States, a typical ratio of research and development for an industrial company is about 3.5% of revenue. A high-technology company such as a computer manufacturer might spend 7%, but anything over 15% is remarkable and usually gains a reputation for being a high-technology company. Companies in this category include pharmaceutical companies such as Merck & Co. (14.1%) or Novartis (15.1%) and engineering companies like Ericsson (24.9%). Generally, such firms prosper only in markets whose customers have extreme needs, such as medicine, scientific instruments, safety-critical mechanisms (aircraft) or high-technology military armaments [4].

Saudi R&D

It is very important to state, from the outset, that the situation in Saudi Arabia is a bit awkward when it comes to conducting R&D, and this is primarily due to the following reasons:

1   There is no systematic process for measuring the economic impact of R&D spending.
2   Practically, there are no product centers in Saudi Arabia.
3   The focus on the R&D process in Saudi Arabia is on supply, not on demand.
4   There are no government mandates to compel private-sector companies to create demand for Saudi R&D.
5   Saudi Arabia has had no military (defense or offence) research program of any magnitude.
6   There are no real Saudi agendas for R&D in Saudi Arabia; mostly, the R&D agenda is an amalgamation of whatever is scientifically attractive at the time of setting the agenda.
7   There is no Saudi-specific R&D, even where it has been demonstrated that challenges are Saudi specific.
8   There have been no grand-scale national R&D projects in Saudi Arabia, à la the Apollo project.

9   Saudi Arabia is a relatively young country with no strong pull from the industry for local R&D, coupled with a scattered R&D workforce that tend to weigh more in favor of higher degrees than associate degrees.

With the world's largest oil company, and with one of the largest petrochemical companies and the worlds' number-one seawater desalination capacity, one would expect to see Saudi Arabia among global leaders in oil, petrochemical and desalination R&D. The fact remains that Saudi Arabia is not a leader in R&D in any of these three fields.

In what follows, we will briefly visit some of the factors that contributed to R&D in Saudi Arabia being what it is today.

Military research

Almost every country with a successful research program owes its inception to military research, with only a handful of countries being the exception. The reason military research programs have a great possibility to beget successful non-military research programs is that they enjoy all the necessary elements of successful R&D components, namely:

1   Unified goal
2   Unified command
3   Committed and talented R&D workforce
4   Ample resources
5   Strict timelines
6   Careful oversight

Successful military R&D programs are too many to enumerate, but they also have some unique characteristics in their management approach, namely the interface between the military command and the R&D team is usually civilian, which ensures that R&D is conducted with an R&D approach that is scientific, rigorous and productive. Even in countries where there were no spillover effects from military to civilian applications of research, well-defined military R&D was carried out successfully.

This does not necessarily constitute a recommendation for Saudi Arabia to roll out military research; it merely cites a fact that is normally not considered in the general discourse on R&D in Saudi Arabia.

Saudi Arabia's R&D agenda

The leading R&D institution in Saudi Arabia is King Abdulaziz City for Science and Technology (KACST) [20]. KACST provides R&D funding to other entities in Saudi Arabia, enters into joint R&D work in-country and internationally, conducts research at its various research institutes and sends Saudi nationals to obtain masters and PhDs in areas relevant to its line of work.

The areas of focus that KACST identified as the National R&D Agenda for Saudi Arabia include:

1   Technology transfer and localization in strategic sectors, divided into three themes [20]:

I   The first theme – global leadership: this theme includes sectors that the Kingdom has a competitive advantage in:

1   Energy
2   Water
3   Oil
4   Gas
5   Minerals
6   Advanced materials

II   The second theme – self-reliance: this theme includes sectors in which the Kingdom is spending large amounts of money:

7   Health and medicine
8   Information and communications technology (ICT)
9   Agriculture
10   Building and construction
11   Transportation and logistics
12   Environment
13   Nuclear science
14   Applied physics

III The third theme – national security: this theme includes military and national security sectors:

15   Space and aeronautics
16   Defense
17   Security

2   Technical Leaders Preparation Program: "KACST has established 15 centers, distributed throughout the world, in collaboration with big research institutions and universities in the field of scientific and applied research. These centers work on research in the strategic areas that are important for the development and prosperity of the national economy." These programs include [20]:

- Center for Complex Engineering Systems in collaboration with MIT
- Center of Excellence for Aeronautics and Astronautics in collaboration with Stanford University
- Center of Excellence in Integrated Nanosystems in collaboration with Northwestern University
- Center for Advanced Materials and Manufacturing in collaboration with the University of Cambridge

- Center of Excellence for Green Nanotechnologies in collaboration with the University of California, Los Angeles
- Center of Excellence for Telecom Applications in collaboration with the University of California, San Diego
- Center of Excellence of Nanomaterial for Clean Energy Applications in collaboration with the University of California, Berkeley
- Center of Microwave Sensor Technology in collaboration with the University of Michigan
- Solid State Lighting Center of Excellence in collaboration with the University of California, Santa Barbara and King Abdullah University for Science and Technology
- Center of Excellence for Earth and Space Science in collaboration with the California Institute of Technology
- Decision Support Center in collaboration with Boeing

3   National Research Partnerships, including [20]:

1   Saudi Energy Efficiency Center
2   KACST-SEC Joint R&D Center for the Distribution Sector
3   Joint Research Center for Desalination Using Renewable Energy
4   Joint Center for Wildlife Research

A quick tally of the previous finds that KACST is leading the national R&D agenda in more than two dozen areas of research.

There is no doubt that the majority of the previously mentioned fields of research are important, and, of the topics that KACST has committed Saudi Arabia to work on and invest in, several are among the top research areas that the world is focusing on, namely [11]:

1	Advanced materials	✓
2	Agriculture/food	✓
3	Automotive	✗
4	Commercial aerospace	✓
5	Communications	✓
6	Energy	✓
7	Environmental	✓
8	Instrumentation	✓
9	Life science/health care	✓
10	Military/defense	✓
11	Pharmaceutical/biotech	✓

The questions are: where shall we focus and where do we want to excel? Can we afford to spread our government R&D funding as shown previously?

Today, the United States is the world leader in the previous 11 categories, except automotive, with Germany, Japan and China at a distant second. Where should Saudi Arabia aim to be and in which research area? We cannot be leaders in all of the previous areas that KACST is investing in.

Saudi-specific R&D?

A national identity of R&D may appear, at face value, an alien concept. But it may just be one of the key reasons we have not had any meaningfully successful and sustainable R&D program that produced results and solutions in Saudi Arabia.

Diabetes research in Saudi Arabia was funded by the government through various agencies, but most notably KACST. That was the closest we had to conducting Saudi R&D. To appreciate the magnitude and severity of diabetes in Saudi Arabia, I quote the following paragraph in its entirety [21]:

> It is believed that around 6 Million Saudis are Pre-diabetic/diabetics with an estimated cost per year of around 36 Billion Riyals. Figures suggest that up to 30% of over 40 year old Saudi population may suffer from diabetes, costing the government $800 a month/patient in treatment. This together with the assessment that 50% of the population is considered overweight or obese indicates the vulnerable number of future diabetics is set to rise. It is estimated that the burden of Diabetes may exceed SR 120 billion by 2035.

Author was personally but indirectly involved in the diabetes research through reviewing and editing a significant number of reports and papers produced through KACST funding in the early to late 1990s. Author has observed was that the diabetes research conducted in Saudi Arabia then largely was one of diagnostics, which was necessary, but remained in this realm and never progressed beyond diagnosis.

Aside from medical research, we have carried out and funded R&D in Saudi Arabia that is technology specific, and we made no significant contribution, largely because we have very little technical workforce to support R&D everywhere in Saudi research institutions compared to other global leading institutions, in addition to lack of focus. The situation is slightly better at large companies such as SABIC and Saudi Aramco, yet even there, we are barely recognizable based on the R&D output generated domestically.

National research programs

John F. Kennedy's famous statement in the early 1960s about putting a man on the moon and returning him safely before the end of the decade is often quoted with admiration, but largely ignored whenever Saudi Arabia, and similar nations, attempt to forge national agendas for R&D.

Has Saudi Arabia's leadership declared a mission with a specific and timely goal for Saudi Arabia that cannot be arrived at without R&D? If it is a national research program that we are after, then it is insufficient for this national program to be declared by the R&D boss, irrespective of who he might be.

In conclusion, it is believed that Saudi Arabia has not had:

- A focused military R&D program
- A truly focused Saudi-specific R&D agenda
- A critical mass of R&D workforce
- A strong demand for R&D from the industry and private sectors
- A significant number of successful product centers
- Any national research programs launched and monitored by the highest authority in the Kingdom
- A set of tools to inform us how much economic impact our spending on R&D is creating

What we have carried out in Saudi Arabia is scattered research, with hardly any development, that resulted in a significant number of publications, some of which are of very high quality. This is what we have done in the past, and, based on the mandate and the resources available, Author actually believe that we have done okay. In addition, we have not been involved in or created incentives for the private sector to generate value-added R&D.

This is the era of the national transformation as defined by Vision 2030 **[22]**. It is critical and urgent to rethink how R&D is to be conducted in and for Saudi Arabia, if R&D will meaningfully act as a catalyst for achieving the Vision.

In what follows, Author attempt to construct a matrix of answers that may, collectively or separately, provide part of the answer to how can R&D play its vital role in supporting Vision 2030.

Proposed R&D actions for Saudi Arabia

In what follows, Author will attempt to put together various ideas, with the eventual goal of constructing a matrix of solutions, for how to transform the way we conduct R&D in Saudi Arabia, with the aim of supporting Vision 2030. The proposed actions are:

1   Develop and roll out a structured approach to measure the economic impact of R&D spending in Saudi Arabia. This will require a dedicated national agency to carry out this task, and Author believes that the most qualified entity would be the General Authority for Statistics **[23]**. Input, output, outcome and impact of R&D are to be measured and reported quarterly.
2   Increase R&D spending in Saudi Arabia to reach 3% of the GDP by 2030.
3   Set up an R&D-dedicated fund to be capitalized through:

    a   0.5% of the profits from all fully or partially state-owned corporations in Saudi Arabia.
    b   1% of the profits from all Saudi commercial banks.

4 Set up a dedicated endowment-based R&D fund and encourage NGOs and donors to capitalize the fund and contribute to setting up its R&D agenda.

5 Create demand or R&D in Saudi Arabia through:

    a A mandate on all fully or partially state-owned corporations to develop and announce a list of challenges that require R&D solutions, and invite only Saudi institutions doing R&D to participate through open competition.

    b Mandate the same on all companies, inside or outside Saudi Arabia, in which the Public Investment Fund (PIF) is a shareholder, to submit a similar list to the one cited in (a).

6 Mandate the establishment of product centers at all leading Saudi corporations.

7 Carefully integrate the development of homegrown R&D talent with attracting international talent in focused areas.

8 Create an ecosystem for startups, with focus on the following [10]:

    a Attract international startups to develop technologies in the focus areas, which will fast-track the development of technologies and solutions competitively.

    b Provide initial angel and VC funding and tolerate a high rate of startup failure initially.

    c Create open technology incubators, where all brainpower can develop in centralized facilities that promote connectivity.

    d Mandate big technology consumers, such as fully and partially state-owned enterprises, to provide a secure entry point for home-grown technologies to be demonstrated.

9 Mandate that all leading Saudi universities, research centers and corporations adopt and report on the utilization of the following R&D tools:

- Crowdsourcing
- Hackathons
- Open science
- Prize competitions
- Student team contests

10 Create a program of focused military R&D guided by and reporting to the newly established Saudi Arabia military industries.

11 Incentivize startups and the private sector to participate meaningfully and to provide technology solutions [10].

12 Create a government venture capital fund to fund technology-focused startups [10].

13 Establish a dedicated Ministry for Science and Technology.

All of the previous ideas are necessary, Author believes, to usher in a new R&D ecosystem for launching a new R&D era in Saudi Arabia. However, the previous enablers will not yield results if the two most important determinants for successful R&D in and for Saudi Arabia are not successfully and carefully developed:

1 A focused Saudi-specific national agenda.
2 A set of a few focused national research programs.

And, above all, what Saudi Arabia requires is a talented, capable and enabled R&D workforce.

The steady-state R&D model, necessary for supporting Vision 2030, needs to be built on a national agenda, enables the development of local R&D skills, utilizes the novo-R&D tools of decentralization and diversification, leverages directed funding in a dynamic approach to address short- and medium-term partial or incremental goals and smartly attracts the best minds globally using carefully developed tools and methodologies.

References

1 Aramco Trading Annual Report. (2018). https://aramcotrading.com/Data/FileManager/files/Annual_Report_2018.pdf
2 Al-Abdrabbuh, S. (2013). Sabic takes innovation to next level with four new technology centers set for opening this year. www.sabic.com/en/news/3898-sabic-takes-innovation-to-next-level-with-four-new-technology-centers-set-for-opening-this-year
3 Sabic Growth Through Transformation Annual Report. (2018). https://www.sabic.com/assets/en/Images/SABIC-AR-English-2018_tcm1010-18629.pdf
4 Wikipedia. Research and development. http://en.wikipedia.org/wiki/Research_and_development
5 Wikipedia. Research. http://en.wikipedia.org/wiki/Research
6 https://en.wikipedia.org/wiki/New_product_development
7 Private communication with Dr. Ahmed Nabil Abo-khatwa, 2017.
8 Private communication with Dr. Jill Engel-Cox, 2016.
9 Kenneth, K. (2013). *The PDMA Handbook of New Product Development* (3rd ed.). Hoboken, NJ: John Wiley & Sons Inc. p. 34.
10 Private communication with Dr. Basel Abu Sharkh, 2017.
11 https://www.rdworldonline.com/UNESCO Institute for Statistics (uis.unesco.org). ID: GB.XPD.RSDV.GD.ZS
12 Van Noorden, R. (2017). Israel edges out South Korea for top spot in research investment. *Nature*. www.nature.com/news/israel-edges-out-south-korea-for-top-spot-in-research-investment-1.21443
13 The World Bank. (2017). Research and development expenditure (% of GDP). UNESCO Institute of Statistics. https://data.worldbank.org/indicator/GB.XPD.RSDV.GD.ZS
14 OECD. (2020). Gross domestic spending on R&D. https://data.oecd.org/rd/gross-domestic-spending-on-r-d.htm
15 R&D Magazine. (2016). *2016 Global R&D Funding Forecast.* www.iriweb.org/sites/default/files/2016GlobalR%26DFundingForecast_2.pdf
16 Mervis, J. (2017). Data check: U.S. government share of basic research funding falls below 50%. *Science*. www.sciencemag.org/news/2017/03/data-check-us-government-share-basic-research-funding-falls-below-50

17 Cornell University, INSEAD, & WIPO. (2017). *Global Innovation Index 2017: Innovation Feeding the World.* www.wipo.int/publications/en/details.jsp?id=4193
18 Leader of the pack. (2017). *Nature.* www.nature.com/articles/549S62a
19 www.strategyand.pwc.com/innovation1000
20 www.kacst.edu.sa/eng/Pages/default.aspx
21 Strategic Priorities for Advanced Medical and Health Research. www.kfupm.edu.sa/deanships/dsr/en/Documents/NSTP/MedicalAndHealth.pdf
22 http://vision2030.gov.sa/en
23 www.stats.gov.sa/en

6 Economic transformation through incubation and entrepreneurship (in light of Vision 2030)

Muhammad Babar Khan, Sadia Iqbal and Irfan Hameed

Literature review

Entrepreneurship education and cultural barriers in KSA

Entrepreneurship is one of the most lucrative milestones and can trigger economic transformation and development in various countries globally. Keeping this in mind, with special emphasis on small to medium-sized enterprises (SMEs), promotion and reinforcement of entrepreneurship is considered the most important step in both developing and developed countries [1].

In the past few years, there has been a sudden boom in the market in which women's active participation in business activities seems to have increased in the Gulf Cooperation Council dramatically. This in turn has brought about a revolution and has affected all the countries of the world in the context of development and globalization [2, 3]. However, it is still clear that men outnumber women in almost all business fields. Despite the inescapable fact that women are usually more knowledgeable and their participation exceeds that of men in various fields of business, with many succeeding in owning their own businesses, men still are in a dominant position as far as the size and type of business is involved.

In order to achieve long-term entrepreneurial goals, two aspects of culture, collectivism versus individualism, have usually been observed as the most central trait in studying successful outcomes of cultures [4]. Saudi Arabia's culture follows collectivism, as people practice strong unity and possess concrete loyalty throughout their lives, collectivism having been infused in them since birth [5]. Early research on entrepreneurship postulated that collectivist cultures produce fewer entrepreneurs compared to individualist cultures. Hence, in order to produce more entrepreneurs, it is necessary to keep a sound balance between both types of culture [6]. The productivity and efficiency of an organization are enhanced with the help of entrepreneurship, but how is still a pressing question [7]. In Saudi Arabia, students acquiring higher education are not very eager to take up entrepreneurship due to their country's collectivist culture, their lack of entrepreneurial education and basic educational background versus the education provided to European and U.S. students. According to extensive observational research, entrepreneurial intentions help in forecasting entrepreneurial actions [8]. The importance of entrepreneurship education has been greatly emphasized by researchers, and, as a result, it is now on its way to becoming part of the curriculum in all academic institutes, including schools and training programs [9]. Malaysia is also among those countries that project their growth through entrepreneurship education, and universities within GCC countries as well as internationally have incorporated this education into their curricula since its birth [10–12].

Countries all over the world practice different cultures and lifestyles. The culture of Saudi Arabia is very different from other cultures, as it is greatly influenced by religion. There are various cultural barriers in Saudi Arabia, and having a better understanding of them can help provide more security and success for an organization [13]. Management decisions, behavior and styles are affected by Saudi Arabian culture [14].

Language is the most substantial way one communicates with others. Communication is a two-way street, and if there is a language barrier between two communicating countries, there is a serious issue between cultures without any solution. Arabic is very different from other languages, especially English, which is mostly used by technology suppliers, and technology is the need of the time for any country. Differences between cultures because of languages can cause major frustration because it sends a clear message of not being understood by others and may lead to miscommunication. This, in return, may prove quite risky, as in order to translate Arabic to English, a word-to-word translator may be required, which may not break the language barrier, as IT coding and programming are often in English [15].

Gender discrimination is yet another barrier in Saudi entrepreneurial education. Saudi Arabian women are allowed to work with men in organizations as long as they don't interact with them. Saudi Arabian women therefore prefer working in all-female settings like girls' schools, universities, banks, women's development programs and other places that deal with only women so that there is no chance of communicating with men [16].

The year 2010 marked a revolution for Saudi Arabia in terms of entrepreneurship and innovation. According to a publication of the National U.S.-Arab Chambers of Commerce, by the end of 2010, the Kingdom had set a goal to be on the list of the world's top ten most competitive nations whose major reliance is on a vibrant economy driven by today's creative and upcoming young entrepreneurs. Saudi Arabia's business is composed of 92% small and medium-sized enterprises (SMEs), and there are significant indicators that point to the fact that Saudi Arabia will produce the business leaders of the next generation [17].

According to H.E. Amr Al-Dabbagh, Governor of the Saudi Arabian General Investment Authority (SAGIA), if the Kingdom is committed to becoming one of the most competitive nations in the world, it is essential that it nurture its small and medium-sized enterprises, as they are the economy's oxygen and backbone [17].

The Kingdom is on its way to undergoing a major transformation from an oil-based economy to a knowledge-based economy. This diversification is linked to many reasons, of which fluctuation in oil prices plays the most vital role. To expedite this transformation, the Kingdom should invest more in entrepreneurship education, schools, colleges, universities and health services. Economic growth and human capital development are linked through entrepreneurship education, which actually leads to a knowledge-based economy, which is Saudi Arabia's Vision 2030. This way, the Kingdom's culture will become more sustainable [18]. Keeping this in mind, the King Abdullah University of Science and Technology (KAUST), with its Innovative Industrial Collaboration Program (KICP), is working toward fostering strong ties with local, global and regional businesses that possess a keen interest in building up entrepreneurship links and participating in the Kingdom's transition to a knowledge-based economy [17]. KAUST is playing a vital part in recruiting the best intellectuals from within and outside the Kingdom globally to participate in scientific research. This type of collaboration would facilitate creating new leading-edge companies and more entrepreneurial facilities and will expedite the Kingdom's achievement of a knowledge-based society, which has been a longtime vision of the Kingdom of Saudi Arabia [17].

Extremely low literacy rates were experienced in the Arab countries in the mid-1990s, particularly among women, especially in rural areas. According to UNESCO statistics, in 1995, illiteracy rates in these nations were between one-fifth and one-half of the state's population [19]. In order to address this problem, King Abdullah has invested a significant amount towards education, with a special emphasis on women's education. According to Minkus-McKenna, Saudi Arabia university enrollment is 58% women, with the majority found in diversified fields from all walks of life [20]. Despite all the flexibility, women still face threats in acquiring freedom of education in Saudi Arabia but this is changing with the modernization of society [21, 22]. This has forced Saudi women to occupy only 15% of the Saudi workforce, leaving 85% of women at home, as they are unable to fight cultural and socio-economic constraints [23].

For the socio-economic development of women, availability of higher education and easy access to the same are two major factors that need to be taken into consideration. Women are allowed access to higher education, but colleges and universities have unseen barriers like social empowerment that restrict their learning experiences and their implementation of learning in practical life, leaving them without human capital development. Sexism in educational institutes is practiced, with separate classrooms for men and women [24].

Due to constraints and accessibility, some Saudi women have been known to develop low self-esteem, loss of self-confidence and a poor image of themselves, which in turn builds more barriers for them in pursuing higher education and entrepreneurship [25]. In order to address these struggles, constraints and challenges faced by Saudi women in the business sector on an everyday basis, the Al-Sayedah Khadijah Bint Khuwailid First Businesswomen Center was established with the purpose of providing aid to Saudi women in entrepreneurship. This business center's sole purpose is to tackle sensitive issues like gender discrimination and other cultural issues so that women have access to a strong support system and networking opportunities. This has helped in eradicating sex segregation issues to a great extent. The center has instilled the importance of education in Saudi women and taught them to balance the demands of family life along with work, building their self-confidence at the same time **[25]**.

Entrepreneurial education is a current need. Most developed countries are heavily investing in entrepreneurial education at the university, high-school and primary-school levels to encourage economic transformation **[26–28]**. In 1945, Harvard University initiated entrepreneurial education in order to kindle a new spirit in the United States' economic transformation **[29]**. In Europe, entrepreneurial education is taught through four different routes: 1) as a subject to start a business; 2) as an additional subject for those who want to pursue entrepreneurship; 3) as one of the topics that lead to innovation, development of confidence and skills to initiate a start-up and 4) last, not as a formal but as an informal academic course.

According to the Women's Institute of Management in 2012, women entrepreneurs were subjected to a shortage of peer support networks as compared to men, who had comparatively strong peer support networks **[30]**. For women entrepreneurs to create strong network opportunities, various industry and women's entrepreneurship associations have been established so that they may share experiences and exchange knowledge with people in their surroundings. This will help them acquire practical tips for their startups. These associations conduct seminars, motivational workshops and human capital development sessions to groom women entrepreneurs. Women, however, may not get an opportunity to be a part of such associations because they are burdened with family responsibilities and business **[31–33]**. This results in less interaction and fewer networking possibilities, restricts women entrepreneurs' knowledge of their surroundings and hampers exchange of ideas; thus, in a nutshell, it may make a difference in the sluggishness and growth of small and medium-sized enterprises or startups owned by women entrepreneurs. In 1980, Malaysia marked 7% of employers as women, whereas in 1984, 8% of working Malaysian women were entrepreneurs and employers. Furthermore, 16% were classified as "self-employed" workers. In 1990, this percentage increased by only 8.5%, with men still ruling the roost compared to women in employer status **[34]**. Women occupied less than 10% of the total employers' share compared to men **[35]**. Thus, if one extrapolates, the conclusion is that Malaysia also shares almost the same status of gender discrimination and constraints as Saudi Arabia and even Asia as a whole.

Skill development through entrepreneurial education

The economy of any country is directly linked to the development of entrepreneurship in that community, and several studies have been carried out to support this. According to a study conducted by Wei-Loon in 2012 **[36]** which concerned entrepreneurial intentions of public universities in Turkey **[37]** and student motivation for entrepreneurship in Romania **[38]**, the development of entrepreneurship is crucial to improve the economic sector of a country. This study and many other related studies point to the fact that entrepreneurship education is the need of the times which will ultimately enhance the growth of entrepreneurs, especially among college and university students. An educated workforce will ensure higher productivity, which will lead to a strengthened economy and more innovation [39]. Higher productivity ultimately leads to higher income, which is proof of substantial success achieved through entrepreneurial education along with human capital development [40, 41]. The drivers which govern entrepreneurial intentions are perceived behavioral controls, norms and attitudes [42].

Formal and informal entrepreneurial education findings point to certain contradictions which are essential for one to study in order to become an actual entrepreneur. According to Syahrina et al. [43] and Collins et al. [44], formal entrepreneurial education provided by higher education institutions leads to a satisfactory increase in the production quantity of entrepreneurs. This type of education reduces unemployment, boosts the economic sector and at the same time enhances entrepreneur graduates' production [45]. The graduates actually become job creators rather than job seekers. In the case of informal education, as suggested by Abidin et al. [46], entrepreneurial activities are at their peak, as this type of education proves more effective and directs graduates towards entrepreneurial targets. Informal education aims to transform an individual into a lucrative entrepreneur based on personal experiences and self-determination [47]. A good example of an informal entrepreneurial education is a family business in which every individual encapsulates experience from the surroundings based on self-determination and personal experiences. Different studies have been presented by different researchers, but, in a nutshell, both types of education are essential for transforming graduates into entrepreneurs.

Several researchers have conducted various studies to detect college students' entrepreneurial competencies. The aim of these studies was to analyze entrepreneur qualities in terms of entrepreneurial skills, behaviors and various other psychological characters. According to Arashteh et al.'s research results in 2012 [48], analysis of students' personality characteristics at the Islamic Azad University of Sari concluded that the students possessed positive entrepreneurial features. Luca and Cazan in 2011 [49] identified significant relationships between entrepreneurial potential and personality variables like creativity, entrepreneurial skills, internal locus of control and resource organization. On the other hand, Chiru's research in 2012 [50] took this finding to a new level, where he analyzed students' acquired business skills and psychological factors like personal motivation, risk acceptance, self-confidence and so on with respect to higher and middle educational institutes.

Oosterbeek et al. in 2008 [51] described ten varieties of entrepreneurial competencies, including need for achievement, need for power, need for autonomy, self-efficacy, social orientation, risk-taking propensity, endurance, market awareness, creativity and flexibility.

Rasmussen, Mosey and Wright in 2011 **[52]** investigated three different competencies which can play a vital role in access to future resources and emerging spin-offs' future credibility. These competencies include the entrepreneurial team's ability to exchange with industry partners, ability to attract external project champions from among industry personnel and ability to gain others' trust so as to acquire resources from them. All these competencies are linked in turn to one core prerequisite: a positive attitude towards entrepreneurship, which includes technology commercialization, a current need **[52]**. Similar findings were reached by Rasmussen and Borch in 2010 **[53]**. According to their findings, the competencies found had a special focus on 1) exploring opportunities leading to business ideas pertaining to the university, 2) external resource allocation and 3) balancing the interests of the university organization and commercial spin-off **[53]**. Vohora, Wright and Lockett in 2004 **[54]** summarized these findings that pointed to the inescapable fact that universities lack the necessary resources essential for spin-offs, technology commercialization is a major lack in academics and disunity of interests may lead to worsened growth of spin-off companies by stakeholders **[54]**.

Universities are building blocks for creativity and innovation, leading to the emergence of colossal amounts of university spin-offs every year. Sadly, not all of these creative spin-offs survive in the long term, as they fail to achieve the targets set for them in their development's early stage, as pointed out by Vohora, Wright and Lockett in 2004 **[54]**.

Etzkowitz in 2008 **[55]** pointed out that a university supporting entrepreneurship is based mainly on four building blocks: 1) academic leadership, an essential ingredient to administer a strategic vision; 2) authentic control of resources, which includes all legal accessibilities like available equipment, intellectual properties acquired as a result of research, buildings and so on; 3) abilities on an organizational level, which will assist in technology transfer by means of various variables, including licensing, patenting and business incubation; and, lastly, 4) the most vital building block is the ethos of entrepreneurship: the moral beliefs that make up an entrepreneurial community established by people who are faculty, students and leaders. Nevertheless, not all universities focus on the previous four pillars; instead, their main priority is teaching and research, as they do not tend to possess any interest in marketing innovations **[55]**.

However, there are a few articles that address the phenomenon of economic transformation and skill development through entrepreneurial education in Saudi universities and their counter-programs. King Abdullah University of Science and Technology's founding president is of the opinion that the risk-takers of this new generation should be encouraged, as entrepreneurship is all about risk taking **[56]**. According to President, people opting for KAUST possess adventurous qualities like cultural and intellectual curiosity and professionalism, and these skills play a prominent role in entrepreneurship building, as they prepare individuals for gutsy start-ups in the future **[56]**. According to the president and CEO of the National U.S.–Arab Chamber of Commerce (NUSACC), in Saudi Arabia today, the economic landscape is gradually being reshaped by a new breed of talented entrepreneurs, including men and women who are precariously leaping over the boundaries of risk-taking and accepting challenges to confront the ingredients of risk and value creation in the Arab world.

According to SAGIA Governor Amr-Al Dabbagh, Saudi Arabia is rapidly making progress in creating a business-minded culture which aims to be the backbone of creativity, innovation and entrepreneurial initiatives. Furthermore, he added that SAGIA is truly steadfast in making the Kingdom of Saudi Arabia one of the nations most ready to meet challenges in the world [56]. In order to achieve this long-term goal, emerging growth economies must be nurtured by the Kingdom of Saudi Arabia, as they serve as the oxygen for the economy of the country [56].

Professor Choon Fong Shih, founding president and former professor of electrical engineering at the King Abdullah University of Science and Technology, claimed that KAUST has state-of-the-art students who are tech savvy, intellectual and entrepreneurially smart, along with a competent faculty. Additionally, it has the required funding to enable students and faculty to indulge in the development of key technologies in major sectors like clean water, renewable energy, environmental and food resources. The biggest lack in the field of science and technology is not only funds but the absence of entrepreneurial people, which is the strength of KAUST as well as Saudi Arabia [56]. Amer Kayani, counselor for commercial affairs, U.S. Embassy, Riyadh, in an interview with the U.S. Arab Chamber of Commerce, added that the Saudi government has committed to spending USD 400 billion over the next decade on infrastructure projects and a knowledge-based economy which will particularly focus on education and technology, which are the essential ingredients, along with financial services [56].

Bayan Gardens School is yet another venture of Saudi Arabia, located in the Eastern Province in Al Khobar. This venture is the brainchild of the director, Ms. Yasmeen Husain, and her entrepreneurial family and was established in 1999. The vision of this venture is to create an innovative approach towards education. Since 1999, Bayan Gardens School has been making leaps and bounds towards quality education as a bilingual school and a good-English curriculum school. A unique thing about this venture is the implementation of its innovative program, TREP$, which will shortly push the envelope of students' intellectual capacity from grades 4 to 8 in the form of entrepreneurship education to develop their skills in the area of starting their own business [56]. According to Husain, quality education is the focal point which drives people to give their best shot, at the same time enabling them to become creative and innovative. "What you reap is what you sow." These students will thus cultivate a firm ground for entrepreneurship if the Kingdom cultivates them with the seeds of quality education, especially entrepreneurial education [56].

EDUCON Educational Services is an educational consulting service established in 2005 in Saudi Arabia. The aim of this service is to promote education by arranging English-language programs to promote human capital development, identify academic degree programs in foreign universities for students to enable them to acquire a quality education and facilitate summer exchange camps for students aged 8 to 16. In its initial phases, EDUCON faced many challenges, as only small colleges and universities would sign up with it. Another challenge for EDUCON was working with students who were doubtful about choosing their careers. EDUCON has recently created a niche in the educational consulting market, as its vision is to help students reach their long-term educational goals by providing them with state-of-the-art services and perfectly relating to their student clientele [56].

So, in a nutshell, Saudi Arabia is ready to travel the road to skill development and entrepreneurship.

Entrepreneurship theories

James Truslow Adams [57] built his dream on his theory which states that life should be an equal-opportunity recipe for all, with rich and full chances for everyone according to their abilities and achievements. Building on the same, Schumpeter [58] stated his theory of innovation, which suggests that entrepreneurs are a combination of sheer hard work and countless dreams so they have an entirely different world of desires which facilitates them to create kingdoms of their own. At the same time, they get joy from innovating new things, which presents the true essence of entrepreneurship. According to him, the theory of innovation is linked to economic development theory, which has five characteristics: new product development, new method application, new market opening, new source acquisition and the proposition of new industries. The theory of innovation serves as a backbone for entrepreneurial concepts [58]. Apart from the five characteristics stated by Schumpeter [58], there is another characteristic of immense importance: motivation. According to the learned need theory [59], there are three motivation drivers: affiliation, power and achievement, irrespective of age, gender, culture, caste or creed. It was further suggested that start-ups always involve risk; therefore, the motivation driver achievement is present and entrepreneurs should understand that challenges and risks in entrepreneurship are backed by the ingredient of achievement. On the other hand, an entrepreneur's risk must be accurately calculated with strong support from analysis and certainty. The second motivation driver, affiliation, is basically an internal drive in human beings which pushes them to acquire admiration from others. This affiliation driver is linked to another aspect, collaboration, and this aspect is of vital importance with affiliation because it rejuvenates people's motivation. Individuals can therefore relate to collaboration and affiliation because these two aspects enable an individual to come up with something new and innovative [59].

The third important motivation driver in the learned need theory is power. Power is an internal characteristic of an individual which he/she can enjoy and win on an individual level. According to this theory, power comes in two forms: individual and institutional. It is recommended that power be a motivational driver so that an individual using it positively may form different teams and achieve challenges in a more effective manner. This may further motivate an individual to achieve risky challenges in line with both the individual and institutional aspects of power, and at the same time, they may receive gratification through feedback from society as a whole **[59]**.

Other authors **[60, 61]** have also suggested that achievement is accessed via success; it is also a needed factor for failure prevention. People who strive for achievement love challenging tasks; they may make leaps and bounds to accomplish difficult tasks and work tirelessly to develop their human capital and consider success their foremost duty. The basic instinct of an entrepreneur is gauged by an effective entrepreneurship curriculum which in turn helps them transform themselves into successful businesspeople.

According to McMullen and Shepherd's theory of entrepreneurial action **[62]**, entrepreneurial activity is a result of a strong belief that the decision to become an entrepreneur is linked to an individual's desire to attain an original goal and the feasibility of the same. Education plays a vibrant role in this decision-making. Prior research has also demonstrated that entrepreneurship education is of crucial importance, and through this education, an individual will be polished to such an extent that he/she will find entrepreneurial activities more passionate, desirable and practical **[63, 64]**, which will further enhance his or her career. Entrepreneurial careers have seen a sudden boom in the market because of entrepreneurship education awareness, enabling students to transfer their knowledge and motivational skills **[65–67]**, along with further helping them showcase their entrepreneurial learning **[68, 69]**.

All these theories contribute to the buzzword "sustainable entrepreneurship," which seems to be a combination of entrepreneurship theory and environmental and welfare economics theory **[70]**. For sustainable development, it is crucial that existing knowledge have a special extension of entrepreneurial education, as new information should be added to one's existing knowledge with time so that one may compete in the real world. This will further enable students to empower the masses and keep their personal lives fully tuned to a sense of sustainable development.

Saudi success stories

Saudi Arabia is well on its way to entrepreneurial success and transforming its economy. SMEs are playing an important role in transforming the economy because they are the means of creating job opportunities and triggering growth and innovation in the country **[71]**. For a knowledge-based economy, SMEs are the main driving forces. This section will focus on successful small and medium-sized enterprises, as these are the main ingredients which have been the focal point of a successful economic transformation and knowledge-based economy for Saudi Arabia.

Brains Contracting Ltd. Company was founded in 2002. Initially, it was launched with 40,000 SR, and in 2009, it took a dip to 20 million SR and came to be known in the Eastern Province as one of the premier maintenance companies. The company provides facility management and technical services in the Eastern Province to the government, hospitals, universities, private entities and the oil and gas sector **[71]**. Fully acknowledging the hurdles one has to cross to become a successful entrepreneur, the chairman of Brains, Saleh Bin Jahlan, mentors "young to-be entrepreneurs" through the Chamber of Commerce **[71]**.

Midrar Development, a Jeddah-based company, was established in 2007. With more than 100 years of experience, this management company is an expert in real estate management and consulting services in Saudi Arabia. This company was provided incubation by Siraj Capital, committed to giving support to Saudi Arabia and Middle East and North Africa (MENA)-based entrepreneurs who have the vision to convert something small into the "next big thing." Midrar proved to be a lucrative company because it was able to pay back all the capital invested at the end of the first fiscal year. By the second year, its dividends had increased four times as compared to the first year **[72]**. In a nutshell, this company added another feather to the proud economic transformation cap of Saudi Arabia.

EDUCON Educational Services is one of the small and medium-sized enterprise (SMEs) founded in Saudi Arabia providing educational consulting services. Founded in 2005, this company faced a lot of difficulty at the initial stage, as no one would register with it because it didn't have an established reputation. It was a challenge to work with students who were doubtful about their careers. EDUCON made it its vision to find a solution. It partnered with various international education and networking links and starting cementing itself in the industry. In no time, with sheer hard work, it expanded and made a mark in the educational consulting market. It was ranked fifth in the Saudi Fast Growth 100 list in 2010, which has helped EDUCON grow and reach this level **[73]**.

Lomar is a fashion brand which designs thobes, an ankle-length garment worn by men. Lomar was not a planned company, but in 2009, its revenue crossed SR 18 million (USD 4.78 million). The success story of Lomar is full of effort, and getting it to four stores was not an easy job. All the owner's start-ups failed, and in 1994, he, along with his family, headed to Houston to pursue graphic design. Three years later, he returned and along with his wife started designing and selling innovative thobes from home, and by the time he co-founded Lomar with his wife, their sales had crossed USD 399,000. He is on his way to becoming an international brand, and Lomar tholes are used by the major universities of Saudi Arabia, one of which is KAUST. For the past three years, graduates of KAUST have been wearing Lomar-designed graduation robes. Lomar was recognized by Saudi Fast Growth 100 as one of the fastest-growing SMEs and was ranked 13th in 2008 and 21st in 2009 **[74]**.

The Prince Salman Bin Abdul Aziz Young Entrepreneurs Awards were established in 2006 to back up young and aspiring entrepreneurs so as to encourage their entrepreneurial spirit and put them on track to be the future leaders of Saudi Arabia. This award basically gives credit to the youth of Saudi

Arabia for the role they play as young entrepreneurs in transforming the Kingdom's economy. These awards are divided into six categories: industry, service, trade, technical, agricultural and leadership. This award is available for those who are between 18 and 40 and have made a contribution to the Kingdom's economy in terms of a start-up or project in any of the previous six categories with at least a year track record. According to Prince Salman Abdul Aziz, young entrepreneurs should take success step by step; they should not rush but instead renew their entrepreneurial spirit, as they are the pillars of the Kingdom **[75]**.

Hypothesis justification

Entrepreneurship education

Vision 2030 revolves around entrepreneur education, as perceived from the literature review. It is a fact that in order to contribute to the economy of a country and bring positive change to venture productivity, consumers and employees should have sound knowledge of entrepreneurship. Formal and informal education both play an important role in a venture's success and should be acquired simultaneously **[76]**. The stated hypothesized model depicts three dependent variables, innovativeness, need for achievement and motivation, which are closely related to three mediating variables, commitment, challenge and need for cognition.

Innovativeness or creativity is the most important ingredient for starting a new venture. It is the creation of a new product or idea or sole development of a new market space (also called blue-ocean strategy) to capture a lucrative market share **[77]**. Innovativeness enables an entrepreneur to create blue oceans and step out of the red oceans pool. Red oceans are all the industries in existence today – the known market space. In red oceans, industry boundaries are defined and accepted, and the competitive rules of the game are known. Blue oceans lead to demand creation and finally to high profitable growth **[77]**, which is the key ingredient for the progress of a start-up and eventually the economy of a country. The new and creative ideas an entrepreneur puts into the new venture result in making him a much better and more effective entrepreneur **[76, 78]**. The transition from a manager to an entrepreneur requires innovativeness in every step as an entrepreneur's most important personality trait **[76, 78]**.

The need for achievement is the second dependent variable in the hypothesized model. The need for achievement is a forward step towards persistence and goal achievement, which are essential for an individual to excel in any field. One will have nothing on one's entrepreneurship plate if there is no hunger for achievement. Individuals will work harder and even climb mountains if they have the desire to achieve something, because this pushes them towards excellence and accomplishment. If there is a need to achieve something, an individual will find new solutions to accomplish his long-term goal, which will eventually lead to new ideas (required to drive entrepreneurship).

An entrepreneur should possess this important personality trait in order to become successful **[76, 79]**.

Motivation drives the individual on the road of action; it is the most vital ingredient and actually inspires an individual to perform in a particular way. Motivation can be categorized in two ways, intrinsic and extrinsic. Both types should be a mandatory part of one's personality. Intrinsic motivation is driven by internal factors such as inner satisfaction, loyalty, sincerity and so on, whereas extrinsic motivation is linked to organizational rewards, appreciation and the like. Motivation, whether intrinsic or extrinsic, should be inculcated in an entrepreneur because it is linked to the hard work, greater productivity and increased efficiency mandatory for success **[80, 81]**.

Commitment as a predictor

The very first step towards entrepreneurial activities is an individual's commitment to his responsibilities, which enables him to position his venture on the road to success. Without the ingredient of commitment instilled in one's personality, it is impossible to achieve any task. Commitment is achieved through entrepreneurship education, which is essential for students, as it teaches them sincerity and loyalty and makes them more reliable. Although entrepreneur education has long been taught in all educational institutes around the globe, the impact of commitment through entrepreneurship still needs to be fully investigated across a myriad of research domains to find out whether it leaves a lasting impression on an individual's practical life **[82]**. The ability to predict entrepreneurial commitment can be measured through the ingredient of *self-efficacy* **[83]**. Now let's see what relationship the commitment variable shares in our hypothesis model with the three dependent variables.

H1a: Commitment mediates the positive relationship between entrepreneurship education and innovativeness.

According to this hypothesis, entrepreneurship education enables students to become better critical thinkers and gives them an outside-the-box approach, leading to innovativeness and creativity. Therefore, commitment gained through entrepreneurship education will enable an entrepreneur to accomplish tasks in teams, resulting in building their innovativeness and making them better critical thinkers.

H1b: Commitment mediates the positive relationship between entrepreneurship education and need for achievement.

According to the learned theory, needs take shape through experiences, and achievement is one of the learned needs which may act as an impulse for creative destruction **[85]**. Therefore, a positive relationship generated via commitment will direct the individual in a positive direction towards entrepreneurship, making one hardworking in one's actions and instilling within one constructive desires to solve problems. Thus, commitment improves one's need for achievement.

H1c: Commitment mediates the positive relationship between entrepreneurship education and motivation.

The positive attitude generated through commitment enables an individual to remain persistent and pushes him to put forth more effort in achieving his or her goal because he/she is confident of receiving intrinsic and extrinsic rewards from the success of his or her venture. This is the reason businesses will flourish as a result of entrepreneurship education for students **[85]**.

Based on the previous arguments, commitment gained by students through entrepreneurship education builds their positive attitude and enables them to attain new skills like innovativeness, need for achievement and motivation.

Challenge as a predictor

Institutions, in conducting entrepreneurial courses, should not only instill entrepreneurial skills in students but also strengthen their entrepreneurial self-efficacy. One's sense of self-efficacy may play a vital role in how one approaches challenges **[86]**. A risk-taking tendency among entrepreneurs will make more room for experiments leading to innovativeness. High-need achievers also tend to take challenges in a positive way so that they may achieve success in their venture and satisfy their desire to gain **[84]**. Therefore, entrepreneurial education is necessary to become a successful entrepreneur because it enables one to learn the capability of taking on challenges in starting a new venture. Furthermore, challenges teach them to await intrinsic and extrinsic rewards they might get from facing challenges. Thus, we may hypothesize:

H2a: Challenge mediates the positive relationship between entrepreneurship education and innovativeness.
H2b: Challenge mediates the positive relationship between entrepreneurship education and need for achievement.
H2c: Challenge mediates the positive relationship between entrepreneurship education and motivation.

Need for cognition as a moderator

Need for cognition is defined by the way people perceive environmental stimuli, which helps them to organize and use information from their environment **[87]**. Researchers have based their research on the idea that the thinking process of an individual is influenced by the cognitive process through which individuals acquire information **[88–90]**. This research can help one see that entrepreneurs think and process information differently from non-entrepreneurs **[88–90]**. According to the hypothesized model:

H3a: Need for cognition moderates the positive relationship between entrepreneurship education and commitment, such that a person high in need for cognition is more inclined towards commitment and vice versa.

This means that a person low in need for cognition will be less inclined towards commitment and in turn will possess less desire for innovativeness, need for achievement and motivation. On the other hand, a person high in need for cognition will be more inclined towards commitment and in turn will possess more desire for innovativeness, need for achievement and motivation.

H3b: Need for cognition moderates the positive relationship between entrepreneurship education and challenge, such that a person high in need for cognition is more inclined towards challenge and vice versa.

This means that a person low in need for cognition will be less inclined towards challenge and in turn will possess less desire for innovativeness, need for achievement and motivation. On the other hand, a person high in need for cognition will be more inclined towards challenge and in turn will possess more desire for innovativeness, need for achievement and motivation.

This shows that a person with a high need of cognition will be more confident and directed towards more problem-focused styles of coping **[91]**.

The hypothesized model based on all previous hypotheses is shown in Figure 6.1.

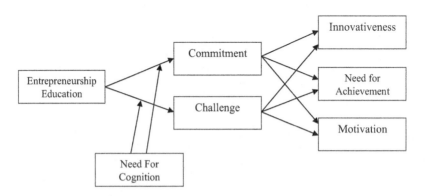

Figure 6.1 Hypothesized model

Research methodology

Participants

The target population of the study was undergraduates (pursuing their last semesters) and graduates of King Saud University and King Abdullah University of Science & Technology (KSA). The classes were selected randomly as clusters. To ensure seriousness, we contacted them during classes with due permission of faculty. An established measurement scale (self-administered) was distributed for all survey questions. Respondents' anonymity was ensured, and they were asked not to disclose their IDs, contact details or names. This was according to the guidelines of Podaskoff et al. [92] for reducing the threat of common method bias in data. From 650 distributed questionnaires, 623 usable responses were selected to utilize for final data analysis. The mean age of respondents was 22 years, and the majority of respondents were male. There were 22.3% students working and running their own businesses; the remaining were all full-time students.

Hypothesis testing

SPSS 20 (IBM Corp: Armonk, New York, USA, 2011) was used for the analysis of data. In the subsequent tables, short forms of the variables are used, where Inn stands for innovation, NFA for need for achievement, Mot for motivation, E_E for entrepreneurship education, Com for commitment and Cha for challenge.

The coefficient of correlation is 0.479, which states that entrepreneurship education and commitment have a moderate relationship with innovativeness. The coefficient of determination is 0.229, which means that 22.9% of the model is explained by independent variables and the rest by unknown variables (Table 6.1, Model I).

In the first case, the significance value is 0.005, which is less than 0.05, so there is a relationship between commitment and innovativeness. In the second case, the significance value is 0.000, so there also exists a relationship between entrepreneurship education and innovativeness (Table 6.2, Model I).

The hypothesis that commitment mediates the positive relationship between entrepreneurship education and innovativeness is accepted because the lower

Table 6.1 Model summary (testing Hypotheses 1a to 1c)

	R	R-squared	Mean squared error (MSE)	F	Degree of Freedom (df1)	Degree of Freedom (df2)	Probability (p)
Model I	0.479	0.229	0.442	92.292	2	621	0.000
Model II	0.506	0.257	0.340	96.061	2	621	0.000
Model III	0.286	0.082	0.402	27.683	2	621	0.000

Table 6.2 Model (testing Hypotheses 1a to 1c)

		Coeff	SE	T	Probability (p)	Lower level of Confidence Interval (LLCI)	Lower level of Confidence Interval (ULCI)
Model I	Constant	2.711	0.227	11.926	0.000	2.264	3.157
	Com	0.081	0.029	2.837	0.005	0.025	0.137
	E_E	0.444	0.036	12.317	0.000	0.373	0.515
Model II	Constant	2.912	0.213	13.658	0.000	2.493	3.331
	Com	0.155	0.030	5.184	0.000	0.097	0.214
	E_E	0.369	0.034	10.862	0.000	0.302	0.436
Model III	Constant	4.423	0.217	20.411	0.000	3.997	4.848
	Com	0.119	0.027	4.384	0.000	0.066	0.173
	E_E	0.168	0.034	4.881	0.000	0.100	0.235

Table 6.3 Indirect effect of X on Y (testing Hypotheses 1a to 1c)

		Effect	Boot SE	Boot Lower level of Confidence Interval (LLCI)	Boot Lower level of Confidence Interval (ULCI)
Model I	Com	0.023	0.008	0.007	0.040
Model II	Com	0.050	0.012	0.029	0.076
Model III	Com	0.034	0.009	0.019	0.056

limit of the confidence interval is 0.007 and the upper limit is 0.040; thus, both values are positive and zero does not lie between the upper and lower limits of the confidence interval (Table 6.3, Model I).

The coefficient of correlation is 0.506, which states that entrepreneurship education and commitment have a moderate relationship with need for achievement. The coefficient of determination is 0.257, which means that 25.7% of the model is explained by independent variables (Table 6.1, Model II). In the first case, the significance value is 0.000, which is less than 0.05, so there is a relationship between commitment and need for achievement. In the second case, the significance value is 0.000, so there also exists a relationship between entrepreneurship education and need for achievement (Table 6.2, Model II). The hypothesis that commitment mediates the positive relationship between entrepreneurship education and need for achievement is accepted because the lower limit of the confidence interval is 0.029 and the upper limit is 0.076; thus, both values are positive and zero does not lie between the upper and lower limits of the confidence interval (Table 6.3, Model II).

The coefficient of correlation is 0.286, which states that entrepreneurship education and commitment have a weak relationship with innovativeness. The coefficient of determination is 0.082, which means that 08.2% of the model is explained by independent variables (Table 6.1, Model III). In the first case, the significance value is 0.000, which is less than 0.05, so there is a relationship between commitment and motivation. In the second case, the significance value is 0.000, so there also exists a relationship between entrepreneurship education and motivation (Table 6.2, Model III). The hypothesis that commitment mediates the positive relationship between entrepreneurship education and motivation is accepted because the lower limit of the confidence interval is 0.019 and the upper limit is 0.056; thus, both values are positive and zero does not lie between the upper and lower limits of the confidence interval (Table 6.3, Model III).

The coefficient of correlation is 0.495, which states that entrepreneurship education and challenge have a moderate relationship with innovativeness. The coefficient of determination is 0.245, which means that 24.5% of the model is explained by independent variables and the remaining by unknown variables (Table 6.4, Model I).

In the first case, the significance value is 0.006, which is less than 0.05, so there is a relationship between challenge and innovativeness. In the second case, the significance value is 0.000, so there also exists a relationship between entrepreneurship education and innovativeness (Table 6.5, Model I).

The hypothesis that challenge mediates the positive relationship between entrepreneurship education and innovativeness is accepted because the lower limit of the confidence interval is 0.005 and the upper limit is 0.067; thus, both values are positive and zero does not lie between the upper and lower limits of the confidence interval (Table 6.6, Model I).

The coefficient of correlation is 0.516, which states that entrepreneurship education and challenge have a moderate relationship with need for achievement. The coefficient of determination is 0.266, which means that 26.6% of the model is explained by independent variables (Table 6.4, Model II). In the first case, the significance value is 0.000, which is less than 0.05, so there is a relationship between challenge and need for achievement. In the second case, the significance value is 0.000, so there also exists a relationship between entrepreneurship education and for achievement (Table 6.5, Model II). The hypothesis that challenge mediates the positive relationship between entrepreneurship education and need for achievement is accepted because the lower limit of the confidence interval is 0.040 and the upper limit is 0.092; thus, both values are positive and zero does

Table 6.4 Model summary (testing Hypotheses 2a to 2c)

	R	R-sq	Mean squared error (MSE)	F	Degree of Freedom (df1)	Degree of Freedom (df2)	Probability (p)
Model I	0.495	0.245	0.440	90.475	2	621	0.000
Model II	0.516	0.266	0.335	101.128	2	621	0.000
Model III	0.258	0.066	0.418	19.776	2	621	0.000

Table 6.5 Model (testing Hypotheses 2a to 2c)

		Coeff	SE	T	Probability (p)	Lower level of Confidence Interval (LLCI)	Lower level of Confidence Interval (ULCI)
Model I	Constant	2.511	0.248	10.143	0.000	2.024	2.997
	Cha	0.097	0.035	2.737	0.006	0.027	0.167
	E_E	0.456	0.039	11.699	0.000	0.379	0.532
Model II	Constant	2.793	0.216	12.923	0.000	2.368	3.217
	Cha	0.182	0.031	5.897	0.000	0.122	0.243
	E_E	0.358	0.034	10.513	0.000	0.291	0.424
Model III	Constant	4.495	0.241	18.627	0.000	4.021	4.969
	Cha	0.073	0.035	2.120	0.035	0.005	0.141
	E_E	0.189	0.038	4.987	0.000	0.115	0.264

Table 6.6 Indirect effect of X on Y (testing Hypotheses 2a to 2c)

		Effect	Boot SE	Boot Lower level of Confidence Interval (LLCI)	Boot Lower level of Confidence Interval (ULCI)
Model I	Cha	0.033	0.015	0.005	0.067
Model II	Cha	0.061	0.013	0.040	0.092
Model III	Cha	0.025	0.012	0.004	0.050

not lie between the upper and lower limits of the confidence interval (Table 6.6, Model II).

The coefficient of correlation is 0.258, which states that entrepreneurship education and challenge have a weak relationship with motivation. The coefficient of determination is 0.066, which means that 06.6% of the model is explained by independent variables (Table 6.4, Model III). In the first case, the significance value is 0.035, which is less than 0.05, so there is a relationship between challenge and motivation. In the second case, the significance value is 0.000, so there also exists a relationship between entrepreneurship education and motivation (Table 6.5, Model III). The hypothesis that challenge mediates the positive relationship between entrepreneurship education and motivation is accepted because the lower limit of the confidence interval is 0.004 and the upper limit is 0.050; thus, both values are positive and zero does not lie between the upper and lower limits of the confidence interval (Table 6.6, Model III).

The coefficient of correlation is 0.293, which states that entrepreneurship education, need for cognition and interaction effect have a weak relationship with student's commitment level. The coefficient of determination is 0.086, which means that 08.6% of the model is explained by independent variables (Table 6.7, Model I).

In the first case, the significance value is 0.000, so there is a relationship between need for cognition and commitment. In the second case, the significance value is 0.000, so there is a relationship between entrepreneurship

Table 6.7 Model summary (testing Hypotheses H3a and H3b)

	R	R-squared	Mean squared error (MSE)	F	Degree of Freedom (df1)	Degree of Freedom (df2)	Probability (p)
Model I	0.293	0.086	0.851	22.305	3.000	620.000	0.000
Model II	0.369	0.136	0.606	24.991	3.000	620.000	0.000

education and commitment. The moderation effect has been shown by "int_1" (i.e., E_E X NFC), and the *p*-value is 0.001, which is again less than 0.05, so need for cognition acts as a moderator between entrepreneurship education and commitment (Table 6.8, Model I).

The standard deviation below the mean is −0.751, the mean value is 0.000, and above the mean is 0.751. For low levels of need for cognition, the effect size is 0.130, which is insignificant; for medium need for cognition levels, the effect size is 0.294, which is significant, and for high levels of fortitude, the effect size is 0.457, which is also significant. So, as we move from low to high levels of need for cognition, the effect size increases and even becomes significant, so there exists a perfect moderation effect of need for cognition between entrepreneurship education and commitment (Table 6.9, Model I).

The coefficient of correlation is 0.369, which states that entrepreneurship education, need for cognition and interaction effect have a weak relationship with student's challenge level. The coefficient of determination is 0.136, which means that 13.6% of the model is explained by independent variables (Table 6.7, Model II).

In the first case, the significance value is 0.000, so there is a relationship between need for cognition and challenge. In the second case, the significance value is 0.000, so there is a relationship between entrepreneurship education and challenge. The moderation effect has been shown by "int_1" (i.e., E_E X NFC), and the *p*-value is 0.153, which is more than 0.05, so need for cognition does not act as a moderator between entrepreneurship education and challenge level of students (Table 6.8, Model II).

The standard deviation below the mean is −0.750, the mean value is 0.000, and above the mean is 0.750. For low levels of need for cognition, the effect size is 0.365, which is significant; for medium need for cognition, the level effect size is 0.311, which is significant, and for high levels of need for cognition, the effect size is 0.256, which is also significant. So, as we move from low to high levels of need for cognition, the effect size decreases, as need for cognition does not act as a moderator between entrepreneurship education and challenge (Table 6.9, Model II).

When there is low need for cognition and low entrepreneurship education, commitment is also low, and when entrepreneurship education is high but need for cognition is low, commitment is still low, which shows that with need for cognition, there is a positive result. When need for cognition is high and entrepreneurship education is low, commitment is low, but when entrepreneurship education is high and need for cognition is high, commitment is also high. Thus, need for cognition strengthens the positive relationship between entrepreneurship education and commitment (Figure 6.2).

Table 6.8 Model (testing Hypotheses H3a and H3b)

		Coeff	SE	T	Probability (p)	Lower level of Confidence Interval (LLCI)	Lower level of Confidence Interval (ULCI)
Model I	Constant	5.002	0.039	129.134	0.000	4.926	5.078
	NFC	0.182	0.054	3.391	0.001	0.077	0.288
	E_E	0.294	0.053	5.521	0.000	0.189	0.398
	int_1	0.218	0.066	3.326	0.001	0.089	0.346
	Interactions: int_1 = E_E X NFC						

		Coeff	SE	T	Probability (p)	Lower level of Confidence Interval (LLCI)	Lower level of Confidence Interval (LLCI)
Model II	Constant	5.349	0.034	156.672	0.000	5.282	5.416
	NFC	0.182	0.047	3.919	0.000	0.091	0.274
	E_E	0.311	0.057	5.486	0.000	0.199	0.422
	int_1	-0.072	0.051	-1.430	0.153	-0.172	0.027
	Interactions: int_1 = E_E X NFC						

Table 6.9 Conditional effect of X on Y (testing Hypotheses H3a and H3b)

	NFC	Effect	SE	T	Probability (p)	Lower level of Confidence Interval (LLCI)	Lower level of Confidence Interval (ULCI)
Model I	-0.751	0.130	0.070	1.852	0.065	-0.008	0.268
	0.000	0.294	0.053	5.521	0.000	0.189	0.398
	0.751	0.457	0.075	6.140	0.000	0.311	0.603

	NFC	Effect	SE	T	Probability (p)	Lower level of Confidence Interval (LLCI)	Lower level of Confidence Interval (LLCI)
Model II	-0.750	0.365	0.062	5.933	0.000	0.244	0.486
	0.000	0.311	0.057	5.486	0.000	0.199	0.422
	0.750	0.256	0.074	3.454	0.001	0.111	0.402

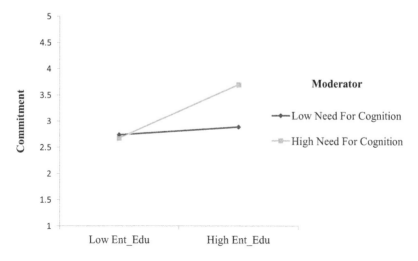

Figure 6.2 Interaction effect (Hypothesis H3a)

When there is low need for cognition and low entrepreneurship education, the challenge level of the student is low, and when entrepreneurship education is high but need for cognition is low, challenge is high. When need for cognition is high and entrepreneurship education is low, the challenge level of the student is low, but with high entrepreneurship education and high need for cognition, challenge is also high. Thus, need for cognition does not act as moderator between entrepreneurship education and challenge level of students (Figure 6.3).

Conclusions

This study provides significant insight that entrepreneurship education moderated with challenge and commitment provides the required skills to be a successful entrepreneur, which contributes to the development of the country. It was found that commitment and challenge mediated by entrepreneurship education produce motivation, need for achievement and innovativeness. All hypotheses were accepted due to their moderate relationship with dependent variables, except H3b, which was rejected due to its weak relationship. Hence, those predictors appreciably contribute to the theories of entrepreneurship mentioned in the literature section.

Hence, the finding presents a clear picture to policy makers and academics to consolidate both informal and formal entrepreneurial education to help students become innovative entrepreneurs. In previous findings, researchers presented either formal or informal education's impact on entrepreneurial intentions, but in our study, we have presented the variable of informal education mediated with the formal education variable, and it shows a strongly positive impact for determining high entrepreneurial tendency in university graduates.

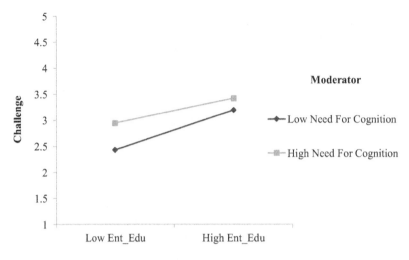

Figure 6.3 Interaction effect (Hypothesis H3b)

Discussion

The relationship of entrepreneurial intentions is discussed in this chapter; these are produced by human capital acquired in the academic journey. We discussed in detail the consequences of entrepreneurial intentions derived by formal and informal entrepreneurial education in the literature section. *Global Entrepreneurship Monitor* recently reported that a broad array of entrepreneurial ideas should be encouraged to support SMEs in the GCC. An educated workforce can be produced with the help of entrepreneurial education and financial support of the government, which can lead to a strengthened economy, innovation and high productivity [92]. In the shadow of Vision 2030, Saudi Arabia is well on its way to entrepreneurial success and transforming its economy. SMEs are already supported by the government and playing a vital role in transforming the economy, as they are the means of creating job opportunities and triggering growth and innovation in the country. Some SME success stories have been discussed in the literature.

Vigorous endeavors are required to reassess the structure of entrepreneurial courses to reach the right potential in academic arenas. This will help students develop problem-solving and analytical skills, and we believe it will bestow independent thinking capabilities with the ability to design systems. Devising a collective approach to entrepreneurial education is needed. We advise the government to fund students for their small projects at school and the college level to enhance their risk-taking propensity, which will encourage and lead them to become entrepreneurs. Funding at the school level may provide the understanding to enjoy success at a young age and overcome the fear of failure, which will lead to shaping them into entrepreneurs. If any successful idea emerges, it could be taken to the next level after funding by several funding agencies, which KSA already has, and we have discussed them in the section on success stories. On the other hand, if a student faces failure, at least he will have experience to face the fear of failure, which is the first step towards success. In Vision 2030, it has already been addressed how the country will encourage entrepreneurs through business-friendly directives with easy access to funding.

Motivation is the crucial ingredient to activate dormant curiosity. Thus, success stories of entrepreneurs should be a part of the curriculum at early school ages. This will influence the cognitive behavior of students to become entrepreneurs instead of job seekers. Successful entrepreneurs should be called to share their stories in schools and to interact with students. This will help students idealize those entrepreneurs and get inspiration, which will influence them to become the same as their favorite entrepreneurial personality. For entrepreneurial education, entrepreneurs from industry with adjunct classrooms may form an entrepreneurial lab due to their industry experience. Moreover, career counseling should be a part of the academic realm, as it helps identify the qualities of any individual.

References

1 Durbin, S. and Conley, H. (2010). Gender, intersectionality and labour process theory. In *Working Life: Renewing Labour Process Analysis*. pp. 182–204. Retrieved from http://eprints.uwe.ac.uk/12537/1/gender_intersectionality_and_LP_theory.docx.

2 Metcalfe, B.D. and Mimouni, F. (eds.). (2011). *Leadership Development in the Middle East*. Cheltenham, UK and Northampton, MA: Edward Elgar.

3 Women Matter 2014. (2014). *GCC Women in Leadership—From the First to the Norm: Unlocking Women's Potential to Enhance Organizational Effectiveness in the Gulf Cooperation Council (GCC) States*. Retrieved from www.mckinsey.com/~/media/McKinsey Offices/Middle East/Latest thinking/GCC_Women_In_Leadership_FINAL.ashx.

4 Morris, M.H., Davis, D.L., and Allen, J.W. (1994). Fostering corporate entrepreneurship: Cross-cultural comparisons of the importance of individualism versus collectivism. *Journal of International Business Studies* 25, 65–89.

5 Hofstede, G. (1994). *Cultures and Organizations. Software of the Mind: Intercultural Cooperation and Its Importance for Survival*. London, UK: Harper Collins.

6 Morris, M.H., Avila, R.A., and Allen, J.W. (1993). Individualism and the modern corporation: Implications for innovation and entrepreneurship. *Journal of Management* 19, 595–612.

7 El-Gohary, H., O'Leary, S., and Radway, P. (2012). Investigating the impact of entrepreneurship online teaching on science and technology degrees on students attitudes in developing economies: The case of Egypt. *International Journal of Online Marketing* 2, 29–45.

8 Kautonen, T., van Gelderen, M., and Fink, M. (2015). Robustness of the theory of planned behaviour in predicting entrepreneurial intentions and action. *Entrepreneurship Theory and Practice* 39, 655–674.

9 Hattab, T., Albouy, C., Lasram, F.B.R., Somot, S., Le Loc'h, F., and Leprieur, F. (2014). Towards a better understanding of potential impacts of climate change on marine species distribution: A multi scale modelling approach. *Global Ecology and Biogeography* 23, 1417–1429.

10 Hashim, M.K. (2002). *Small and Medium-Sized Enterprises in Malaysia Role and Issues*. Sintok, Malaysia: University Utara Malaysia Press. ISBN:9832479231.

11 Armanurah, M., Abdul Razak, A., and Syahrina, A. (2012). Kepentingan pendidikan keusahawanan kepada organisasidan Negara. In *Proceedings of the National Conference on Skills and Competencies in Education*, Selangor, Malaysia. pp. 101–106. (In Malayan)

12 Mahmood, R., Foster, S.A., and Logan, D. (2010). The GeoProfile metadata, exposure of instruments, and measurement bias in climatic record revisited. *International Journal of Climatology* 26, 1091–1124.

13 Alkahtani, H., Dawson, R., and Lock, R. (2013). The impact of culture on Saudi Arabian information systems security. In Georgiadou, E., Ross, M., and Staples, G. (eds.), *Proceedings of the 21st International Conference on Software Quality Management (SQM 2013), Quality Comes of Age*, Southampton. pp. 201–210.

14 Atiyyah, H.S. (1993). Management development in Arabic countries: The challenges of the 1990s. *Journal of Management Development* 12, 3–12.

15 Nikzad, N. (2013). *Arabic Translation: The Importance of Breaking the Language Barrier*. Retrieved 5 August 2013, from www.selfgrowth.com/articles/arabic-translation-the-importance-of-breaking-the-languagebarrier

16 Sabbagh, S. (1996). *Arab Women: Between Defiance and Restraint*. Northampton, MA: Olive Branch Press.

17 US-Arab Trade Line. (Spring 2010). A publication of the National U.S.-Arab Chambers of Commerce. XVIII(1).

18 Hameed, I., Khan, M.B., Shahab, A., Hameed, I., and Qadeer, F. (2016). Science, technology and innovation through entrepreneurship education in the United Arab Emirates (UAE). *Sustainability* 8, 1280.

19 Mazawi, A.E. (2002). Educational expansion and the mediation of discontent: The cultural politics of schooling in the Arab states. *Discourse: Studies in the Cultural Politics of Education* 23(1), 59–74.

20 Minkus-McKenna, D. (2009). *Women Entrepreneurs in Riyadh, Saudi Arabia*. University of Maryland University College Working Paper Series. Retrieved from www.wamda.com/web/uploads/resources/UMUC_WP-2009-02.pdf

21 Dechant, K. and Lamky, A.A. (2005). Toward an understanding of Arab women entrepreneurs in Bahrain and Oman. *Journal of Developmental Entrepreneurship* 10(2), 123–140.

22 Mazawi, A.E. (2002). Educational expansion and the mediation of discontent: The cultural politics of schooling in the Arab states. *Discourse: Studies in the Cultural Politics of Education* 23(1), 59–74.

23 Vaid, I.Y. (2011). Saudi women and entrepreneurship opportunities in architecture and interior design: Bright future for new graduates. *Middle East Studies Online Journal* 3(6), 445–459. Retrieved from www.middle-east-studies.net/wpcontent/uploads/2011/08/perspectives3-Entrepreneurship.pdf

24 Mtango, S. (2004). A state of oppression? Women's rights in Saudi Arabia. *Asia-Pacific Journal on Human Rights & the Law* 5(1), 49–67.

25 Rawaf, H.S. and Simmons, C. (1991). The education of women in Saudi Arabia. *Comparative Education* 27(3), 287–296.

26 Katz, J.A. (2003). The chronology and intellectual trajectory of American entrepreneurship education 1876–1999. *Journal of Business Venturing* 18, 283–300.

27 Sánchez, J.C. (2013). The impact of an entrepreneurship education program on entrepreneurial competencies and intention. *Journal of Small Business Management* 51, 447–465.

28 Huber, L.R., Sloof, R., and van Praag, M. (2014). The effect of early entrepreneurship education: Evidence from a field experiment. *European Economic Review* 72, 76–97.

29 Mitra, J. and Manimala, J.M. (2008). Higher education's role in entrepreneurship and economic development. *Entrepreneurship and Higher Education*, 45–64.

30 Xavier, S.R., Ahmad, S.Z., Nor, L.M., and Yusof M. (2012). *Women as Executives and Entrepreneurs*. Retrieved 9 February 2012, from www.winnet.org.my/. Elsevier Ltd.

31 Kim, K. (2007). Shifting family involvement during the entrepreneurial process. *International Journal of Entrepreneurial Behavior & Research* 13(5), 258–277. Emerald Group Publishing Limited.

32 Amzad, H. (2009). Factors influencing women business development in the developing countries: Evidence from Bangladesh. *International Journal of Organizational Analysis* 17(3), 202–224. Emerald Group Publishing Limited.

33 Weeks, J.R. (2009). Women business owners in the Middle East and North Africa: A five-country research study. *International Journal of Gender and Entrepreneurship* 1(1), 77–85. Emerald Group Publishing Limited.

34 Women's Aid Organisation (WAO). (2001). *Women's Equality in Malaysia Status Report.* Retrieved 7 June 2011, from www.wao.org.my/news/20010301statusreport.htm

35 Jamilah, A. (1992). *Women & Development in Malaysia.* Kuala Lumpur: Pelanduk Publications (M) Sdn. Bhd.

36 Wei-Loon, K., Sa'ari, J.R., Majid, I.A., and Ismail, K. (2012). Determinants of entrepreneurial intention among millennial generation. *Social and Behavioral Sciences* 40, 197–208.

37 Yildirim, N. and Askun, O.B. (2012). Entrepreneurship intentions of public universities in Turkey: Going beyond education and research? *Social and Behavioral Sciences* 58, 953–963.

38 Brancua, L., Munteanub, V., and Gligorc, D. (2012). Study of student motivations for entrepreneurship in Romania. *Social and Behavioral Sciences* 62, 223–231.

39 Gennaioli, N., La Porta, R., Lopez-de-Silanes, F., and Shleifer, A. (2013). Human capital and regional development. *The Quarterly Journal of Economics* 128, 105–164.

40 Becker, G. (1964). *Human Capital: A Theoretical and Empirical Analysis With Special Reference to Education* (3rd ed.). Chicago, IL: University of Chicago Press.

41 Mincer, J. (1958). Investment in human capital and personal income distribution. *Journal of Political Economics* 66, 281–302.

42 Schlaegel, C. and Koenig, M. (2014). Determinants of entrepreneurial intent: A meta-analytic test and integration of competing models. *Entrepreneurship Theory and Practice* 38, 291–332.

43 Syahrina, A., Armanurah, M., Habshah, B., Norashidah, H., and YengKiat, O. (2013). Tracer study of bachelor in entrepreneurship program: The case of University Utara Malaysia. *International Journal of Educational Research* 1, 1–10.

44 Collins, L., Hannon, P.D., and Smith, A. (2004). Enacting entrepreneurial intent: The gap between students' needs and higher education capabilities. *Education and Training* 48, 454–463.

45 Muhammad, A., Akbar, S., and Dalziel, M. (2011). The journey to develop educated entrepreneurs: Prospects and problems of Afghan businessmen. *Education and Training* 53, 433–447.

46 ZainalAbidin, M., Golnaz, R.I., Amin, M.A., and Ezhar, T. (2011). Work culture and developing agri-entrepreneurial skills among farmers. *The American Journal of Economics and Business Administration* 3, 490–497.

47 Grilo, I. and Irigoyen, J.M. (2006). Entrepreneurship in the EU: To wish and not to be. *Small Business Economics*. 26, 305–318.

48 Arasteh, H., Enayati, T., Zameni, F., & Khademloo, A. (2012). Entrepreneurial personality characteristics of university students: A case study. *Social and Behavioral Sciences* 46, 5736–5740.

49 Luca, M.R. and Cazan, A.M. (2011). Involvement in entrepreneurial training and personality. *Social and Behavioral Sciences* 30, 1251–1256.

50 Chiru, C., Tachiciu, L., & Ciuchete, S.G. (2012). Psychological factors, behavioural variables and acquired competencies in entrepreneurship education. *Social and Behavioral Sciences* 46, 4010–4015.

51 Oosterbeek, H., van Praag, M., and Ijsselstein, A. (2008). *The Impact of Entrepreneurship Education on Entrepreneurship Competencies and Intentions: An Evaluation of the Junior Achievement*

Student Mini-Company Program. Tinbergen Institute Discussion Paper No. TI 2008 038/3. Faculty of Economics & Business, University of Amsterdam, and Tinbergen Institute.

52 Rasmussen, E., Mosey, S., and Wright, M. (2011). The evolution of entrepreneurial competencies: A longitudinal study of university spin-off venture emergence. *Journal of Management Studies* 48(6), 1314–1345. doi:10.1111/j.1467-6486.2010.00995.x.

53 Rasmussen, E. and Borch, O. (2010). University capabilities in facilitating entrepreneurship: A longitudinal study of spin-off ventures at mid-range universities. *Research Policy* 39(5), 602–612. doi:10.1016/j.respol.2010.02.002.

54 Vohora, A., Wright, M., and Lockett, A. (2004). Critical junctures in the development of university high-tech spinout companies. *Research Policy* 33(1), 147–175. doi:10.1016/s0048-7333(03)00107-0.

55 Etzkowitz, H. (2008). *The Triple Helix—University-Industry-Government Innovation in Action.* New York, NY: Routledge. p. 164.

56 US-Arab Trade Line. (Spring 2010). A publication of the National U.S.-Arab Chambers of Commerce. XVIII(1).

57 The American Dream. Retrieved 21 July 2016, from www.loc.gov/teachers/classroom-materials/lessons/Americandream/students/thedream.html.

58 Sweezy, P.M. (1943). Professor Schumpeter's theory of innovation. In *The Review of Economic Statistics.* Cambridge, MA: The MIT Press. pp. 93–96.

59 McClelland, C.A. (1961). The acute international crisis. *World Politics* 14, 182–204.

60 Atkinson, R.C. and Shiffrin, R.M. (1968). Human memory: A proposed system and its control processes. *Psychology of Learning and Motivation* 2, 89–195.

61 Shelly, A.B. and Seung, Y.C. (2008). Factors that influence informal learning in the workplace. *Journal of Workplace Learning* 20, 229–244.

62 McMullen, J.S. and Shepherd, D.A. (2006). Entrepreneurial action and the role of uncertainty in the theory of the entrepreneur. *The Academy of Management Review* 31(1), 132–152.

63 Athayde, R. (2009). Measuring enterprise potential in young people. *Entrepreneurship: Theory & Practice* 33(2), 481–500.

64 Souitaris, V., Zerbinati, S., and Al-Laham, A. (2007). Do entrepreneurship programmes raise entrepreneurial intention of science and engineering students? The effect of learning, inspiration and resources. *Journal of Business Venturing* 22(4), 566–591.

65 Huber, L.R., Sloof, R., and Van Praag, M. (2014). The effect of early entrepreneurship education: Evidence from a field experiment. *European Economic Review* 72, 76–97. Institute for Management Development, 2011. World Competitiveness Yearbook (Lausanne).

66 Peterman, N.E. and Kennedy, J. (2003). Enterprise education: Influencing students' perceptions of entrepreneurship. *Entrepreneurship: Theory and Practice* 28(2), 129–144.

67 Sánchez, J.C. (2013). The impact of an entrepreneurship education program on entrepreneurial competencies and intention. *Journal of Small Business Management* 51(3), 447–465.

68 Cunha, F. and Heckman, J. (2007). The technology of skill formation. *American Economic Review* 97(2), 31–47.

69 Huber, L.R., Sloof, R., and Van Praag, M. (2014). The effect of early entrepreneurship education: Evidence from a field experiment. *European Economic Review* 72, 76–97. Institute for Management Development, 2011. World competitiveness yearbook (Lausanne).

70 Dean, T.J. and McMullen, J.S. (2007). Toward a theory of sustainable entrepreneurship: Reducing environmental degradation through entrepreneurial action. *Journal of Business Venturing* 22, 50–76.

71 US-Arab Trade Line. (Spring 2010). A publication of the National U.S.-Arab Chambers of Commerce. XVIII(1), 19.

72 US-Arab Trade Line. (Spring 2010). A publication of the National U.S.-Arab Chambers of Commerce. XVIII(1), 19–20.

73 US-Arab Trade Line. (Spring 2010). A publication of the National U.S.-Arab Chambers of Commerce. XVIII(1), 21.

74 US-Arab Trade Line. (Spring 2010). A publication of the National U.S.-Arab Chambers of Commerce. XVIII(1), 21–22.

75 US-Arab Trade Line. (Spring 2010). A publication of the National U.S.-Arab Chambers of Commerce. XVIII(1), 40.

76 Hameed, I., Khan, M.B., Shahab, A., Hameed, I., and Qadeer, F. (2016). Science, technology and innovation through entrepreneurship education in the United Arab Emirates (UAE). *Sustainability* 8, 1280.

77 Kim, W.C. and Mauborgne, R. (2005). *Blue Ocean Strategy, How to Create Uncontested Market Space and Make the Competition Irrelevant.* Boston, MA: Harvard Business School Press.

78 Kogan, N. and Wallach, M.A. (1960). Certainty of judgment and the evaluation of risk. *Psychological Reports* 6, 207–213.

79 Agarwal, R. and Prasad, J. (1998). A conceptual and operational definition of personal innovativeness in the domain of information technology. *Information Systems Research* 9, 204–215.

80 McMullan, W.E., Long, W.A., and Wilson, A. (1985). MBA concentration on entrepreneurship. *Journal of Small Business & Entrepreneurship* 3, 18–22.

81 Zimmerman, B. and Schunk, D.H. (2011). *Handbook of Self-Regulation of Learning and Performance.* New York, NY: Taylor & Francis.

82 Tasnim, R. and Singh, H. (2016). "What, exactly, is entrepreneurial commitment?": Modeling the commitment of successful entrepreneurs. *Journal of Applied Management and Entrepreneurship* 21(3), 6–35.

83 Sinclair, R.F. and Bruce, R.A. (2009). Determining entrepreneurial commitment in the pre-entrepreneur (summary). *Frontiers of Entrepreneurship Research* 29(6), Article 18.

84 Sweezy, P.M. (1943). Professor Schumpeter's theory of innovation. In *The Review of Economic Statistics.* Cambridge, MA: The MIT Press. pp. 93–96.

85 Ihmeideh, F.M., Al-Omari, A.A., and Al-Dababneh, K.A. (2010). Attitudes toward communication skills among students'-teachers' in Jordanian public universities. *Australian Journal of Teacher Education* 35, 1–11.

86 Chen, C.C., Greene, G.P., and Crick, A. (1998). Does entrepreneurial self-efficacy distinguish entrepreneurs from managers? *Journal of Business Venturing* 13(4), 295–316.

87 Sánchez, J.C., Carballo, T., and Gutiérrez, A. (2011). The entrepreneur from a cognitive approach. *Psicothema* 23, 433–438.

88 Baron, R.A. and Markman, G.D. (1999). Cognitive mechanisms: Potential differences between entrepreneurs and non-entrepreneurs. In Reynolds, P.D., Bygrave, W.D., et al. (eds.), *Frontiers of Entrepreneurship Research.* Wellesley, MA: Babson College.

89 Krueguer, J. and Evans, M. (2004). If you don't want to be late, enumerate: Unpacking reduces the planning fallacy. *Journal of Experimental Social Psychology* 40, 586–598.

90 Neisser, U. (1967). *Cognitive Psychology.* Englewood Cliffs, NJ: Prentice Hall.

91 Deniz, G., Erten, G., Kücüksezer, U.C., Kocacik, D., Karagiannidis, C., Aktas, E., Akdis, C.A., and Akdis, M. (2008). Regulatory NK cells suppress antigen-specific T cell responses. *Journal of Immunology* 180, 850–857.

92 Podsakoff, P.M., MacKenzie, S.B., Lee, J.Y., and Podsakoff, N.P. (2003). Common method biases in behavioral research: A critical review of the literature and recommended remedies. *Journal of Applied Psychology* 88, 879–903.

7 Vision 2030 and the National Transformation Program

Muhammad Babar Khan and Sadia Iqbal

Opening the doors to the world of Saudi Arabia

The Kingdom of Saudi Arabia (KSA) is a land of rich assets, which has enabled it to take a leading position in the world of transformation. It is correctly said that "leaders aren't born, they are made," and they are made just like anything else, through hard work. That's the price we will have to pay to achieve that goal or any other goal. This is the success story behind Saudi Arabia, which has embarked upon its transformation journey on its leader's back. Prince Mohammad Bin Salman Bin Abdulaziz Al-Saud's relentless efforts have further enabled Saudi Arabia to become the heart of the Arab and Islamic world. The country has now made a start in becoming a global investment powerhouse and global hub, crafting a strong bond between three continents, Asia, Europe and Africa. The leader's aspirations to turn the tables for KSA have pioneered a successful global model of excellence on all fronts, which is clearly visible through the lens of transformation in the Kingdom.

For industrial sectors, KSA is considered a strategic roadmap and the land of opportunities for economically sound business. The beauty of Saudi Arabia lies in its hospitality and being a springboard for energy-intensive industries which otherwise would not survive because of their high electricity consumption. Additionally, it is considered one of the world's most thriving and fastest-growing industrial sectors, along with being the 18th-largest economy in the world. It constitutes the largest market in the Middle East–North Africa, along with enjoying a lucrative share of over 424 million consumers at the very heart of a fast-growing region. It shares its borders with eight countries, along with the addition of two of the world's busiest shipping routes: the Red Sea and the Arabian Gulf.

The global map identifies various flavors of culture and lifestyle for every country. As Saudi Arabia is greatly influenced by Islam, it has a very different culture. This includes various cultural barriers in Saudi Arabia such as language, gender discrimination, education for women, women's empowerment and so on. All these barriers have led to low self-esteem in some Saudi women, along with the absence of a very important ingredient: confidence, as all these barriers restrict women from meeting their full potential, resulting in poor use of their skills. The struggles, constraints and challenges faced by Saudi women led to the establishment of various centers with a special focus on women's entrepreneurship, providing them a strong support system and networking opportunities. These centers and associations place special emphasis on conducting motivational workshops and seminars to provide human capital development to women entrepreneurs. All these initiatives proved to be icing on the cake, led to an overall improvement in the Kingdom to a great extent and created a pathway for women's entrepreneurship and empowerment. These transformations took the shape of documentation in the form of Vision 2030, which is comprehensive in all aspects and in light of which the Kingdom is well on its way to transform from an oil-based economy to a knowledge-based economy.

Vision 2030

Vision 2030 is a roadmap to the Kingdom's economic development vision. Under its umbrella are three key pillars, which are the building blocks to a sound economy the Kingdom can use to move towards a knowledge-based economic transformation. These pillars need to be focused on with great determination and aspiration, as all successful visions can be achieved if they are carried on a strong back. These three pillars are:

1   To become the cornerstone of the Arabic and Islamic world.
2   The determination to become a global investment powerhouse.
3   To transform the Kingdom's unique location into a global hub connecting three major continents: Asia, Europe and Africa.

This vision is based on three themes: a vibrant society, a thriving economy and an ambitious nation. All these themes combine to form the three pillars of Vision 2030 and further occupy a place to accomplish the Saudi National Strategic Vision. The *vibrant society* theme is the most spirited theme to achieve the Kingdom's strategic vision and the basic foundation for economic prosperity. A vibrant society revolves around three core objectives: a vibrant society with strong roots, a vibrant society with fulfilling lives and, last, a vibrant society with strong foundations.

A *vibrant society with strong roots* is packaged with clear goals that need to be achieved by 2030. In keeping with this theme, the government of KSA aspires to make it a priority to conserve the historical heritage of the Kingdom. The Saudi government has pledged to build Saudi heritage sites and cultural museums registered with UNESCO. These registrations are strategically envisioned to more than double by 2030. These goals further include increasing the Kingdom's capacity for welcoming Umrah visitors from 8 million to 30 million every year. The vision to achieve these goals for a vibrant society with strong roots revolves around commitments first to honor and serve the number of Umrah pilgrims in the best possible way and second to build the largest Islamic Museum.

The *vibrant society with fulfilling lives* pillar aspires to stimulate a far better culture and ambience. It further aims to provide a healthy and balanced lifestyle, as this is a very important goal in order to achieve a sustainable and fulfilling life. Additionally, to gain immense pride, this objective focuses on developing cities with high levels of security and development. Last, to preserve environmental and natural resources to fulfill the Kingdom's Islamic, moral and human duties; by 2020, KSA aspires to be equipped with 450 registered clubs and professionally organized amateur clubs that will provide a state-of-the-art variety of cultural and entertainment activities with a diversified economic transformation for people from all walks of life within the Kingdom.

A *vibrant society with a strong foundation* focuses on providing special care to KSA's families, developing children's characters from infancy via the educational and academic system. Empowering society with all the basic essentials of life and building a state-of-the-art health care system is another important chapter of a vibrant society with a strong foundation. Furthermore, raising the Kingdom's position from 26th to 10th in the social capital index and increasing the average life expectancy of citizens from 74 years currently to 80 years are some of the goals to be achieved, along with building a strong health care system equipped with the state-of-the-art technology for every citizen.

A *thriving economy* with rewarding opportunities is the second important theme of the Kingdom's National Strategic Vision. It focuses on human capital development and state-of-the-art education for all in accordance with the market needs. This will mean economic opportunities for entrepreneurs and large, small and medium-sized enterprises. Additionally, this would open new doors for employment opportunities, unlocking the economic sectors and making way for economic diversification.

A *thriving economy with rewarding opportunities* concentrates on lowering the rate of unemployment by 2030. In the context of rewarding opportunities, KSA also aspires to bring about a revolution in the gross domestic product (GDP) via small and medium-sized enterprises (SMEs), along with a smooth path for women's empowerment in the workforce. To accomplish this, a strong education system is required to contribute to economic growth, along with a significant role for small and medium-sized enterprises. Another goal attached is to establish new business incubators, specialized training institutions and new venture capital to aid entrepreneurs in building networking opportunities, which will in turn facilitate economic growth.

A *thriving economy with investment for the long run* concentrates on diversifying the economy in various additional sectors apart from oil and gas to meet the sustainability mark. KSA is aware of the fact that it is a challenging task, as oil and gas are major pillars of economic growth, but it has a strong long-term plan to overcome any challenges ahead. As the 18th largest economy of the world, Saudi economy has contributed to job creation in innumerable sectors and aspires to go a long way by 2030. Diversifying the economy has become the need of the time, as the global economy is experiencing a slowdown and countries need to invest all their resources in diversifying economic growth and unleashing the power of their promising economic sectors.

For this, the vision is to participate in large international and technological companies around the world in order to enter various sectors as market makers and take a leadership position in state-of-the-art funding, asset management and investment. For all this to be accomplished, an advanced financial and capital market formation is mandatory, open to the world, which will open new doors for funding opportunities along with stimulating economic growth. A *thriving economy with investment for the long run* commitments include localized defense industries, a mining sector with a major contribution to the national economy at full potential and a renewable energy market, which the Kingdom aspires to grow threefold by 2030.

A *thriving economy open for business* marks a new initiative for opening yet more Saudi Arabian doors for business so as to boost the country's productivity and ensure a safe transition to becoming the largest economy in the world. For this be achieved, the business environment must be improved, along with rehabilitating economic cities, establishing special zones in exceptional and competitive locations and, furthermore, increasing the competitiveness of Saudi Arabia's energy sector.

The *thriving economy open for business* objectives are to accelerate to the top ten from the 25th position on the Global Competitiveness Index. Saudi Arabia further aspires to increase foreign direct investment in terms of GDP along with increasing the private sector organization from a GDP of 40% to 65%. For this, Saudi Arabia needs to focus on a well-developed and state-of-the-art restructured King Abdullah financial district, a flourishing and vibrant retail sector and an infrastructure which is digitally developed for business opportunities.

A *thriving economy leveraging its unique position* aims to maximize the benefits from its strategic geographic location at the heart of the important international trade routes in the midst of three continents, Asia, Africa and Europe. This will enable Saudi Arabia to increase the export of its products and will further make way for distinctive logistical offers along with stimulating a new phase of industrialization. To achieve this, the goals involve raising the Kingdom's global ranking from 49 to 25, ensuring that the Kingdom is a regional leader and raising the share of non-oil exports in non-oil GDP from 16% to 50%. To leverage its unique position, the Kingdom aspires to make special plans for building a unique, regional logistical hub; establishing new business partnerships regionally and internationally via enhanced logistic services and also to support its national companies.

The *ambitious nation* theme is the third vital theme which rests on a proficient and high-performing government pillar. In order to see KSA as an ambitious nation, it is essential that the Kingdom make sure that the private sector, citizens and the non-profit sector take ownership of their responsibilities. To do so, the Kingdom should provide them with the right environment and enable them to take a step towards meeting challenges and seizing opportunities.

An ambitious nation effectively governed focuses on the fact that in order to keep pace with rising expectations and jump-start challenges, the government of any nation needs to meet trials by evolving and improving tirelessly and continuously. Furthermore, for an ambitious nation effectively governed, the nation needs to embrace transparency and the highest level of governance in all sectors, along with upholding extraordinary standards of accountability. Under this umbrella, the Kingdom aspires to commit to efficient spending and balanced finances by applying zero taxes on all citizens' incomes and basic goods. This will give a lift to the economic sector, as this way, citizens will be able to efficiently balance their budgets, allowing maximization and diversification of their revenue resources. The nation also aspires to protect vital resources by building safe and sufficient strategic food reserves in order to provide shelter in case of emergencies. Engaging everyone is, again, an important aspect of effectively governing an ambitious nation. This goal aims to bring everyone onto the same page, from government agencies to citizens and the private sector, to deepen their communication channels. This way, citizens will get a chance to give their perspective, enabling government agencies to bring about change in the quality of services and serve them better from every angle. Organizing oneself is the need of the time. For this goal to be achieved, it is necessary for the Kingdom to speed up decision-making and become agile.

To achieve this, it is essential that human capital development be promoted through the King Salman program, making way for shared services across government agencies. Additionally, an increment in spending efficiency (QAWAM) is essential, along with notable progress in effective e-government.

An ambitious nation responsibly enabled focuses on the fact that the nation Saudi Arabia aspires to build is not possible without a collective national effort and the contribution of everyone. Its focal point is that everyone needs to take responsibility to contribute and fulfill roles, irrespective the sector they belong to, public, private or non-profit. This includes being responsible for one's life and future, with major concentration on developing one's own self and working tirelessly to become active and independent members of society. Second, it includes being responsible in business so that ventures participate in contributing to developing society and the country, apart from just focusing on generating profits. This will in turn facilitate contributing to social responsibility and creating a sustainable economy, enabling both young men and women to build their professional careers. Third, it includes being responsible to society and in turn developing compassion, empathy and cooperation for others in all sectors. This is a very important ingredient which needs to be practiced in order to bring about a revolution for an ambitious nation. To achieve this, a more impactful and long-lasting non-profit sector is required, which will provide state-of-the-art high-quality training to staff and promote a culture of volunteering with full-time careers in the sector.

How to achieve Vision 2030

Vision 2030 is comprehensive and ambitious in every aspect for Saudi Arabia. The road map to achieve Vision 2030 will lead to a much better and brighter future for the country and citizens as a whole. This includes various transformative programs which will facilitate achieving Vision 2030. Some of these programs include the following.

The Government Restructuring Program

Governments all over the world are striving to continuously restructure and align their systems in accordance with their national priorities. In line with the same culture, Saudi Arabia turns the tables by eliminating supreme councils and instead giving way to the establishment of Council of Political and Security Affairs hand in hand with the Council of Economic and Development Affairs. The establishment of these councils has proved the icing on the cake, resulting in speedy strategic development and decision-making along with fruitful performance. This will go a long way, as Saudi Arabia is determined to make a clear pathway to a smooth transformation journey based on its clearly defined priorities.

The Strategic Directions Program

According to this approved program which is determined by government agencies, Saudi Arabia has taken the initiative to revise roles so as to align them with its future economic and social needs. Each agency's programs, plans and relevant performance indicators have been comprehensively analyzed, along with detailed studies and benchmarks for effective decision-making which will prove fruitful for decades to come and assist Saudi Arabia in achieving Vision 2030.

The Fiscal Balance Program

This program is in line with the establishment of the Council of Economic and Development Affairs. After the establishment of this council, Saudi Arabia began a hunt to examine its existing capital expenditures along with their approval mechanisms and measured economic impact. This in turn resulted in the formation of new committees and the introduction of novel departments particularly tasked for taking necessary action on expenditures. This all added another feather to the revenue cap of Saudi Arabia with a 30 percent increment in diversified sectors other than the oil-based sector. New measures are in the pipeline as Saudi Arabia aspires to continuously diversify its economy in the coming years.

The Project Management Program

This program falls under the umbrella of the Council of Economic and Development Affairs. Since there is a wave of transformation and reform in Saudi Arabia's agencies, there is a dire need to harness this momentum and adopt an effective approach to project management. Furthermore, this has led to the establishment of expert project management offices (PMOs) in government agencies and the Council of Economic and Development Affairs, along with a central delivery unit. This will ensure that all efforts are well coordinated and organized to achieve Vision 2030.

The Regulations Review Program

According to this program, Saudi Arabia intends to bring all laws, including company law, non-governmental organization law, laws concerning fees law on non-used lands, Awqaf law and many others in line with the Kingdom's priorities. This program is vital, as, according to this program, the review of all laws is under process so that old ones which have been in force since the past decade may be rectified and new ones enacted so as to facilitate the smooth functioning of Vision 2030.

The Performance Measurement Program

It is a fact that for success, proper performance measurement principles must be enacted in order to evaluate activities, including government agencies and their programs, initiatives and executives. This will ensure that all activities are in line with the Kingdom's Vision 2030, and performance measurement principles will furthermore prove to be a weapon to eradicate or correct any program or activity which may prove to be a weak spot. To this end, the Kingdom has made special arrangements to establish the Center for Performance Management of Government Agencies so that these efforts continue on a long-term basis in order to promote transparency and accountability.

Vision 2030 also includes executive programs to make a significant impact on implementation and ensure complete realization of Saudi Arabia's vision for 2030. Some of these executive programs include the following.

The Saudi Aramco Strategic Transformation Program

Saudi Aramco is Saudi Arabia's national petroleum and natural gas company and the world's largest oil and gas company by revenue. According to the strategic transformation program, Saudi Aramco will undergo a major transformation, as it has the ability to lead other sectors as well as gas and oil. The sweeping transformative program will position it as a leader in more sectors by leaps and bounds.

The Public Investment Fund Restructuring Program

Saudi Arabia has worked hard to restructure its funds, and now its focus is on refining the fund's investment capabilities, which will enable it to manage a much broader portfolio of new and current assets. Saudi Arabia aims to transform these funds into the world's largest sovereign wealth fund and is working on a comprehensive plan to achieve this long-term goal which will prove fruitful for Vision 2030.

The Human Capital Program

Human capital development is the need of the day, and it is essential that this ingredient be thoroughly nurtured to polish human talent. Saudi Arabia has launched a full-fledged program which will adhere to the needs of human talent and help them reach avenues which are only possible via extra skills. The key roles which this program will play include measuring, assessing and analyzing the efficiency of the civil service. Additionally, this includes supporting government agencies and their staff, studies, consultations and strategic partnerships which relate to human capital development.

The National Transformation Program

This program has been outlined so that the government agencies of Saudi Arabia may groom themselves in order to examine their roles and implement the initiatives necessary to deliver on national priorities. For this, they are striving to identify opportunities which will enable them to create relationships with the private sector as well. Additionally, they aspire to implement explicit initiatives which will have very clear performance indicators.

The Program for Strengthening Public Sector Governance

Under the umbrella of this program, Saudi Arabia aims to eliminate the roles of government agencies which are redundant and, furthermore, streamline procedures along with continuously restructuring these agencies with flexibility. The Kingdom will ensure that agencies are delivering on their own directives, along with accountability for every new challenge which comes their way, along with adaptability. This will lead to the establishment of a strategic management office under the Council of Economic and Development Affairs. The main focus of this office will be to put special emphasis on bringing all government programs in line with the same platform and to ensure that they are properly aligned with the national vision. This office will also ensure there are no duplications between agencies' policies and programs and also make sure that there are no gaps within policies. Furthermore, to support decision-making, the Kingdom will establish a decision support system under the same program based on analytical and evidence-based information.

The Privatization Program

Saudi Arabia aspires to establish a comprehensive privatization program under the wings of which additional sectors will be determined. For this to be successful, the Kingdom will make use of international best practices and transfer their knowledge so that it will be able to achieve its goals in a fully balanced and purely scientific manner.

The Strategic Partnerships Program

This program aims to build up new strategic partnerships globally with economic partners for the Kingdom in accordance with the twenty-first century. This is essential in order to acquire alignment with the national vision and become a trade hub for connecting Asia, Africa and Europe.

The National Transformation Program 2020

The National Transformation Program is designed to achieve the ambitious goals of Saudi Arabia's Vision 2030 and identify the challenges of economic and development sectors faced by government bodies. This program will help establish strategic objectives based on Vision 2030 and address challenges in accordance with precise targets. To measure and monitor performance, each year, this program will continuously analyze the initiatives and plans deployed to achieve Vision 2030 goals. This program was launched across 24 government bodies in the economic and development sectors in its first year with a plan to expand its coverage annually to cover more government bodies. See figure 7.1 for the key performing indicators.

Objectives of the National Transformation Program

The National Transformation Program aspires to fulfill the commitments of Vision 2030 in terms of spending efficiently and achieving fiscal balance through the following objectives:

- Identifying the strategic objectives and targets of participating entities.
- Translating strategic objectives into initiatives for participating entities.
- Promoting joint action towards the achievement of common national goals.

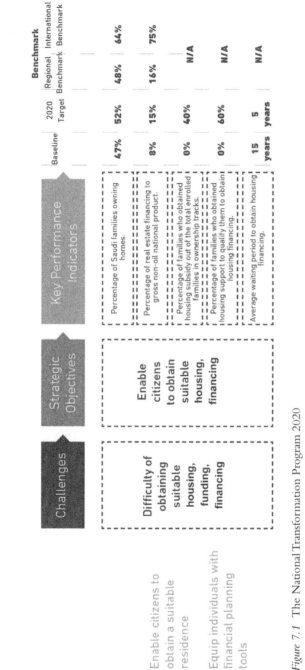

Figure 7.1 The National Transformation Program 2020

Promoting joint action towards the achievement of common national goals includes the following areas:

- Contributing to job creation
- Strengthening partnerships with the private sector
- Maximizing local content
- Digital transformation

For sustainable work achievement and maximized impact, the National Transformation Program has a number of enabler employers to help professionalism reach a higher level and ensure a much smoother workflow. These areas include:

- Transparency
- Institutionalization
- Specialized support

Operating model of the National Transformation Program

The National Transformation program is a joint venture of the Council of Economic and Development Affairs and 24 participating government entities who have worked hand in hand to formulate and launch this program. Other activities include initiative planning, efforts coordination and high-quality realistic outcome as a contribution of the Ministries of Interior and Foreign Affairs. The operating model of the National Transformation Program includes the following five phases, which are themselves significant challenges:

Phase One: Identifying the Challenges Faced by Each Government Entity in Fulfilling the Vision and Establishing 2020 Interim Targets

Phase Two: Developing Initiatives Designed to Reach the Strategic Objective

Phase Three: Developing Detailed Implementation Plans for the Initiatives

Phase Four: Promoting Transparency in the Publication of Targets and Outcomes

Phase Five: Auditing, Continually Improving, Launching New Initiatives and Adding New Participating Entities

Participating entities of National Transformation Program 2020

The National Transformation Program includes 24 participating entities for now. New entities are expected to be added per Vision 2030 and Council of Economic and Development Affairs decisions. The current participating entities include:

- **Ministry of Justice:** This includes 7 strategic objectives, 21 indicators and 9 targets to be achieved.

- **Ministry of Finance:** This includes 6 strategic objectives, 12 indicators and 12 targets to be achieved.
- **Ministry of Economy and Planning:** This includes 6 strategic objectives, 13 indicators and 7 targets to be achieved.
- **Ministry of Health:** This includes 15 strategic objectives, 17 indicators and 16 targets to be achieved.
- **Ministry of Communications and Information Technology:** This includes 10 strategic objectives, 17 indicators and 17 targets to be achieved.
- **Ministry of Commerce and Investment:** This includes 7 strategic objectives, 10 indicators and 9 targets to be achieved.
- **Ministry of Municipal and Rural Affairs:** This includes 7 strategic objectives, 25 indicators and 24 targets to be achieved.
- **Ministry of Civil Services:** This includes 5 strategic objectives, 11 indicators and 11 targets to be achieved.
- **Ministry of Culture and Information:** This includes 4 strategic objectives, 10 indicators and 9 targets to be achieved.
- **Ministry of Environment, Water and Agriculture:** This includes 16 strategic objectives, 35 indicators and 35 targets to be achieved.
- **Ministry of Energy, Industry and Mineral Resources:** This includes 15 strategic objectives, 24 indicators and 24 targets to be achieved.
- **Ministry of Labor and Social Development:** This includes 13 strategic objectives, 37 indicators and 37 targets to be achieved.
- **Ministry of Housing:** This includes 3 strategic objectives, 11 indicators and 11 targets to be achieved.
- **Ministry of Education:** This includes 8 strategic objectives, 20 indicators and 19 targets to be achieved.
- **Ministry of Transportation:** This includes 9 strategic objectives, 15 indicators and 15 targets to be achieved.
- **Ministry of Haj and Umrah:** This includes 5 strategic objectives, 15 indicators and 10 targets to be achieved.
- **Saudi Commission for Tourism and National Heritage:** This includes 4 strategic objectives, 16 indicators and 16 targets to be achieved.
- **Sports Authority:** This includes 4 strategic objectives, 7 indicators and 5 targets to be achieved.
- **Royal Commission for Jubail and Yanbu:** This includes 9 strategic objectives, 12 indicators and 10 targets to be achieved.
- **King Abdul Aziz City for Science and Technology:** This includes 7 strategic objectives, 12 indicators and 12 targets to be achieved.
- **King Abdullah City for Atomic and Renewable Energy:** This includes 4 strategic objectives, 8 indicators and 8 targets to be achieved.
- **Institute of Public Administration:** This includes 2 strategic objectives, 4 indicators and 4 targets to be achieved.
- **Saudi Arabian General Investment Authority:** This includes 5 strategic objectives, 12 indicators and 11 targets to be achieved.
- **Saudi Food and Drug Authority (SFDA):** This includes 6 strategic objectives, 7 indicators and 5 targets to be achieved.

The strategic goals of the participating entities

- **Ministry of Justice:**

  The seven strategic objectives are:

  1   Improve judicial services and institutional excellence.
  2   Limit the flow of lawsuits to the courts.
  3   Improve judicial ranking locally and internationally.
  4   Develop and expand judicial assets.
  5   Improve notarization service performance.
  6   Strengthen real-estate security.
  7   Reduce execution time.

- **Ministry of Finance:**

  The six strategic objectives are:

  1   Strengthen public financial governance.
  2   Increase non-oil revenues.
  3   Raise the efficiency of spending on salaries and wages.
  4   Improve the efficiency of spending on government programs and projects.
  5   Achieve sustainability of public debt.
  6   Safeguard state assets (real estate and personal property).

- **Ministry of Economy and Planning:**

  The six strategic objectives are:

  1   Privatize some government services and assets.
  2   Diversify the GDP.
  3   Improve planning and implementation efficiency.
  4   Increase the efficiency of government subsidy programs.
  5   Grow the private sector.
  6   Activate the environmental dimension as a pillar of sustainable development.

- **Ministry of Health:**

  The 15 strategic objectives are:

  1   Increase private sector share of spending through alternative financing methods and service provision.
  2   Increase the efficient utilization of available resources.
  3   Improve the efficiency and effectiveness of the healthcare sector through the use of information technology and digital transformation.
  4   Increase training and development both locally and internationally.
  5   Increase the attractiveness of nursing and medical support staff as a preferred career path.

6 Improve healthcare provision before hospitalization and in the main hospitals (ER and ICU).

7 Improve integration and continuity in service provision by developing primary care.

8 Improve the infrastructure, facility management and safety standards in healthcare facilities.

9 Attain acceptable waiting times across all stages of service delivery.

10 Improve governance in the health system in order to enhance accountability with regard to quality issues and patient safety.

11 Adopt a national plan for emergency response to public health threats per international standards.

12 Identify additional sources of revenue.

13 Improve public health services, with a focus on obesity and smoking.

14 Improve the quality of life and healthcare service provided to patients outside hospitals.

15 Improve quality and safety principles as well as skills of service providers.

- **Ministry of Communications and Information Technology:**

The ten strategic objectives are:

1 Rehabilitate specialized Saudi human capital and employment of this capital to reduce the gap between supply and demand in the ICT sector.

2 Accelerate the restructuring and regulation of the postal sector.

3 Develop and activate smart government transactions based on a common infrastructure.

4 Provide critical resources, especially frequency spectrum for telecommunication and information technology services.

5 Provide broadband services to all KSA regions by stimulating investment in infrastructure and developing tools, technical and regulatory frameworks.

6 Support e-commerce.

7 Bridge the digital gap in the skills of ICT users.

8 Increase the IT industry's contribution to the non-oil GDP.

9 Reduce the percentage of revenue leakage to the IT industry abroad.

10 Complete the transformation of the Saudi Postal Corporation to a commercially viable company.

- **Ministry of Commerce and Investment:**

The seven strategic objectives are:

1 Guarantee fair trade between the consumer and the seller.

2 Build consumer confidence in products sold in the market.

3   Increase the culture of entrepreneurship.
4   Increase the contribution of small and medium-sized enterprises to the gross domestic product.
5   Increase the creation of job opportunities in small and medium enterprises.
6   Strengthen and increase the awareness of the consumer relating to rights and products.
7   Increase the competitiveness of locally produced products and services.

- **Ministry of Municipal and Rural Affairs:**

The seven strategic objectives are:

1   Continuously enhance quality of life by providing cities with public facilities and infrastructure of high quality and efficiency.
2   Achieve sustainable and balanced urban development and improvement of the level of quality of life in cities and regions of the Kingdom.
3   Achieve increasing levels of financial self-sufficiency and high-quality sustainable institutional performance.
4   Improve land management system, protect government land and provide accurate spatial information.
5   Provide fast, high-quality services.
6   Improve efficiency of project and program execution.
7   Provide a healthy local urban environment.

- **Ministry of Civil Services:**

The five strategic objectives are:

1   Improve work culture in government sector.
2   Improve ministry clients' satisfaction and enhance employee engagement level.
3   Increase efficiency of salary and compensation expenditure.
4   Improve human capital efficiency.
5   Improve strategic partnerships among government entities.

- **Ministry of Culture and Information:**

The four strategic objectives are:

1   Develop an environment that stimulates cultural activities.
2   Increase awareness regarding the government's decisions and achievements.
3   Enhance the Kingdom's image locally and internationally.
4   Develop media industry and related industries and strengthen their competitiveness internationally.

- **Ministry of Environment, Water and Agriculture:**

The 16 strategic objectives are:

1 Contribute to ensuring sustainable food security for the Kingdom.
2 Monitor and control spread of cross-border veterinary diseases.
3 Monitor and control spread of cross-border agricultural pests.
4 Optimize the use of renewable water resources for agricultural purposes.
5 Develop sustainable, highly efficient production systems for plants, livestock and fishery and increase the value added of these target products to contribute to the diversification of the Kingdom production base.
6 Develop national parks.
7 Improve land utilization and management in the agricultural sector.
8 Achieve organizational development and privatization.
9 Preserve vegetation of pastures and forests.
10 Improve financial efficiency.
11 Improve service quality.
12 Boost water storage resources and security.
13 Improve the efficiency of municipal and agricultural consumption.
14 Increase local content.
15 Expand service coverage.
16 Reduce service connection time.

- **Ministry of Energy, Industry and Mineral Resources:**

The 15 strategic objectives are:

1 Increase non-oil commodities exports.
2 Strengthen the capabilities, infrastructure and procedures of exporters.
3 Enhance market accessibility and promote strategic markets.
4 Increase the contribution of the mining sector in the national economy.
5 Increase the efficiency of fuel utilization in the electricity sector.
6 Incentivize the private sector to manufacture goods, provide services locally and encourage both public and private sectors to rely on local products and services.
7 Maximize the use of available hydrocarbon and mineral resources in less-developed regions with non-existing industries.
8 Enhance the primary sources and security of electricity supplies.
9 Improve the quality of electricity service and increase service coverage.
10 Achieve institutional development and privatization of the electricity sector to optimize financial efficiency.

11   Compensate reserves, maintain petroleum production capacity and increase the volume of gas supplies through the development of exploration and reserves activities.

12   Reduce fuel consumption emissions.

13   Increase the refining capacity to meet growth in demand.

14   Grow strategic sectors in manufacturing in collaboration with all key stakeholders.

15   Allocate required enablers to ensure execution governance of ministry initiatives.

- **Ministry of Labor and Social Development:**

The 13 strategic objectives are:

1   Establish an integrated system for family protection.

2   Build capacity and improve governance of third sector entities.

3   Transform beneficiaries who receive ministry support to productive members of society (Tamkeen).

4   Develop quality standards and technical professional accreditation.

5   Enable volunteer work.

6   Direct efforts to secure proper housing for social security beneficiaries in desperate need of housing.

7   Expand the third sector and direct its efforts towards developmental activities.

8   Provide suitable jobs for citizens.

9   Create a safe and attractive work environment.

10   Raise Saudis' skill level to match labor market needs.

11   Raise the efficiency of services and programs offered through centers, hostels and institutions.

12   Increase the capacity of technical and vocational training institutions and link it to the labor market needs.

13   Raise the quality of services provided.

- **Ministry of Housing:**

The three strategic objectives are:

1   Improve performance of the real estate sector and increase its contribution to the GDP.

2   Stimulate the real estate supply and raise productivity to provide residential products with appropriate price and quality.

3   Enable citizens to obtain suitable housing financing.

- **Ministry of Education:**

The eight strategic objectives are:

1   Provide education services for all student levels.

2   Improve recruitment, training and development of teachers.

3   Improve the learning environment to stimulate creativity and innovation.
4   Improve curricula and teaching methods.
5   Improve students' values and core skills.
6   Enhance the educational system's capability to address national development requirements and to meet labor market demands.
7   Develop creative financing methods and improve the educational system's financial efficiency.
8   Increase private sector participation in the education sector.

- **Ministry of Transportation:**

  The nine strategic objectives are:

  1   Minimize the rate of transportation accidents.
  2   Improve the legislative environment of the transportation sector.
  3   Improve efficiency of transportation infrastructure.
  4   Increase usage of public transportation.
  5   Increase reliance on self-funding.
  6   Increase percentage of private sector participation in financing and operating transportation projects.
  7   Improve environment for port management.
  8   Improve efficiency of railways.
  9   Improve efficiency of ports.

- **Ministry of Haj and Umrah:**

  The five strategic objectives are:

  1   Provide the opportunity for the largest number of Muslims possible to perform Hajj and Umrah.
  2   Implement effective strategic partnerships with the private sector.
  3   Raise awareness among pilgrims and Umrah visitors.
  4   Raise awareness among workers in the Haj and Umrah system.
  5   Establish a mechanism to improve the level of coordination between all entities concerned with decisions and special procedures affecting the Hajj and Umrah ecosystems.

- **Saudi Commission for Tourism and National Heritage:**

  The four strategic objectives are:

  1   Establish and develop tourism destinations as well as integrated entertainment cities and islands for all family members and encourage the private sector to invest in and operate them.
  2   Protect and develop awareness of national heritage sites and encourage private investment and operation.
  3   Increase and organize events and festivals that appeal to the various segments of society.
  4   Increase and develop hospitality facilities and tourism services.

- **Sports Authority:**

  The four strategic objectives are:

  1   Increase the percentage of exercise and physical activity (regularly).
  2   Develop the next generation of young people, increase their pride and national pride and improve their outlook and satisfaction with the presidency programs.
  3   Improve investment of sports and youth facilities for the presidency.
  4   Enable and ensure the sustainability of elite athletes to achieve high-level performance in the international arena to win medals in different games.

- **Royal Commission for Jubail and Yanbu:**

  The nine strategic objectives are:

  1   Attract diverse and integrative industries with higher added value.
  2   Expand and diversify financial resources.
  3   Increase the efficiency of asset usage and operational processes.
  4   Increase the volume of investments and industrial production.
  5   Provide a competitive investment environment to attract new investments.
  6   Improve the quality of education outputs and provide a qualified national workforce to investors in the cities.
  7   Maintain and enhance existing infrastructure and public utilities.
  8   Preserve, protect and develop the environment.
  9   Improve the standard of living, security, health and recreation.

- **King Abdul Aziz City for Science and Technology:**

  The seven strategic objectives are:

  1   Enhance the infrastructure and facilities necessary for the development of local content.
  2   Establish emerging technology companies with added value to contribute to the increase of local content.
  3   Strengthen the capability of small and medium-sized companies to contribute to the increase of local content.
  4   Provide technical consulting services to government sectors.
  5   Localize and develop technology in large domestic spending sectors.
  6   Support research and development to ensure the sustainability of the local content development system.
  7   Support local content through development of nationally qualified professionals

- **King Abdullah City for Atomic and Renewable Energy:**

The four strategic objectives are:

1   Enable atomic energy to contribute to the national energy mix in accordance with local requirements and international obligations.
2   Enable renewable energy to actively contribute in the national energy mix.
3   Increase local content in the industrial and service value chains and localize expertise in the technologies of both sectors, atomic and renewable energy, and invest it commercially.
4   Qualify needed human capital for the atomic and renewable energy sectors.

- **Institute of Public Administration:**

The two strategic objectives are:

1   Improve human capital efficiency.
2   Improve effectiveness of administrative organizations in the public sector.

- **Saudi Arabian General Investment Authority:**

The five strategic objectives are:

1   Improve administrative and procedural environments to enable significant investments.
2   Improve infrastructure needed to ensure ease of doing business.
3   Increase the percentage of local content.
4   Develop a unified national investment vision to promote and direct investments supporting the national economy.
5   Excel in investor services and improve their level of satisfaction.

- **Saudi Food and Drug Authority (SFDA):**

The six strategic objectives are:

1   Capitalize on KSA's Islamic position to establish the SFDA as the global reference for Halal food and products.
2   Establish control over the medicine supply chain.
3   Ensure sufficient supply of basic medicines.
4   Excel at controlling products within SFDA jurisdiction.
5   Intensify consumer communication to improve awareness of SFDA services.
6   Improve registration, licensing, inspection, release and policy enforcement with respect to the investors within all SFDA sectors (food, drugs, medical products and equipment).

Conclusion

Thus, in a nutshell, Vision 2030 and the National Transformation Program 2020, hand in hand, will help the Kingdom bring about a revolution and transform the economy from an oil-based to a knowledge-based economy in terms of research, innovation and entrepreneurship. Soon the Kingdom will rule the roost in comparison to all GCC countries and will be called a hub for providing state-of-the-art education to men and women without any discrimination, and it will lead in research, innovation and entrepreneurship for decades to come in light of Vision 2030 and the National Transformation Program 2020.

Conclusion

This research encompasses the core areas discussed in Saudi Arabia's Vision 2030 and the National Transformation Program 2020. The largest oil-producing country, KSA, founded in 1932, the center of the two Holy Mosques in Mecca and Medina and bordering almost eight Arab states, including two large coastal borders, became a high-income economy with a high human development index with oil discovery. Almost a decade ago, aggressive steps began to be taken to break the long-established economic link with oil. In Vision 2030, the emphasis is on engaging more Saudi nationals in all sectors of life. Steps have been taken to induct Saudi women into public life and education. To promote the importance of sports and culture, the Kingdom is to establish the biggest quality culture, sports and entertainment city by 2022. To attract Saudi nationals, 45 diverse programs are planned to keep them in the Kingdom instead of traveling abroad. Saudi women were allowed to drive in 2017, a physical education program for girls was launched and Saudi women were allowed to watch a football match in the stadium. To reduce dependency on oil and diversify its economy by developing public sector services, that is, health, education, infrastructure, tourism and recreation other than Mecca and Medina, the Kingdom made plans to strengthen economic growth and investment activities and encourage non-oil based trade within the country through goods and consumer products. The 2030 Vision has three main pillars:

- To maintain the status of the country as the "heart of the Arab and Islamic worlds."
- To become a global investment powerhouse.
- To transform the country's location into a connection hub between three continents (Asia, Europe and Africa).

Vision 2030 includes plans to develop economic and other opportunities for the upcoming years. To meet its goals, the vision is to participate in large international and technological programs and companies around the world in order to participate in various sectors as market markers and take on a leadership position in state-of-the-art funding, asset management and investment. One part of the vision is the National Transformation Program (NTP), which is followed by national goals like job creation, partnership with the private sector, maximizing local content and digital transformation. Vision 2030 will focus on many aspects that need to be transformed to see Saudi Arabia as an international business platform. The National Transformation Program for instruction has different advances, vital objectives and targets to reinforce schools and colleges, inquire about organizations, prepare foundations and do innovative work with the aim of enhancing undergraduates' abilities and polishing them for conclusive goals. It likewise will attempt to enhance educational programs on global premises, enhance staff and their preparation at prestigious establishments that will provide better administration to students and set them up to accomplish Vision 2030 for the Kingdom and eventually satisfy the requirements of the targets and market requests. A portion of the work process charts were introduced and demonstrated how the NTP is working with respect to educational change.

Three targets are summarized as:

• A vibrant society.
• A thriving economy.
• An ambitious nation with a non-oil economy.

Vision 2030 features a flourishing economy which gives chances to all by building an instructional framework aligned with advertised needs and opening monetary doors for the business visionary, the small enterprise and additionally the huge company.

Eighty major projects are planned under Vision 2030. A few are:

• National Transformation Program
• Red Sea luxury resort project
• Entertainment sector
• NEOM northwest of Saudi Arabia; includes land within Egypt and Jordan

The Ministry of Economy and Planning (MoEP) reports that there have been a few difficulties, for example, poor scholastic execution of undergraduates and lack of able educators, and performance among schools and colleges of instruction, the preparing administrations and life-long learning (LLL) were additionally below the level of expected effectiveness. Low work profitability and a high unemployment rate were found among adolescents (male and female). Technical and vocational training (TVET) is a clear need for young and mature workers.

The Saudi economy's challenges so far have been petroleum exports and the non-Saudi workforce. It needs to prepare national youth as a workforce and diversify its economic avenues. Saudis have to engage in using renewable groundwater resources for agriculture, as the residual groundwater was depleted in 2012. Renewable energy dependency will also move to solar power. The

Kingdom has many high-standard universities and educational and technical institutes. The new vision shows the following:

- Irtiqaa and Tatweer programs.
- Parental induction in school boards.
- Academic partnership with international educational institutions.
- Education and industry collaboration.
- Sustainable academic development and entrepreneurship.

King Abdul-Aziz City of Science and Technology aims to foster innovation and promote a knowledge-based nation. The institution supports the following sectors:

- Energy
- Water
- Oil, gas and mining technology
- Advanced materials
- Health
- Communication and information technology
- Agriculture
- Building and construction
- Transportation and logistics services
- Environment
- Space and aeronautics
- Defense and security
- Nuclear science and applied physics

Saudi Arabia is on the road to success to become the number-one choice for international business by focusing on each sector to be developed so that younger generations can have easy access to those opportunities. On the other hand, in recent years, Saudi Arabia has faced a lot of problems in the transformation of the Kingdom due to barriers faced by the people that have left them behind from other developed countries. The most important barriers are:

- Gender discrimination
- Cultural barriers
- Language barriers

Due to these factors, youngsters, especially females, have stepped back to present themselves on a bigger platform. Some barriers have led to low self-esteem in some Saudi women along with the absence of a very important ingredient confidence. However, new measures by the government is uplifting it and women are actively participating and contributing in the development of Saudi Arabia.

In addition, the Kingdom is well on its way to transform from an oil-based economy to a knowledge-based society. Vision 2030 includes some initiatives to achieve or build a knowledge-based society; the most important element is promoting young entrepreneurs to motivate them to do their best. Saudi Arabia should take serious steps to promote or develop platforms that help them present their innovative and unique ideas and work on them. Saudi Arabia wants to build an environment such that young graduates stop seeking jobs and instead build job opportunities for themselves and others. An emphasis on small and medium-sized enterprise (SME) promotion and a reinforcement of entrepreneurship are needed.

- Promote collectivism in business activities.
- Grow through entrepreneurship education.
- Provide hypothetical models to promote and implement successful entrepreneurship.

The King Abdullah University of Science and Technology (KAUST) is a co-educational graduate school near Jeddah that aims to achieve reforms that will enable the Kingdom to attract promising graduates from all over the world. This outward-looking perspective sets the tone for much of the Vision. It is reflected in the strategic objectives of the NTP, which include:

- Improving recruitment, training and development of teachers.
- Improving the learning environment to stimulate creativity and innovation.
- Improving curricula and teaching methods.
- Improving students' values and core skills.
- Developing financing methods and improvements in financial efficiency.
- Educating students to address national development requirements and labor market demands.
- Encouraging private sector participation in the education sector.

One of the most important problems observed from early childhood development is that there is less motivation to become an independent entrepreneur, and the early stage of studies also does not include such subjects because they are focusing on Arabic and Islamic culture. Saudis are being nationalist by promoting the Arabic language, which makes it difficult to interact with other international agencies, and students are facing difficulty interacting internationally. The English language should be focused on for their future development. To compete with other developed countries, a student should be bilingual, while learning more than two languages so that he/she can communicate with competing countries. At the same time, universities or institutes should focus on entrepreneurial activities and engaging students to participate and to bring up the new ideas to serve their country to develop business industries, market areas and platforms so that others are also motivated to be successful entrepreneurs. Universities should take the initiative to have entrepreneurs as guest speakers who are already working in their fields so that students will get to know about the risks and failures in the market to be faced in the future, because just having an idea will not make them a successful entrepreneur: they have to face market challenges and take small steps to build their own businesses. Many times it's been noted that students are not ready to accept failure and cannot manage risk, or they do not want to take any risks in business because they are afraid of failure. There should be risk management and motivational sessions to guide them in the right way or prepare them for the real world outside the four walls of the university. Saudi Arabia, working with these factors and universities like King Abdullah University of Science & Technology (KAUST) and King Saud University, is also focusing on these problems and overcoming them in these upcoming years, with the National Transformation Program, while providing opportunities to build an education system aligned with the market needs and creating economic opportunities for entrepreneurs. The fundamental objective of building up the NTP program in Saudi Arabia is getting a strong position in all fields to make sense of the general course, arrangements, objectives and target to achieve the objectives of Vision 2030. The Vision likewise incorporates a number of areas, key goals, targets, result-oriented pointers and responsibilities that are to be accomplished by the public, private and non-profit sectors.

Universities in Saudi Arabia are now implementing educational reforms, and they are collaborating with international institutes and governmental sectors so that students can study well and also have opportunities to get to know more about the industry and improve education with innovative ideas. University and industry collaboration is important for different beneficial reasons. Developing countries face greater challenges for such collaboration to promote university-industry relations. University and industry collaboration is also important for skill development for the nation, adoption of knowledge and acquisition and promotion of entrepreneurship. The motive is to overcome the gap between the outcome of higher education and the needs of the job market. In the year 2030, the Kingdom aims to have at least five Saudi universities among the top 200 universities in the international rankings. This will probably help students to get the best results in global indicators. Some factors they will focus on are character development, literacy and skill development to raise the standards. They will promote working with the public sector to generate the needed outcomes for the professional world and to develop opportunities for jobs in every field. They are also improving the quality of education with professional and qualified teachers and faculty and engaging parents in children's education. According to research, women are more active in working fields than men, but men are still given a higher priority in engineering education. It is vital that privately owned businesses and colleges work together for common gain. The essential point of organizations is to implement open development systems for better access, to collect information and finally to cooperate with colleges. The key mission of colleges has moved past the custom of instructing and research toward making better sense of the requirements for industry and contributing straightforwardly to monetary development and improvement. In many universities, men have more courses than women. Women are scoring higher than men. Likewise, in offices, there are far fewer women than men. Also, women seem to be more productive, innovative and active in their fields. These cultural boundaries are the biggest drawback for Saudis and are hindering the Kingdom in developing more rapidly. Arab states with the most contributed-to universities are engaging and reforming in these fields. Education is the most essential thing for the country to be successful in the future, and this education is not just for book learning but also teaches cultural values and educates us in right and wrong. Due to this, Saudi women are being empowered and allowed to drive and work in offices with their male counterparts. It is said that if we educate a woman, then she is the one from whom the whole generation will be educated, not just with the curriculum but in behavioral studies as well that will help to overcome the illiteracy rate in the state. Universities are not only promoting entrepreneurial activities but also working in the fields of science and technology and doing research on different topics that help to explore more in the fields of science, technology, health and medicine and make developments in these areas. Saudis are not only focusing on educational reforms but also in the entertainment area, which will help those in the Kingdom spend time with their loved ones. Also, it is promoting tourism, as Saudi Arabia is called "the Land of the Two Holy Mosques" in reference to Al-Masjid al-Haram (in Mecca) and Al-Masjid an-Nabawi (in Medina), the two holiest places in Islam.

According to research and development, "inventive work embraced on systematic study to expand the load of learning, including information of man, culture and society, and the utilization of this supply of learning to devise new applications." Instead of just focusing on educational reforms and promoting entrepreneurial activities, it's important for any country also to work with its R&D departments. Through these R&D institutes, the country will be competitive with developed states and other global institutions. In Saudi Arabia, particularly, it needs to know about R&D, and certain statistics are cited to demonstrate how little it is spending on R&D as compared to others. Many state agencies, universities, companies and non-governmental organizations are oriented towards R&D activities. R&D is spreading across the entire globe with much faster development and unique innovations. Likewise, Saudi Aramco operates 11 research centers and technology institutes worldwide. Saudi Arabia proposed to spend more on R&D projects. The performance of any country's R&D can be seen through innovation. On the global innovation index, Saudi Arabia stands at 55th, while others such as the Netherlands, the United States and the United Kingdom are the top innovative countries. In terms of quality of research, Saudi Arabia stands 30th globally. Compared to other countries around the world, Saudis are facing a bit of an unusual situation when it comes to conducting R&D. The reasons are as follows:

- No systematic process for measuring the economic impact of R&D spending
- No Research labs, product center or R&D center of global high-tech giants

- R&D process focus in Saudi Arabia is by supply, not by demand
- Less military (defense and offense) research projects
- Limited grand-scale national R&D projects

The leading R&D institution in Saudi Arabia is King Abdul Aziz City for Science and Technology (KACST). KACST provides R&D funding to other entities in Saudi Arabia.

The areas of focus that KACST identified as the national R&D Agenda for Saudi Arabia include technology transfer and localization in strategic sectors, divided into three themes:

- Global leadership: this theme includes sectors that the Kingdom has a competitive advantage in:

  1 Energy
  2 Water
  3 Oil
  4 Gas
  5 Minerals
  6 Advanced materials

- Self-reliance: this theme includes sectors in which the Kingdom is spending large amounts of money:

  7 Health and medicine
  8 Information and communications technology (ICT)
  9 Agriculture
  10 Building and construction
  11 Transportation and logistics
  12 Environment
  13 Nuclear science
  14 Applied physics

- National security: this theme includes military and national security sectors:

  15 Space and aeronautics
  16 Defense
  17 Security

KACST has committed Saudi Arabia to work on and invest in several items on the top list of research areas that the world is focusing on, namely:

1	Advanced materials	✓
2	Agriculture/food	✓
3	Automotive	✗
4	Commercial aerospace	✓
5	Communications	✓
6	Energy	✓

 7 Environmental   ✓
 8 Instrumentation   ✓
 9 Life science/healthcare ✓
10 Military/defense   ✓
11 Pharmaceutical/biotech   ✓

Besides medical research, it has carried out and subsidized R&D in Saudi Arabia that is innovation focused, and it made no noteworthy commitment, to a great extent because it has next to no specialized workforce to help R&D in Saudi research organizations compared to other worldwide driving foundations, notwithstanding the absence of core interests. The circumstance is marginally better in organizations, for example, SABIC and Saudi Aramco, yet even there, it is barely recognized in view of the R&D yield created locally.

Showing dissatisfaction with the R&D in the Kingdom, research suggests the following measures for better R&D.

 1 Develop and roll out a structured approach to measure the economic impact of R&D spending in Saudi Arabia.
 2 Increase R&D spending in Saudi Arabia to reach 3% of the GDP by 2030.
 3 Set up an R&D-dedicated fund.
 4 Set up a dedicated endowment-based R&D fund and encourage NGOs and donors to capitalize the fund and contribute to setting up its R&D agenda.
 5 Create demand or R&D in Saudi Arabia through:

    a A mandate on all fully or partially state-owned corporations.
    b Mandate the same on all companies, inside or outside Saudi Arabia.

 6 Mandate the establishment of product centers at all leading Saudi corporations.
 7 Carefully integrate the development of homegrown R&D talent with attracting international talent in focused areas.
 8 Create an ecosystem for start-ups.
 9 Mandate that all leading Saudi universities, research centers and corporations adopt and report on the utilization of the following R&D tools:

    • Crowdsourcing
    • Hackathons
    • Open science
    • Prize competitions
    • Student team contests

10 Create a program of focused military R&D guided by and reporting to the newly established Saudi Arabia military industries.
11 Incentivize startups and the private sector to participate meaningfully and to provide technology solutions.

12 Create a government venture capital fund to fund technology-focused startups.
13 Establish a dedicated Ministry for Science and Technology.

National Transformation Program 2020 and Vision 2030, hand in hand, helping to transform the oil-based economy to a knowledge-based economy. Kingdom is going to be the hub of state of the art education without gender discrimination. In the light of NTS 2020 and vision 2030, KSA is going to lead research, innovation, and entrepreneurship in the region.

Index